CREATIVITY INSIDE OUT

Learning Through Multiple Intelligences

TERRY MARKS-TARLOW

With a Foreword by Howard Gardner

Innovative Learning Publications

Addison-Wesley Publishing Company

Menlo Park, California • Reading, Massachusetts • New York
Don Mills, Ontario • Wokingham, England • Amsterdam
Bonn • Paris • Milan • Madrid • Sydney • Singapore
Tokyo • Seoul • Taipei • Mexico City • San Juan

Grateful acknowledgment is made to J. T. Steiny for the cartoons that appear on the following pages: xiii, xv, 3, 7, 10, 11, 14, 16, 20, 29, 32, 51, 54, 55, 57, 58, 59, 61, 62, 67, 71, 72, 82, 84, 91, 122, 132, 138, 144, 147, 151, 154, 167, 179.

Photographs on the following pages, unless otherwise noted, courtesy Terry Marks-Tarlow: 2, 4, 12, 40, 43, 77, 83, 88, 98, 106, 110, 112, 147, 148. Personal mandala on page 173 courtesy Terry Marks-Tarlow.

Managing Editor: Cathy Anderson
Project Editor: Mali Apple
Production Coordinator: Claire Flaherty
Production: Novus Design and Communications
Design Manager: John F. Kelly
Design and Art Direction: PCI Design Group/San Antonio, TX
Cover Design and Illustration: Victor Bickmore/Garcia, Bickmore, and Brown

This book is published by Innovative Learning Publications™, an imprint of Addison-Wesley's Alternative Publishing Group.

ISBN 0-201-49044-7

2345678910-ML-99 98 97 96 95

This Book Is Printed
on Recycled Paper

CONTENTS

Unit 1
Creativity Begins with You:
Explorations in Inner Space

Unit 2
Voices Within:
Vocabularies for Self-Expression

Unit 3
The Shape of Things:
Explorations of Outer Space

Unit 4
Putting the Pieces Together:
Quest for Pattern

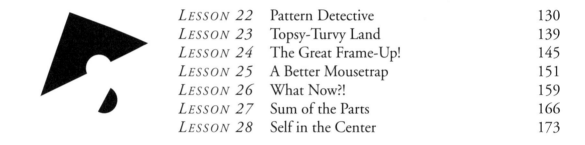

The Creativity Indexes

ACKNOWLEDGMENTS

I have always been attracted to creative enterprises—especially drawing, piano, and dance. I even spent a summer at Rhode Island School of Design, but decided I lacked enough natural talent to pursue a career as an artist. Instead I turned to my other love and earned a doctorate in clinical psychology, later specializing in creativity. I chose to tackle this project because I became convinced that talent is only one of many factors of creative expression. It lags well behind persistence in order of importance. I now know that in trying to become more talented, I impeded my creative expression. Through this curriculum, I hope to pass on this hard-earned pearl to the next generation of students and teachers.

This project originated in 1985 in the Lawndale, California, School District where I consulted as a psychologist for the Gifted and Talented Education (GATE) program. I am indebted to the administration of this district for their courage to experiment with innovative programs. My special thanks to Leona Barnes and David Moorhouse. I am equally indebted to the original committee of GATE and other teachers. Besides showing me what creativity looks like in the classroom, these individuals relentlessly faced the sometimes exciting, other times tedious work of curriculum development. I acknowledge each by name: Lynn Anderson, Judy Bloomingdale, Barbara Charles, Rick Frauman, Laura Kaku, Angie Moller, Helen Reynolds, Brenda Strauch, Jan Tyree, and Carol Wright.

Special thanks to Sherrie Connelly, Caren Finnerman, Janice Roosevelt Gerard, Patricia Greenfield, Jim Haas, Sonia Lisker, Peter Rysavy, Pam Stock, Zach Stock, and Buz Tarlow for comments concerning earlier drafts. Gallery owners Zeneta and John Kertisz, plus all of the artists, have contributed invaluably. Millie Loeb should know I would not have made it to the final draft without her assistance. Last but not least, I extend a heartfelt thanks to a visionary thinker from Addison-Wesley, Stuart Brewster. He had the courage to accept this book on the sole basis of its potential and nourish it over the wild and rocky course of several drafts and many years.

Feedback for the Author

Just as feedback is critical for evaluating and keeping track of students and teacher performance in the classroom, so it is critical to this author. Your responses to the exercises and activities, your creative ideas, your suggestions for improvement, what you liked and didn't like about the curriculum, what you'd like to see in future revisions or editions—all are very important to me. Please write with your feedback to the following address:

TERRY MARKS-TARLOW, PH.D.
1460 SEVENTH STREET, SUITE 304
SANTA MONICA, CA 90401

FOREWORD

In most cultures, throughout most of human history, creativity was simply not tolerated. If individuals wanted to do things in ways that fell outside the normal practices of society, they would be admonished, expelled, or killed. Only in modern times—roughly, since the fifteenth century—and chiefly in the West have creative thought and behaviors been tolerated, let alone encouraged. We are fortunate that we live in a milieu in which "the creative life" remains an option, and we should never take that option for granted.

As a first approximation, I define a creative individual as one who regularly solves problems or fashions products in a domain, in a way that is initially novel but eventually becomes acceptable within a community. This definition calls for a few comments. First of all, creativity is not a flash in the pan. It is a way of living, and people who behave in creative ways do so with some reliability and regularity. Second, people are not creative in general; they are creative in certain domains, where the have talent and interest, and not necessarily in others. Thus, as Terry Marks-Tarlow points out, being creative in music is not the same as being creative in language or with other persons. J. S. Bach is not Virginia Woolf is not Mahatma Gandhi. Third, creativity is never a judgment simply about an individual. Whether something is creative is a judgment that can only be made by individuals and institutions that are knowledgeable about the domain. Thus Sam and Sally may both think that they are equally good poets; and their brains may in fact be identical; but if readers and poets consider Sam's work to be innovative but do not understand Sally's (or vice versa), we can only infer that, for now, Sam is creative and Sally is not.

To my knowledge, *Creativity Inside Out* is the first book that talks about the enhancing of creativity in children from the perspectives of *differences—*differences across children, differences across subject matters. We all know that children differ greatly from one another, and we all know that to be "smart" or "creative" with biology or history is not the same as being "smart" or "creative" with music or sculpture or one's business or social life. Terry Marks-Tarlow shows us—teachers, parents, children of different ages, interested readers of all persuasions—how one can open up the sluices of creativity: how we can be creative with our several sense organs, the different media that are available, the diverse intelligences and sets of intelligences with which each of us is equipped. Perhaps most important, from my perspective as an educator, she shows us how the curricula of schools can be approached in a more creative manner.

No two educators are alike and no two educators will want to use this book in precisely the same way. For those who just like to read and muse, the book can be read through like an adventure story. For those who are looking for neat lessons or exercises to try out, the book is chock-full of simple but effective ideas. For those who like to tinker, there are numerous open-ended suggestions, games, and lessons that cry out for experimentation, for a "creative twist." And for those who are looking for a catalyst, this book encourages reflection upon one's own current practices and offers insights on how they can be more effectively implemented. However one approaches this nutritious book, one cannot help but be struck by the enormous potential for creativity in even the most mundane corners of life. And perhaps, as a result of this book, some individuals will be stimulated to create products that contribute to the life of their community.

Howard Gardner
Harvard Project Zero
Cambridge, Massachusetts

We live in an era of extraordinary confusion. Traditional institutions and values break down faster than new ones emerge. We confront unprecedented cultural diversity and world interdependence.

Creativity is our tool for dealing with these changes. It springs from deep inside us, flowing outward to help us handle new experiences and, most of all, to help us express our individuality.

Creativity Inside Out celebrates individual differences, yet emphasizes unity amidst diversity. It employs communication training, joint goals, teamwork, and cooperative strategies to encourage self-esteem and self-expression.

Although you can adapt the lessons in *Creativity Inside Out* to any grade level, they are specifically geared for grades 4 through 9. Students in these grade levels tend to lose their creative expression unless it is nurtured and guided. *Creativity Inside Out* helps you centralize self-expression in your classroom. You can use the book over the course of a year, or the school district can use it in a coordinated, age-graded fashion over a six-year period.

This curriculum aims to make learning stimulating without sacrificing discipline or rigor. It fits right in with regular curriculum, whether your lesson concerns adjective phrases, Vasco de Gama, or plant biology.

The book contains twenty-eight lessons in four units. Each lesson builds upon previous lessons to explore a different aspect of self-expression. One of the giants in education, Jerome Bruner, recommended such a progression so that students may practice later the concepts introduced earlier. For example, in an early lesson using guided imagery, students float on a cloud to a beautiful place. They learn to open eyes, ears, and other inner senses of imagination. In later lessons, students scale classroom walls as if they were flies and meet a Corlian from the center of the earth. They apply skills they learned to higher-order tasks of problem solving and understanding multiple perspectives. Despite the book's sequencing, you may use lessons flexibly on their own or in any order.

Creativity Inside Out is grounded in research and theory; a detailed account is beyond the scope of this book. The References and Resources section will help guide you to sources for further reading and exploration.

Multiple Intelligences in the Spotlight

Thanks to Howard Gardner (1982), we now know that each of us possesses at least seven entirely different ways to understand the world and to express ourselves: linguistic; spatial; musical; logical-mathematical; body-kinesthetic; and two kinds of social intelligence, intrapersonal (knowledge of self) and interpersonal (knowledge of others). Each intelligence has its own means and modes for expression (see page 36). Each represents an area of expertise with a specific body of knowledge, as well as a way of approaching learning in any domain. *Creativity Inside Out* systematically includes all of the intelligences, using each to stimulate self-expression. Those domains not typically part of traditional Western education—social, musical, body-kinesthetic, and spatial—receive particular emphasis.

Because of the increasing importance of television, film, computers, and other visual-spatial media, this book highlights spatial literacy—the ability to scan, to understand, and in a sense to "read" the images and symbols that surround us. You will find photographs, diagrams, and cartoons in *Creativity Inside Out* to stimulate, to educate, and even to amuse you and your students.

What Is Creativity?

Creativity is original self-expression, natural to all children, achieved through accessing and expressing unique personal and cultural perspectives. Creativity is a maturational process that unfolds through a combination of inborn talent and exposure to encouragement, opportunities, and respected role models. Creativity's fullest bloom occurs when individuals are motivated by internal reasons, such as curiosity, determination, and passion, rather than for external rewards, such as praise, recognition, and good grades. Creativity thrives in the soil where two or more intelligences mix. Here, individuals can shuttle back and forth between different symbol systems, media, and modes of self-expression as best suits their personal, social, and cultural idiosyncrasies.

This definition of creativity is only one among endless possibilities; there are as many ways to conceptualize creativity as there are people and opportunities to do so. While you should hone in on a single definition to guide classroom activities, you should also maintain a broad perspective. Creativity is an open concept—the precise definition is bound to each new context. It differs for each particular era, culture, individual, challenge, and set of resources.

Program Goals

1. Use the fundamental links between creativity, self-esteem, and intrinsic motivation to target basic self-concept in you and your students.

2. Elevate self-expression to a central position in the classroom, where it serves as a springboard for organizing and demonstrating knowledge in all basic curricular areas.

3. Bring out each student's unique combination of skills, multiple intelligences, and capacities for self-expression, using individual activities, cooperative groups, and multicultural perspectives.

The Underlying Approach

In a climate of overworked educators and tight budgets, *Creativity Inside Out* is virtually self-contained. You need little money, special resources, or prior experience to participate in the program. The format is activity oriented and easy to use. The material has no "right" and "wrong" answers, which enhances your students' intrinsic motivation, risk-taking, and freedom of expression. Since the content applies to gifted as well as to slower learners, you can unify rather than divide the classroom. Original self-expression is the right of every student, not just the playground of the youngest or the privilege of the few.

The approach immerses the entire classroom in a creative environment. Since students learn best through role models (John-Steiner 1985), *Creativity Inside Out* targets your creativity as well as that of your students. When you select and adapt lesson Extensions, you tap into your divergent thinking and challenge your fluency and flexibility with the material. The Teacher's Corner sections provide mirrors for self-reflection plus springboards for originality and personal and professional growth. For example, you are invited to examine your body language, to identify your use of personal space, and to sculpt a potential new dimension in life.

You will likely find many of the book's ideas familiar. Because you are human you are already creative by nature, even if you do not think of yourself that way. While this curriculum tries to offer some new ideas, it also attempts to synthesize and systematize age-old ideas in a fresh way to underscore the centrality of self-expression to full learning and a healthy self-concept.

March of the Units

Below is a broad overview of the four units. At the beginning of each unit you will find a brief menu of the seven lessons in that unit, including their major foci and goals.

Unit 1

Creativity Begins with You: Explorations in Inner Space

Since creativity flows from the inside out, this book opens with our inner world, providing a bag of tools for creative self-expression. You teach students to relax, to find the still center from which self-expression emerges, to open inner eyes of imagination, and to sharpen outer eyes of perceptual awareness. You give them the opportunity to scribble and doodle, and "get serious" about play. They learn concentration and observation skills. They experience multiple perspectives. Finally, you encourage students to identify and to respect their own uniqueness, both as individuals and as members of a multicultural world.

Unit 2

Voices Within: Vocabularies for Self-Expression

This unit centers on body, musical, and social intelligences. Lessons cover our need for personal space and different ways of posing, texturing, and moving through physical surroundings. Students use mime and dramatic technique to explore the formal structure of literature, the nature of emotion, and its centrality to creative expression. As the unit progresses into the realm of sound, students make their own instruments from common objects. They explore qualities of sound, such as pitch and beat. Students learn to coordinate sounds with movement—the essence of dance. The final lesson introduces students to notions of multiple intelligences and learning styles based on them.

Unit 3

The Shape of Things: Explorations of Outer Space

This unit places special emphasis on spatial intelligence and communication skills. Students become sensitized to various shapes around them. They build a repertoire from which to fashion creative products and to communicate what they see. Lessons progress from simple to complex shapes, moving from the point to lines, circles, triangles, squares, and three-dimensional space. The unit highlights visual literacy skills, by which we come to "read" the visual cues and vocabulary bombarding us from billboards, television sets, and video games. Students identify, interpret, critique, and produce various shapes and their attributes. In the final lesson, they learn about the importance of precision and feedback to effective communication.

Unit 4

Putting the Pieces Together: Quest for Pattern

The final unit involves what many believe is the heart of the creative process—the discovery, communication, and creation of patterns in the world around us. It offers a cornucopia of patterns, shapes, and intelligences, allowing students to review and to synthesize elements from previous lessons and units. Students explore grouping patterns and patterns of reversal. Frames help isolate figures and demonstrate the importance of context to pattern identification. Students experiment with invention and design, individually and in cooperative groups. They learn problem-solving strategies that address the creativity of everyday life. The book finishes where it began—with the individual, this time in relation to the universe. Students make personal mandalas that articulate values and meet the ultimate, lifelong challenge of self-creation.

***Creativity Inside Out* has been streamlined for busy educators.** Lessons appear in cookbook format with a list of ingredients (materials) and step-by-step instructions.

Anatomy of a Lesson

Each lesson moves from *doing* to *thinking* and *talking*. This progression encourages you and your students to learn first through exploration, then to anchor all experiences intellectually. Lessons immerse students in creative experiences while encouraging you toward greater creative participation as each lesson progresses. You need only follow directions to implement the Preparation and Exercise sections. For the Discussions that follow, you may want to adapt questions according to the maturity of your class. You will need more judgment and ingenuity to select and adapt Extensions. Finally, you can let your originality fly when encountering challenges of the Teacher's Corner.

If you are as busy as this educator, you will appreciate the simple organization of *Creativity Inside Out*. Six indexes will help you to access material easily and place hundreds of ideas at your fingertips instantly.

Introduction

Introduces you to goals, theoretical underpinnings, and classroom uses for each lesson

Materials

Lists both necessary and optional materials for the Exercise.

Exercise

Walks you through the main activity step by step.

Preparation

Outlines any action to take ahead of time.

Discussion

Provides questions for discussing and analyzing creative processes and products

Extensions

Reinforces and expands the skills and concepts learned; lists possibilities for linking the lesson with other basic curricular areas.

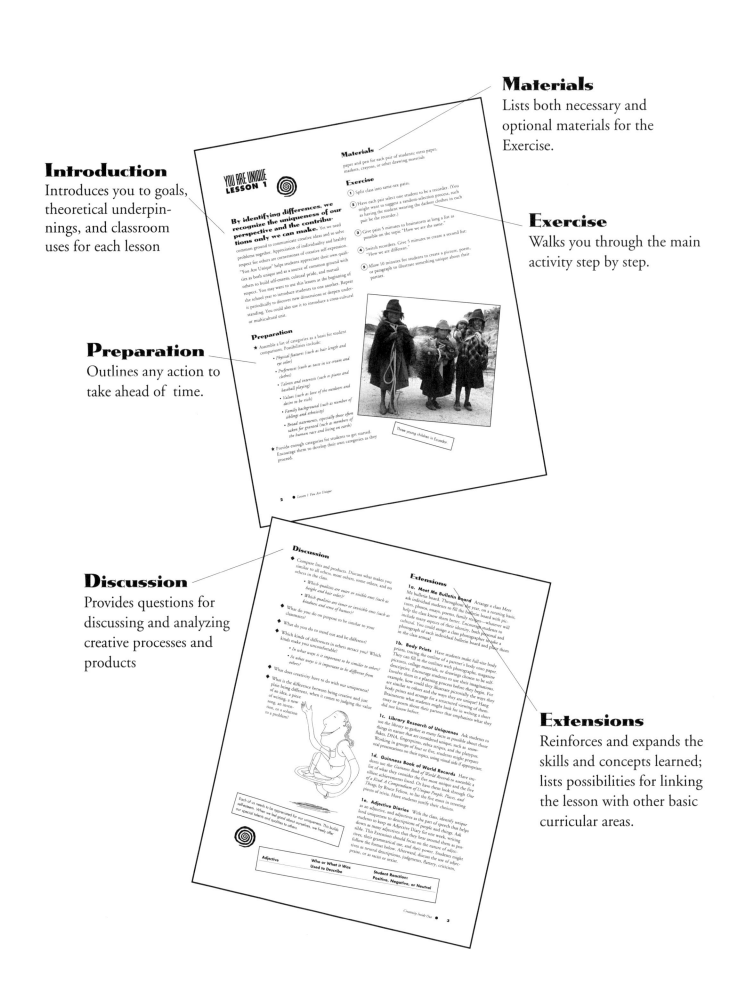

YOU ARE UNIQUE
LESSON 1

By identifying differences, we recognize the uniqueness of our perspective and the contributions only we can make. Yet we need common ground to communicate creative ideas and to solve problems together. Appreciation of individuality and healthy respect for others are cornerstones of creative self-expression. "You Are Unique" helps students appreciate their own qualities as both unique and as a source of common ground with others to build self-esteem, cultural pride, and mutual respect. You may want to use this lesson at the beginning of the school year to introduce students to one another. Repeat it periodically to discover new dimensions or deepen understanding. You could also use it to introduce a cross-cultural or multicultural unit.

Preparation

★ Assemble a list of categories as a basis for student comparisons. Possibilities include:
- *Physical features (such as hair length and eye color)*
- *Preferences (such as taste in ice cream and clothes)*
- *Talents and interests (such as piano and baseball playing)*
- *Values (such as love of the outdoors and desire to be rich)*
- *Family background (such as number of siblings and ethnicity)*
- *Broad statements, especially those often taken for granted (such as members of the human race and living on earth)*

★ Provide enough categories for students to get started. Encourage them to develop their own categories as they proceed.

Materials

paper and pen for each pair of students; extra paper, markers, crayons, or other drawing materials

Exercise

1. Split class into same-sex pairs.
2. Have each pair select one student to be a recorder. (You might want to suggest a random-selection process, such as having the student wearing the darkest clothes in each pair be the recorder.)
3. Give pairs 5 minutes to brainstorm as long a list as possible on the topic "How we are the same."
4. Switch recorders. Give 5 minutes to create a second list: "How we are different."
5. Allow 10 minutes for students to create a picture, poem, or paragraph to illustrate something unique about their partner.

Three young children in Ecuador

2 ● *Lesson 1 You Are Unique*

Discussion

◆ Compare lists and products. Discuss what makes you similar to all others, most others, some others, and no others in the class.
- *Which qualities are outer or visible ones (such as height and hair color)?*
- *Which qualities are inner or invisible ones (such as kindness and sense of humor)?*

◆ What do you do on purpose to be similar to your classmates?

◆ What do you do to stand out and be different?

◆ Which kinds of differences in others attract you? Which kinds make you uncomfortable?
- *In what ways is it important to be similar to others?*
- *In what ways is it important to be different from others?*

◆ What does creativity have to do with our uniqueness? Explain the difference between being creative and just plain being different, when it comes to judging the value of an idea, a piece of writing, a new song, an invention, or a solution to a problem?

Each of us needs to be appreciated for our uniqueness. This builds self-esteem. When we feel good about ourselves, we freely offer our special talents and qualities to others.

Extensions

1a. Meet Me Bulletin Board Arrange a class Meet Me bulletin board. Throughout the year, on a rotating basis, ask individual students to fill the bulletin board with pictures, photos, essays, poems, family recipes—whatever will help the class know them better. Encourage students to include many aspects of their identity, both personal and cultural. You could assign a class photographer to take a photograph of each individual bulletin board and place them in the class annual.

1b. Body Prints Have students make full-size body prints, tracing the outline of a partner's body onto paper. They can fill in the outlines with photographs, magazine pictures, collage materials, or drawings chosen to be self-descriptive. Encourage students to use their imaginations. Involve them in a planning process before they begin. For example, how could they illustrate pictorially the ways they are similar to others and the ways they are unique? Hang body prints and arrange for a structured viewing of them. Brainstorm what students might look for in writing a short essay or poem about their partner that emphasizes what they did not know before.

1c. Library Research of Uniqueness Ask students to use the library to gather as many facts as possible about those things in nature that are considered unique, such as snowflakes, DNA, fingerprints, zebra stripes, and the platypus. Working in groups of four or five, students might prepare oral presentations on their topic, using visual aids if appropriate.

1d. Guinness Book of World Records Have students use the *Guinness Book of World Records* to assemble a list of what they consider the five most unique and the five silliest achievements listed. Or have them look through *One of a Kind: A Compendium of Unique People, Places, and Things*, by Bruce Felton, to list the five most interesting pieces of trivia. Have students justify their choices.

1e. Adjective Diaries With the class, identify *unique* as an adjective, and adjectives as the part of speech that helps lend uniqueness to descriptions of people and things. Ask students to keep an Adjective Diary for one week, writing down as many adjectives that they hear around them as possible. This Extension should focus on the nature of adjectives, their grammatical use, and their power. Students might follow the format below. Afterward, discuss the use of adjectives as neutral descriptions, judgments, flattery, criticism, praise, or as racist or sexist.

Adjective	Who or What it Was Used to Describe	Student Reaction: Positive, Negative, or Neutral

Creativity Inside Out ● 3

(see pages 180-185)

Teacher's Corner

Targets educators for psychological insight and creative growth, personally and professionally.

[sample page inset]

1f. Comparison of Television Parents Ask students to compare and contrast two television dads or moms, such as Bill Cosby, Homer Simpson, Roseanne, or the mom on *The Brady Bunch*. Consider using video excerpts of programs in the classroom. Form a list of outer, visible qualities (such as hair and skin color) and inner, invisible ones (such as honesty and stinginess). Ask students how these television parents compare with their own parents. Ask students to describe the ideal parent.

1g. Comparison of World Leaders Have the class compare and contrast two world leaders who are prominent in the news and look for similarities and differences in how newspapers and other media present these figures. Students might compile a list of adjectives used to describe each of the leaders. They might cut photos or caricatures from newspapers or magazines to study the ways the leaders are visually portrayed.

1h. Imagined Lands Ask students to write a story about a land where a large or small difference among inhabitants threatens to tear them apart. Encourage them to include a solution to the problem and how it was found. Compare and contrast stories. Discuss them as a metaphor for problems of bigotry, racism, scapegoating, prejudice, sexism, and intolerance. Ask if any solutions apply to problems in their classroom, school, or community. To discuss these issues with younger students, you could read to or role-play *The Sneetches*, by Dr. Seuss. Make this Extension more personal by having students draw and discuss the first time they felt different from other people. This can stimulate highly sensitive feelings, such as shame and embarrassment, so handle with care.

1i. Family Folk Art Most areas of the world have their own forms of folk art. Have students find out where their ancestors come from, then research and report on traditional forms of folk art unique to that area. If possible, students should make or bring in samples, slides, or photographs to make reports come alive.

1j. Unique Styles in Art Present a series of poems or passages by writers with very identifiable styles (such as e. e. cummings, Vachel Lindsay, and Zora Neale Hurston). This exercise works best when the writing is on a single subject. As a class, analyze what makes each writer unique. Using slides or video excerpts, present a similar lesson with a few of your favorite artists, perhaps Pablo Picasso, Marc Chagall, Henri Rousseau, or Peter Max. (Inexpensive slides are available through the National Gallery of Art. Write to: Publications Service, National Gallery of Art, Washington, DC, 20565 for their free color slide catalogue.) Or select a fairy tale from the library that is illustrated by different artists. Compare and contrast the approach and style of each. This helps students see there is more than one right answer to an illustration problem.

Folk art can be created anywhere, by anyone.

Teacher's Corner

★ Take a few moments to celebrate yourself by naming three ways you are unique as a person. How can you use each to break away from old habits and enrich your teaching?

★ List every student in the class. Name one quality that makes each individual unique. What are some implications of these individual differences?

★ Shake up your usual routine. Bring more of your unique style to your teaching! Try lesson planning from a pizza parlor. Remember a poem that moved you as a youngster? Wear an article of clothing to school unlike anything you have worn before.

★ Review your class bulletin boards over the past year. Is there anything about them that bears the unique stamp of your signature? Can you come up with four new ideas for bulletin boards?

★ Take a chance! Explore uniqueness through a style of art with which you are unfamiliar, such as glass blowing and scrimshaw. The less formal knowledge you possess about the art or its history, the better, as it enhances the value of personal experience. You become a learner, making it easier to understand the importance of intellectual curiosity and flexibility. By challenging yourself with a new area, you model the student difficulties or frustration. By challenging Students get a boost in self-esteem when they feel on the same plane as you as co-learners.

▲ ● *Lesson 1 You Are Unique*

Tips for Use

There are many different ways to use this book. You can move through it systematically, from start to finish—a good strategy for familiarizing yourself with the material. However, be careful not to drain the pleasure out of the process by becoming too systematic or trying to do everything. Be led by your own passions and interests. Experiment. Have fun. Take risks.

If you have decided to do a creativity exercise, but are not sure what you want to do, try using the flip-through technique: thumb through the pages until you come to something that jumps out and beckons you. Another possibility is to use the six indexes (see pages 180-185). Each index provides a different method for accessing relevant activities.

No matter which method you use, talk about creativity often with your students, even when you are not doing a lesson from this book. Hold an ongoing dialogue about the nature of creativity: what it is, when and why it appears, how to nurture it, and ways it is important to self-esteem and self-concept. Discuss traits that assist the creative process, such as independence of mind, curiosity, playfulness, and risk-taking. Point out internal and external factors that can block self-expression, such as self-consciousness or fear of failure or criticism; lack of support or acceptance by others; and even more inhibiting, ourselves.

Above all, remember that with any complex skill, mastery and confidence come with time and patience. As you become more familiar with the lessons, you will have an easier time using and improvising them. Even master chefs must face a few failed dishes. Try to turn failures upside down, viewing them as risks successfully taken. This is good role-modeling for your students. Whether your direction is forward, backward, or sideways, every single step is vital to the process. When it comes to creativity, it is the process, not the product, that counts.

Thomas Edison made hundreds of attempts until he finally lit the darkness with one of his most famous discoveries—the light bulb. No wonder he said that creativity is 99 percent perspiration and 1 percent inspiration. Isn't it interesting that a lit-up light bulb has come to symbolize a good idea?

As much as you and students want to enjoy and feel stimulated in school, each of you will always struggle with the issue of accountability. You must do your job teaching; students must do their jobs learning. Families and administrators need to be certain both jobs are adequately accomplished. Any serious program of study, whether in the area of creativity or not, must address accountability.

Strategies for Evaluation

You can easily track creativity studies and evaluate student participation and performance. Remember these simple guidelines:

1. There is no right or wrong when it comes to self-expression.

2. Every effort has merit, even failures, especially if risks were taken.

3. Process is just as important to follow and evaluate as product, perhaps even more.

4. Attend to factors other than correctness, including effectiveness of problem solving, communication skills, cleverness of approach, and diligence in effort.

5. Wherever possible, use evaluation for qualitative purposes of description, analysis, and feedback. Stay clear of judgments about good and bad. These inhibit you and the student.

6. Use a combination of strategies to provide as many multimodal evaluation techniques as possible.

Letter Grades—A Last Resort

Avoid assigning letter grades to student work whenever possible in favor of a more descriptive, less quantitative approach. If you must grade, base scores on more than just the beauty or success of the work or the talent of the creator. Grades should primarily address aspects of the production process, such as those listed below in the Creativity Checklists.

Discussion Review

A list of discussion questions follows each of the exercises. These provide a straightforward method to evaluate student experiences. Make observations of student participation during discussion to track progress. Or have students answer these questions more formally, in written form. Use the answers to track understanding or involvement and creative, emotional, intellectual, and academic growth.

Supplement the discussion questions with those of your own, geared specifically toward the particulars of your classroom. If possible, make up questions for each Extension activity you try. This will ensure stronger intellectual anchoring of every activity. Meanwhile you will find out what students have learned and how they connect the Extension to other lessons, subjects, and creativity.

Portfolios

Not every lesson will wind up with a tangible product, but many do. Innovate a system for keeping portfolios, either representative of your class or individual students. Along with actual samples of work, portfolios can contain your observations or snapshots of work that is too cumbersome to keep or that students want to take home. Date all contents, whether originals or photographs, and arrange material chronologically. Then you, your students, families, and administrators will all be able to view, evaluate, and track progress throughout the year.

Portfolios are extremely useful for introducing families and administrators to the fruits of creativity studies and for doing program evaluation. They help identify student learning styles and strengths. They also help identify students for gifted programs based on creative productions (although as you will see in Lesson 7, readers are encouraged to get beyond such labels as "gifted").

Creativity Logbooks

Augment the portfolio system with creativity logbooks. Either have students create their own, or create one for the class. Logbooks you create can contain observations, speculations, ramblings, and doodles that can help you do the tasks listed below.

1. Keep track of creativity lessons and their outcomes. Include which lessons work, which do not, ideas for future improvement, and adaptation of lessons and extensions.

2. Keep observations of the impact of creativity studies on the class. One of the best indicators of high-level learning is the ability to spontaneously translate concepts and ideas learned in one modality to another arena or subject area. You delight in seeing your students spontaneously arriving at their own extensions.

3. Track the progress individual students using random or planned observations. For example, watch and record a student during a two- or three-minute interval.

4. Track the progress of students with learning or discipline problems.

5. Track the progress of cooperative-learning techniques.

6. Make self-assessments of how well your time was used to facilitate student work.

Students can use logbooks for writing, drawing, and doodling. They can refer to them to self-evaluate creativity lessons or to keep track of their reactions to exercises. They can note insights about the creative process, multiple intelligences, and the nature of their own self-expression. Students may keep their logbooks private or share them with you or other students. Although sharing logbooks can be positive—for example, it can help you evaluate students—the process can also inhibit students.

Video- and Audiotaping

You could also use videotape or audiotape to track student work. Record both the process and products of creativity studies. Students love to view what they have done, and tapes of their work often provide a good launching point for discussion, self-reflection, and written analysis to augment the evaluation process. Families delight in seeing the work as well. Administrators will find tapes inspirational in attempts to secure grants and other special funding. If appropriate, add recorded tapes to portfolios.

Creativity Checklists

Use these four checklists (see pages xxi and xxii) to evaluate student process, motivation, products, and interpersonal factors. Adapt them according to your needs.

Using the Creativity Indexes

The indexes, which begin on page 180, will help you access the many activities in *Creativity Inside Out* easily.

Subject Index

This index lists Exercises and Extensions under the following categories:

- Arts
- Creative Writing
- Language Arts
- Multicultural
- Other Social Sciences
- Mathematics
- Sciences

If you are teaching a basic curricular subject—for example, the Industrial Revolution—you could creatively expand the lesson by using this index.

Multiple Intelligences Index

This index will help you access Exercises and Extensions relevant for each intelligence:

- Linguistic
- Spatial
- Kinesthetic
- Knowledge of Self
- Knowledge of Others
- Logical-Mathematical
- Musical

A primary purpose of *Creativity Inside Out* is to enlarge students' learning potential by engaging multiple intelligences. Use this index to familiarize yourself with concepts and to round out classroom activities. You can also use this index to individualize lessons according to learning style based on multiple intelligences (see page 36) and to work with specific learning deficiencies.

For One, For All Index

This index allows you to select Exercises and Extensions based on different student configurations:

- Individual Students
- Independent Research
- Student Pairs
- Cooperative Groups
- Whole Class

Some activities are designed primarily for the individual student; for example, creating a shape poem and keeping a feelings journal. Some activities have students do independent research by going to the library or interviewing others. Another set of activities focuses on student pairs; for example, peer tutoring and mirroring a partner's movements. The category for small cooperative groups includes activities such as invention teams and human machines. Many activities involve the entire class; for example, full-body orchestras and synchronized movement in patterned formation. Independent Research includes any activity that requires extra research by the students, independent of the teacher.

Time and Activity Planner

This index lists Exercises and Extensions under the following categories:

- Beginning of the Year
- Quickies (15 minutes or less)
- About an Hour
- Bulletin Boards
- Field Trips
- Entire Units
- Ongoing or Reusable Activities
- End of the Year

Do you ever find yourself with 10 minutes to spare during the school day and wish you could use it wisely? Try the Quickies section of this index to fill, not kill, extra time. Some of the listings refer to an entire Exercise or Extension, while others refer to one aspect of a multiple-part activity. The Ongoing or Reusable Activities listing refers to projects that extend over time and to teaching tools you can use occasionally, over and over. About an Hour refers to activities that last anywhere from a half hour to a couple of hours, depending on whether you stretch or contract them. Asterisks indicate multiple-part activities that can be spread easily over two or more sessions by subdividing component steps or working in shorter time blocks. Entire Units refers to broader activities than those under About an Hour, though not necessarily as broad as units are traditionally defined. This index also identifies activities that work well at the beginning or the end of the school year.

Special Populations Index

This index lists Exercises and Extensions under the following categories:

- Gifted
- Attention Deficit Disorder
- English as a Second Language

With this index you can access activities for a broad range of student subpopulations. The Gifted category is for challenging students who can handle divergent thinking or higher-order cognition. Attention Deficit Disorder activities draw largely upon multimodal techniques and body intelligence for learning. The list for teachers of English as a

Second Language includes activities that help build vocabulary or contain nonverbal elements from which to anchor verbal cues. There is no category for students with learning disabilities, as these students are such a diverse group. Look at these students in terms of the Multiple Intelligences Profile (see page 73) to discover their specific disability, learning style, and areas of strengths. Then use the Multiple Intelligences index to individualize assignments.

Level Grader Index

The Level Grader index presents three grade-related levels:

- Level I
  (corresponds loosely to grades 4 and 5)
- Level II
  (corresponds loosely to grades 6 and 7)
- Level III
  (corresponds loosely to grades 8 and 9)

If a school district implements *Creativity Inside Out,* it will want to partition the lessons and activities according to developmental levels. This way, students have continuity from year to year without repeating creativity studies. Don't assume activities listed under Level I are too easy for grade 8 or those under Level III are too advanced for grade 4. While certain activities are naturally more basic or advanced than others, you can adapt the majority of them for students at any level.

CREATIVITY CHECKLISTS

Process Checklist	Low				High
Is highly imaginative, thinking rich in detail	1	2	3	4	5
Has originality of ideas	1	2	3	4	5
Notices subtle details	1	2	3	4	5
Has fluency of ideas; sees many possibilities	1	2	3	4	5
Perceives hidden or underlying relationships	1	2	3	4	5
Has flexibility of perspective	1	2	3	4	5
Is nonconforming; does not fear being different	1	2	3	4	5
Modifies, improves, adapts ideas	1	2	3	4	5
Improvises, shows spontaneity	1	2	3	4	5
Shows cleverness or humor	1	2	3	4	5
Has highly developed sensitivity, opinions, or aesthetics	1	2	3	4	5
Derives satisfaction from self-expression	1	2	3	4	5
Applies learning in unusual or unexpected ways	1	2	3	4	5

Motivation Checklist	Low				High
Has interest in challenging self	1	2	3	4	5
Demonstrates curiosity, wants to know why	1	2	3	4	5
Shows interest, energy, and enthusiasm	1	2	3	4	5
Gets excited by new ideas	1	2	3	4	5
Displays diligence and persistence	1	2	3	4	5
Tolerates frustration, overcomes obstacles	1	2	3	4	5
Goes beyond what is taught or required	1	2	3	4	5
Is highly involved in projects, resists interruption	1	2	3	4	5
Initiates own learning	1	2	3	4	5
Is largely inner directed	1	2	3	4	5
Displays independence of thought	1	2	3	4	5

Products Checklist

	Low				High
Prefers new, original ways of doing things	1	2	3	4	5
Is adventurous, takes risks, experiments readily	1	2	3	4	5
Has skill in planning and organizing ideas	1	2	3	4	5
Has high standards of achievement	1	2	3	4	5
Is careful in effort	1	2	3	4	5
Shows depth and detail in products	1	2	3	4	5
Makes good use of environmental resources	1	2	3	4	5
Executes ideas to completion	1	2	3	4	5
Demonstrates unusual skill for developmental level	1	2	3	4	5

Interpersonal Factors Checklist

	Low				High
Cooperates	1	2	3	4	5
Shows leadership skills	1	2	3	4	5
Inspires others easily	1	2	3	4	5
Expresses self honestly and without inhibition	1	2	3	4	5
Has frequent questions or comments	1	2	3	4	5
Communicates ideas effectively	1	2	3	4	5
Makes good use of social resources	1	2	3	4	5
Shows sensitivity in giving feedback	1	2	3	4	5
Response from others is sought and enjoyed	1	2	3	4	5
Readily accepts and learns from feedback	1	2	3	4	5
Displays independence of thought	1	2	3	4	5

UNIT I

Explorations In Inner Space

CREATIVITY BEGINS WITH YOU

YOU ARE UNIQUE
LESSON 1

By identifying differences, we recognize the uniqueness of our perspective and the contributions only we can make. Yet we need common ground to communicate creative ideas and to solve problems together. Appreciation of individuality and healthy respect for others are cornerstones of creative self-expression. "You Are Unique" helps students appreciate their own qualities as both unique and as a source of common ground with others to build self-esteem, cultural pride, and mutual respect. You may want to use this lesson at the beginning of the school year to introduce students to one another. Repeat it periodically to discover new dimensions or deepen understanding. You could also use it to introduce a cross-cultural or multicultural unit.

Preparation

★ Assemble a list of categories as a basis for student comparisons. Possibilities include:

- *Physical features (such as hair length and eye color)*
- *Preferences (such as taste in ice cream and clothes)*
- *Talents and interests (such as piano and baseball playing)*
- *Values (such as love of the outdoors and desire to be rich)*
- *Family background (such as number of siblings and ethnicity)*
- *Broad statements, especially those often taken for granted (such as members of the human race and living on earth)*

★ Provide enough categories for students to get started. Encourage them to develop their own categories as they proceed.

Materials

paper and pen for each pair of students; extra paper, markers, crayons, or other drawing materials

Exercise

(1) Split class into same-sex pairs.

(2) Have each pair select one student to be a recorder. (You might want to suggest a random-selection process, such as having the student wearing the darkest clothes in each pair be the recorder.)

(3) Give pairs 5 minutes to brainstorm as long a list as possible on the topic "How we are the same."

(4) Switch recorders. Give 5 minutes to create a second list: "How we are different."

(5) Allow 10 minutes for students to create a picture, poem, or paragraph to illustrate something unique about their partner.

Three young children in Ecuador.

Discussion

◆ Compare lists and products. Discuss what makes you similar to all others, most others, some others, and no others in the class.

- *Which qualities are outer or visible ones (such as height and hair color)?*

- *Which qualities are inner or invisible ones (such as kindness and sense of humor)?*

◆ What do you do on purpose to be similar to your classmates?

◆ What do you do to stand out and be different?

◆ Which kinds of differences in others attract you? Which kinds make you uncomfortable?

- *In what ways is it important to be similar to others?*

- *In what ways is it important to be different from others?*

◆ What does creativity have to do with our uniqueness?

◆ What is the difference between being creative and just plain being different, when it comes to judging the value of an idea, a piece of writing, a new song, an invention, or a solution to a problem?

Each of us needs to be appreciated for our uniqueness. This builds self-esteem. When we feel good about ourselves, we freely offer our special talents and qualities to others.

Extensions

1a. Meet Me Bulletin Board Arrange a class Meet Me bulletin board. Throughout the year, on a rotating basis, ask individual students to fill the bulletin board with pictures, photos, essays, poems, family recipes—whatever will help the class know them better. Encourage students to include many aspects of their identity, both personal and cultural. You could assign a class photographer to take a photograph of each individual bulletin board and place them in the class annual.

1b. Body Prints Have students make full-size body prints, tracing the outline of a partner's body onto paper. They can fill in the outlines with photographs, magazine pictures, collage materials, or drawings chosen to be self-descriptive. Encourage students to use their imaginations. Involve them in a planning process before they begin. For example, how could they illustrate pictorially the ways they are similar to others and the ways they are unique? Hang body prints and arrange for a structured viewing of them. Brainstorm what students might look for in writing a short essay or poem about their partner that emphasizes what they did not know before.

1c. Library Research of Uniqueness Ask students to use the library to gather as many facts as possible about those things in nature that are considered unique, such as snow- flakes, DNA, fingerprints, zebra stripes, and the platypus. Working in groups of four or five, students might prepare oral presentations on their topics, using visual aids if appropriate.

1d. Guinness Book of World Records Have students use the *Guinness Book of World Records* to assemble a list of what they consider the five most unique and the five silliest achievements listed. Or have them look through *One of a Kind: A Compendium of Unique People, Places, and Things,* by Bruce Felton, to list the five most interesting pieces of trivia. Have students justify their choices.

1e. Adjective Diaries With the class, identify *unique* as an adjective, and adjectives as the part of speech that helps lend uniqueness to descriptions of people and things. Ask students to keep an Adjective Diary for one week, writing down as many adjectives that they hear around them as possible. This Extension should focus on the nature of adjectives, their grammatical use, and their power. Students might follow the format below. Afterward, discuss the use of adjectives as neutral descriptions, judgments, flattery, criticism, praise, or as racist or sexist.

Adjective	Who or What It Was Used to Describe	Student Reaction: Positive, Negative, or Neutral

1f. Comparison of Television Parents

Ask students to compare and contrast two television dads or moms, such as Bill Cosby, Homer Simpson, Roseanne, or the mom on *The Brady Bunch*. Consider using video excerpts of programs in the classroom. Form a list of outer, visible qualities (such as hair and skin color) and inner, invisible ones (such as honesty and stinginess). Ask students how these television parents compare with their own parents. Ask students to describe the ideal parent.

1g. Comparison of World Leaders

Have the class compare and contrast two world leaders who are prominent in the news and look for similarities and differences in how newspapers and other media present these figures. Students might compile a list of adjectives used to describe each of the leaders. They might cut photos or caricatures from newspapers or magazines to study the ways the leaders are visually portrayed.

1h. Imagined Lands

Ask students to write a story about a land where a large or small difference among inhabitants threatens to tear them apart. Encourage them to include a solution to the problem and how it was found. Compare and contrast stories. Discuss them as a metaphor for problems of bigotry, racism, scapegoating, prejudice, sexism, and intolerance. Ask if any solutions apply to problems in their classroom, school, or community. To discuss these issues with younger students, you could read or role-play *The Sneetches,* by Dr. Seuss. Make this Extension more personal by having students draw and discuss the first time they felt different from other people. This can stimulate highly sensitive feelings, such as shame and embarrassment, so handle with care.

1i. Family Folk Art

Most areas of the world have their own forms of folk art. Have students find out where their ancestors come from, then research and report on traditional forms of folk art unique to that area. If possible, students should make or bring in samples, slides, or photographs to make reports come alive.

Folk art can be created anywhere, by anyone.

1j. Unique Styles in Art

Present a series of poems or passages by writers with very identifiable styles (such as e. e. cummings, Vachel Lindsay, and Zora Neale Hurston). This exercise works best when the writing is on a single subject. As a class, analyze what makes each writer unique. Using slides or video excerpts, present a similar lesson with a few of your favorite artists, perhaps Pablo Picasso, Marc Chagall, Henri Rousseau, or Peter Max. (Inexpensive slides are available through the National Gallery of Art. Write to: Publications Service, National Gallery of Art, Washington, DC, 20565 for their free color slide catalogue.) Or select a fairy tale from the library that is illustrated by different artists. Compare and contrast the approach and style of each. This helps students see there is more than one right answer to an illustration problem.

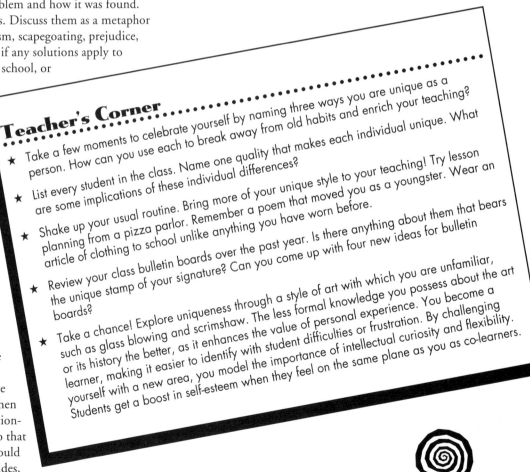

Teacher's Corner

★ Take a few moments to celebrate yourself by naming three ways you are unique as a person. How can you use each to break away from old habits and enrich your teaching?

★ List every student in the class. Name one quality that makes each individual unique. What are some implications of these individual differences?

★ Shake up your usual routine. Bring more of your unique style to your teaching! Try lesson planning from a pizza parlor. Remember a poem that moved you as a youngster. Wear an article of clothing to school unlike anything you have worn before.

★ Review your class bulletin boards over the past year. Is there anything about them that bears the unique stamp of your signature? Can you come up with four new ideas for bulletin boards?

★ Take a chance! Explore uniqueness through a style of art with which you are unfamiliar, such as glass blowing and scrimshaw. The less formal knowledge you possess about the art or its history the better, as it enhances the value of personal experience. You become a learner, making it easier to identify with student difficulties or frustration. By challenging yourself with a new area, you model the importance of intellectual curiosity and flexibility. Students get a boost in self-esteem when they feel on the same plane as you as co-learners.

FINDING YOUR CENTER
LESSON 2

Inner relaxation is central to emotional, physical, and psychological balance. Through inner focus and quiet, we gain access to the still point at the center of the self. From this stillness creative imagination and its expression flows. In "Finding Your Center" students practice deep breathing and relaxation. You use guided imagery to awaken their sensitivity to body cues. Students learn how to focus internally and to free themselves from outside distractions. You introduce the notion of stress and the importance of its relief for a happy, healthy life. Students will use skills practiced in this lesson to actively tap imagination in later lessons. Use the breathing exercise regularly to gain attention and increase receptivity in general. Use relaxation imagery to improve overall concentration, to calm and center students before tests, and to prepare them for creative tasks.

Preparation

★ Read the Exercise.

★ Pick a quiet place to practice the steps for 5 to 10 minutes. First, take cleansing and centering breaths. Then close your eyes, still your body, and progressively relax all of your muscles.

★ Try this for several days in a row, noticing any difficulties you are having.

★ Repeat the relaxation procedure until you feel comfortable with it. Use your experience to anticipate class difficulties.

Materials

the relaxation script (Exercise step 3)

Exercise

1. Guide the class through three cleansing and one centering breaths as follows:

   a. *Let's start by doing a CLEANSING BREATH. Take a very long, deep inhalation through your nose (slowly raise both arms during inhalation). Now exhale slowly through your mouth (slowly lower both arms during exhalation).* (Repeat three times.)

   b. *Now we will do a CENTERING BREATH. Take another very deep inhalation through your nose (slowly raise both arms during inhalation). Hold your breath as long as you feel comfortable (between 5 and 15 seconds; keep arms high in the air). Now exhale sharply through your mouth, making a* whoosh *sound as you do (quickly lower both arms during exhalation).* (Do one time.)

2. Have students practice eye closure. Some students, particularly young ones, those kinesthetically inclined, or those with Attention Deficit Hyperactivity Disorder, will have difficulty keeping their eyes closed in class. If necessary, start with very brief periods of time—a few seconds—and work toward more extended periods—a few minutes. Discuss the impulse to cheat. Remind the class that closing the eyes does not necessarily mean going to sleep. We can be just as alert and awake with eyes closed as with them open.

3. Read the following relaxation script in a slow, steady pace while students sit upright and listen with eyes closed:

   a. *Deep breathing and guided imagery are important ways we can learn to relax, concentrate, and focus better. It is very important to free ourselves from worries and inner chatter. If the mind is still and empty, it is easier to take in new information. Otherwise, it can be like trying to pour liquid into a cup that is already full. If we focus inside ourselves and clear away all distractions, we are also free to open inner eyes, ears, and other senses of our imaginations.*

   b. *Pay attention to your breathing. Do not try to change it, just breathe normally and naturally. (Pause.) As you take the next several breaths, feel your lungs fill up with air. Breathe in very, very deeply . . . then push all the air out of your lungs each time you breathe out. See how much you can slow down your breathing, letting each breath grow longer, slower, and more relaxed than the last. See how completely you can let yourself melt into each breath so nothing else matters except how much you are able to slow down your breathing. Keep slowing down until each breath gets so long you almost have the feeling you could take that breath forever.*

c. *Now, as you breathe in, imagine your whole body is filling with your favorite color. Feel your favorite color moving into every single part of your body. Start at your toes, breathing the colored light into each toe, one at a time, picturing each one clearly in your imagination. Then breathe the colored light through the rest of your feet and into your ankles. Let the light fill your lower legs. Now move it through your knees, relaxing deeper and deeper all the time. Breathe the colored light through your upper leg until both legs are filled completely with the light. Check to make sure all the places already filled with light are still relaxed, right down to your toes. If you want, you can exhale a different color to let go of tension.*

d. *You may notice that your mind wants to wander. That is all right and very natural. Just gently try to bring yourself back to the words and colors again. If you are having some difficulty relaxing, remember this: learning to still the body and relax the mind is an art and a skill. As with any other skill, it takes practice to learn. It should get easier every time you try.*

e. *Move the light through your lower back and stomach now, letting yourself feel lighter and more relaxed with each breath. Fill the top of your back and shoulders with the light as well, letting go of all muscles there. Move the light through your upper arms, your elbows, and right on down through your lower arms. Breathe the light into your hands now, letting it flow into each finger, one at a time, filling all ten with the color. Finally, fill your neck and head with the light as well, even pressing it through every single piece of hair. Now your whole body, from the top of your head to the tip of your toes, should feel light, relaxed, and filled with color. Let yourself enjoy how nice it is to sit very, very still, filled up with such a beautiful light. (Pause.)*

f. *You can use imagery like this yourself, any time you want, to relax at home or just before a scary test. But for now, continue to enjoy these feelings as you prepare to come back to the room again and open your eyes. When you are ready, open your eyes.*

Discussion

◆ What was the hardest thing about sitting still, closing your eyes, focusing inward, and relaxing? What was easiest?

◆ Did your mind wander? How did you bring it back?

◆ Were some parts of your body easier to relax than others?

◆ What is the difference between being still and being relaxed?

◆ What is stress? Is stress always a bad thing?

◆ Can you name some examples of positive tension? (For example, when mild stage fright or test anxiety lead to a good performance, it is positive tension.)

◆ What are some sources of stress in your environment?

◆ How do *you* tend to hold stress in your body?

◆ Why is it important to try to relax completely when you are stressed?

◆ Is it easier to be creative when you are tense or relaxed? Why?

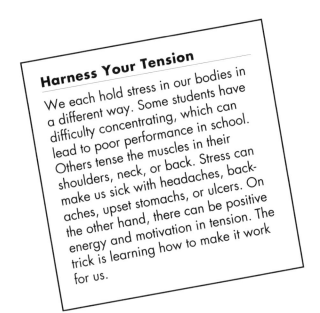

Harness Your Tension

We each hold stress in our bodies in a different way. Some students have difficulty concentrating, which can lead to poor performance in school. Others tense the muscles in their shoulders, neck, or back. Stress can make us sick with headaches, backaches, upset stomachs, or ulcers. On the other hand, there can be positive energy and motivation in tension. The trick is learning how to make it work for us.

Extensions

2a. Still Waters Play this game with younger or Attention Deficit Disorder students. Have the entire class sit as still as possible. Begin by silently tapping the stillest student. Have this student walk around the class, locate and tap the stillest student, then return to his or her seat and rejoin the game. Continue the sequence for a few minutes, as long there is interest and concentration. Remember, in this game even eyeballs count! Discuss the difference between outer and inner stillness. Ask which one students think is more important to relaxation.

2b. Cloud Mobiles With the class, discuss what makes a place or scene relaxing. Have each student draw or paint the most relaxing scenes imaginable on both sides of a precut cardboard (or heavy construction paper) cloud shape. Combine the cloud images of several students into mobiles. Hang them in the classroom for meditation and relaxation. Encourage students to use these or other relaxing scenes in self-guided imagery to calm down before tests or important events.

2c. Calmsters Versus Frenetics Divide the class into two groups: the Calmsters and the Frenetics. Have each group choreograph movements or a dance that reflects the group they are in. The Calmsters should display movements that are slow and controlled, while the Frenetics are fast and chaotic. Form a large circle. Pair one Calmster and one Frenetic at a time to display their movements or dances. Finish with a showdown between the two groups, then reverse the roles. If desired, you or students may choose accompanying music.

One artist's image of a Calmster and a Frenetic

2d. Elevator Music Discuss some places where music is regularly played, such as elevators and shopping malls. Ask students what kind of music is normally chosen. As a class, listen to different kinds of music, such as bluegrass and New Age music. Analyze them for what makes some styles or pieces more relaxing than others. Have students tell you what the music suggests and find movements that fit it. For a multicultural twist use music from other countries, such as African drums and an Indian raga. Ask students which kinds of music they would play in a supermarket when it is busy and they want to hurry customers along, or when it is slow and they want customers to dawdle and buy more items. Think of other situations when you might use music to make the environment more relaxing or stimulating. Play appropriate pieces to make classroom transitions or to help relax students.

2e. Stress Talk Brainstorm expressions in the English language related to stress, tension, and relaxation (such as: "He is a pain in the neck," "What a headache," "I'm as taut as a bow string," "Get off my back"). Ask students to incorporate as many of the expressions as possible into a story about a little boy who was so nervous he just could not relax, and to include a solution that changed the boy's life.

2f. Relax Already! Discuss other ways of reducing stress beside deep breathing and relaxation exercises, such as playing games, sports, and watching a funny show on television. Sometimes children see adults using or abusing alcohol or other substances to reduce stress. As a class, distinguish between healthy and unhealthy ways to relax. Have students, in small groups, make a poster illustrating differences between the two.

2g. Still in There? Investigate degrees of stillness in science. Some things that appear still are not if we take a closer look. Our bodies may be still on the outside, but there is much activity on the inside (our hearts beat, our digestive systems work, and so on). Trees sway in the wind. Even rocks contain a hidden level where atoms in molecules are moving. The earth itself is another example. Watch a time-lapse video of a very slow process that usually appears still, such as a flower growing.

2h. Mechanized Stress Study simple machines, such as a wheel and axle and a fulcrum, that use a still point to do work. Ask students where the points of greatest and least stress are in these and in other more complex machines. Have students use these principles to create machines of their own.

Possible materials include balsa wood, wire, ice cream sticks, plastic foam balls, and cardboard. Together, identify still points and points of least and greatest stress.

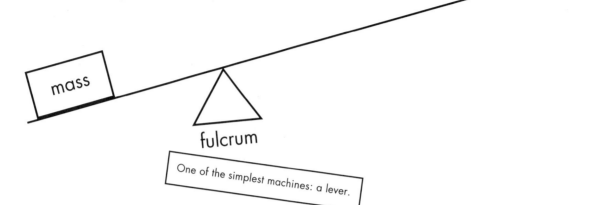

mass

fulcrum

One of the simplest machines: a lever.

2i. Weather You Like It or Not Study different weather patterns related to tension and relaxation, such as high and low pressure systems. Research the still eye of a storm or hurricane. Discuss whether different weather patterns affect the stress level of people. Ask how different weather patterns relate to culture and invention in different parts of the world.

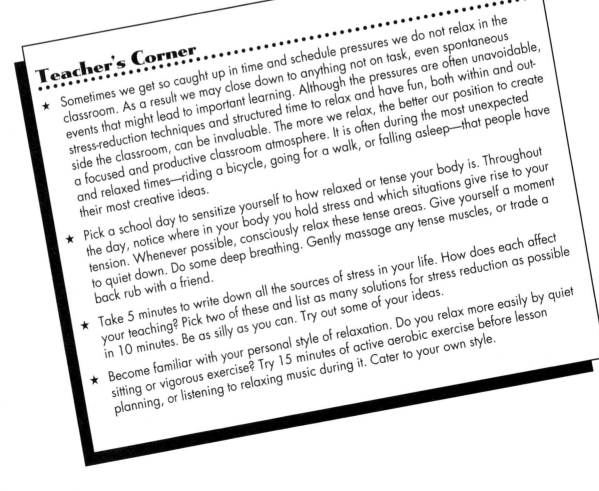

Teacher's Corner

★ Sometimes we get so caught up in time and schedule pressures we do not relax in the classroom. As a result we may close down to anything not on task, even spontaneous events that might lead to important learning. Although the pressures are often unavoidable, stress-reduction techniques and structured time to relax and have fun, both within and out-side the classroom, can be invaluable. The more we relax, the better our position to create a focused and productive classroom atmosphere. It is often during the most unexpected and relaxed times—riding a bicycle, going for a walk, or falling asleep—that people have their most creative ideas.

★ Pick a school day to sensitize yourself to how relaxed or tense your body is. Throughout the day, notice where in your body you hold stress and which situations give rise to your tension. Whenever possible, consciously relax these tense areas. Give yourself a moment to quiet down. Do some deep breathing. Gently massage any tense muscles, or trade a back rub with a friend.

★ Take 5 minutes to write down all the sources of stress in your life. How does each affect your teaching? Pick two of these and list as many solutions for stress reduction as possible in 10 minutes. Be as silly as you can. Try out some of your ideas.

★ Become familiar with your personal style of relaxation. Do you relax more easily by quiet sitting or vigorous exercise? Try 15 minutes of active aerobic exercise before lesson planning, or listening to relaxing music during it. Cater to your own style.

HOW DOODLE YOU DO?
LESSON 3

Scribbles and doodles are common forms of self-expression that are easily overlooked and dismissed. Yet they can be important stepping stones to more serious work. Scribbling gives the class permission to loosen up. Fleshing out scribbles into recognizable forms requires students to work with what they are given, using inner resources to make the most out of a mess. The capacity to transform chaos into order is the creative essence of art as well as science. Both involve using what is available or already known to delve into what is not—to find or make a new order. Improvisation—whether on stage, in music, or everyday life—involves going with the flow, seizing the moment, and risking error. Use this lesson to teach the value of occasional disorder and doodling, of straying from direct goals, and of making mistakes and recovering. Repeat often to loosen up students or to fill in short time cracks.

Preparation

★ Collect and distribute materials.

Materials

large sheets of paper; crayons, felt-tip pens, and/or coffee cans of paint and 1-inch brushes (one per student); lively music (easily turned on and off); pins or tape to hang drawings

Exercise

Choose one or more variation below, or do them in sequence. The first is a good warm-up for the others or for helping the class loosen up before engaging in more serious work.

Variation 1

1. Play Musical Scribble Art. Start the music, and when it starts, have each student start to scribble. Bold strokes work best.

2. Stop the music after 30 to 90 seconds, and have students pass their scribbles to another student, who will spend the rest of the pause observing the work.

3. Start the music again and do a second round, allowing students to add to the scribble art they now have.

4. After a third round, have students return papers to the original artists.

5. Do a final round to put finishing touches on the work.

6. Hang drawings side by side to facilitate discussion.

Variation 2

Do the above exercise with a twist. Have students label the top of their page *Top*. Each time the music stops, rather than pass their sheets on, have students twist their own page a quarter turn clockwise to prepare for the next round. After four turns they will be back to the top. This helps the class learn to fill the entire page. Hang drawings side by side to facilitate discussion.

Variation 3

1. Have each student make three different kinds of scribbles. If possible, select appropriate musical selections.

   - Mad dash doodle *Scribble as if you are in a building that is on fire and madly running around to find a way out. (Provide 30 seconds.)*

   - Slow saunter scrawl *Scribble as if you are strolling around with no particular destination, in a gorgeous meadow on a warm summer's day, taking your time, dawdling, wandering about, and enjoying the sights. (Provide 30 seconds.)*

   - Grasshopper dart *Scribble as if you are a grasshopper being pursued by a butterfly net—hopping in all directions to get away. (Provide 30 seconds.)*

2. Have students label scribble type on the back of each page, then exchange pages with one or more partners.

3. Tell students to take their time with each scribble, opening inner eyes of imagination as they look, until they see something recognizable in the scribble. Once a shape pops out, have students use felt-tip pens or crayons to complete the drawing. Note: Students are bound to work at different speeds, some elaborating in great detail, others simply sketching the idea. Support individual styles and pacing.

4. Hang drawings side by side to facilitate discussion.

Variation 4

Have students make blob art (suggested in *KidsArt,* issue 10, 1988). They first drop a blob of ink on a sheet of white paper. Then they fold or tilt the paper, spreading the ink around in interesting ways. If it is possible in your classroom, students can let the ink run off the edges of the paper. When the ink dries, students finish the artwork by looking at it carefully to see what it suggests to them, then apply contrasting lines with crayons or felt-tip pens to turn it into what they see in the art.

The creative process is often loud, chaotic, ambiguous, and messy. In the classroom, creative self-expression can seem like a big, scary creature who challenges your natural need to keep everything ordered and under control. But remember, this is one beast well worth the struggle.

Discussion

◆ Did this Exercise help loosen you up? How?

◆ What is valuable about loosening up before expressing ourselves creatively?

◆ Which drawings look as if the artists really had fun with them?

◆ Is messiness always a problem? How can it be helpful?

◆ When is it useful to take risks, to be spontaneous, and to take action without worrying what others think or whether we are doing the "right" thing? When can this be a problem?

◆ What is improvisation, and how does it relate to this lesson?

◆ When being creative, why should we stay open to making mistakes or straying from our goals occasionally?

◆ What are some common fears many of us have that prevent us from stepping out and improvising?

◆ At which points do the judgments and reactions of other people interfere with the creative process? When are they helpful?

Improvise

Improvisation is an art form that involves creating and performing on the spur of the moment. Creating with no forethought takes a lot of self-trust. Jazz musicians are famous for improvising solos, playing with the sounds and melodies they hear from fellow performers. Stand-up comics often improvise on material supplied by the audience. They face tremendous risk of looking foolish or having their jokes fall flat.

Extensions

3a. Doodle While You Work
Short doodle lessons make great time fillers! Read or have a student read a poem that contains strong visual imagery, such as "The Highwayman" by Alfred Noyes. Have the rest of the class make doodle drawings while they listen. Hang doodles to compare how they explain and demonstrate features of the poem. Or ask student volunteers to give several-minute impromptu talks on a chosen subject (for example, electricity, hard-boiled eggs, Michael Jackson, democracy). Encourage others to doodle as they listen. Use doodles as the basis for discussion. You can have students do either of these activities in pairs to reduce performance pressure.

The creator of this doodle is a Los Angeles–based educator who travels around the country improvising and teaching kids to doodle in response to serious subjects. Courtesy Jon Pearson.

3b. Doodle Ditty Book
Have students make a Doodle Ditty Book comprised of a running log of doodles, scribbles, and scrawls throughout the day. Or have them put Doodle Ditty pages in Dream Journals (see 4c). Students should date and identify doodles. They can combine doodles with sketches of things they observe; for example, a sketch of their own shoes. Later, they might look at the doodles and sketches of famous artists and scientists, such as Vincent Van Gogh, Leonardo da Vinci, Thomas Edison, and Alexander Graham Bell. Use the "Doodle Digest" sheet (page 14) as a springboard for student imagination. Combine student examples into a class Doodle Digest.

Here is a bare-minimum doodle. What is a bare-minimum doodle? It is one that uses only a few lines to suggest a recognizable form.

3c. Sillier Than Thou
Take a minute or so of class time to let off steam. Have the class all at once act as silly as they possibly can—making faces, unusual sounds, or movements. This is a good way to prepare for more serious work or harness the extraneous energy of overactive students.

3d. Graffiti Fun
Discuss what graffiti is and where and why it appears in the community. Ask students what the difference is between defacement and adornment of public places. Ask if graffiti is ever a positive force. Present examples of graffiti in modern paintings, such as Marcel Duchamp's mustached Mona Lisa, Jean Dubuffet's *Wall with Inscriptions,* and some of the more tasteful works of graffiti artist Keith Haring. Establish a class graffiti bulletin board where anybody can doodle, within appropriate guidelines, as a reward or when the impulse strikes. If desired, relate this bulletin board to a current unit in social studies by making up graffiti that reflects the concerns of people from other eras or cultures under study. Or get permission for students to create a class graffiti or mural made of chalk on a school walkway or outside wall. Take pictures before you wash the doodle art away!

Dada Collage. Gregory Wright, Monochrome No. 1 (detail). Courtesy the artist.

Is this graffiti or art?

3f. Dada Stories Here is a good way to make Dada stories. Have each student supply a single, somewhat uncommon word. Write all the words on the board or distribute them to each student on a sheet of paper. Have students incorporate the entire set into a piece of creative writing. Compare and contrast student stories and essays, and behold how the same ingredients can be combined with such different results.

3e. Dada Posters As a class, study the Dada period of modern art, which included artists Marcel Duchamp, Hannah Höch, and Raoul Hausman. This movement ruptured tradition, sweeping away all artistic principles to date under the banner of anti-art. Tie it in with the historical era in which this movement arose—the chaos following the World War I. Have students make Dadaist-style art or posters using random words, phrases, and sentences combined with pictures cut from magazines and newspapers.

3g. What Do You Mean? Study nonsense poems, such as *The Jabberwocky* by Lewis Carroll. Have students create their own nonsense poems or stories, then trade with others and try to make sense of them. Introduce the concept of *neologisms* into your class, made-up words that have become accepted as legitimate. Play the Neologic Game: Have students work in pairs. One student invents a word, then the other student defines it and uses it in a sentence. Have pairs mix made-up words and their definitions with real ones, trying to stump the rest of the class by passing off a made-up word for a real one.

The Fool

The Fool is an ancient tarot image denoting positive inner forces. In *Free Play*, Stephen Nachmanovitch says the Fool plays a role similar to the wild card in modern card decks, embodying the idea that anything is possible. The Fool represents the spirit of play in myth and literature throughout the world and is allied with the essence of the consciousness of children: acting and speaking freely, without the fear or shame that inhibits many adults.

3h. Bloopers In class, watch a team sporting event, such as basketball and football, and analyze when and how bloopers occur. Or watch a videotape of a blooper show that reveals mistakes and multiple takes in television or film clips. Discuss how the various stars handle their mistakes. Ask students why bloopers make us laugh. Make your own class videotape of bloopers designed to show the value of making mistakes.

3i. Fools Rush In Throughout the world and history, the character of the Fool plays an important role in literature and myth. Do a unit contrasting and comparing the Fool as he appears in various cultures (for example, the Native American gods Trickster and Coyote; the Greek figure Pan; and the jesters, clowns, and buffoons of Renaissance Italy, England, and France). In cooperative groups, have students make up and perform short plays that incorporate some of these figures. Can you find an ongoing role for these characters in your classroom?

Teacher's Corner

★ Many of us are caught in a work ethic that associates productivity with suffering, work with being serious, and play with idleness. Yet history tells us that some of the most brilliant discoveries have occurred when people were not trying, but playing or just fooling around. Gunpowder, the telescope, and the Möbius strip were invented as toys. At least one aeronautic design emerged from spontaneous play with paper airplanes. And plenty of the most creative business environments include recreational facilities to relax and energize their employees.

★ The Greeks understood the close relationship between learning and having fun: their word for education, paideia, was almost identical to the word for play, paidia.

★ Take a moment to reflect upon control versus disorder in your life. Do you always need to have everything in a pre-planned order with details under complete control? Or are you able to tolerate the loud, chaotic confusion that so often accompanies a truly creative experience?

★ Experiment by bringing more of your own silliness and spontaneity into the classroom. Make up a game for learning something new. Improvise. Let yourself get dirty or messy. Make a mistake purposely. Venture into the pit of chaos, fear, and uncertainty in the hopes of re-emerging more creatively.

★ For further inspiration about improvisation in life and art, read *Free Play*, by Stephen Nachmanovitch.

Doodle Digest

Make up a four-line poem about what is going on in the doodle below. Allow yourself to be as silly as possible.

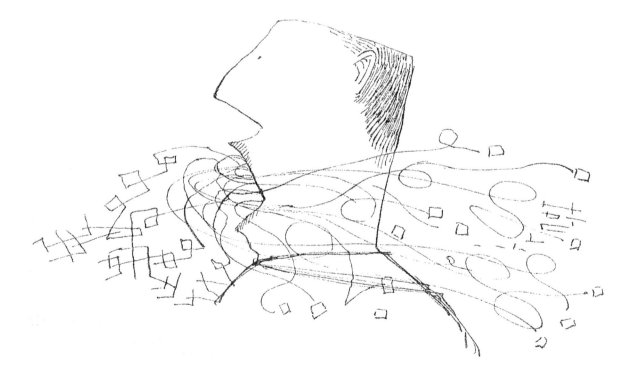

MIND'S "I"
LESSON 4

Perhaps the most extraordinary and distinctive ability humans possess is imagination. We can see, hear, and feel people, places, and future possibilities using inner eyes, ears, and other senses. They allow us to soar across landscapes of our own creation. Imagination often leads to the Aha! experience in discovery. It forms the basis of "in-sight," whether in art, science, or our personal lives. "Mind's 'I'" uses guided imagery to tap the flow of student imagination and to awaken inspiration. Techniques require full-sensory involvement to help sharpen listening skills and facilitate absorption, retention, and comprehension of detail. Students may gain empathy as they visualize themselves in the shoes of another. Use the Exercise to introduce the importance of imagination and Extensions to deepen involvement and understanding of any subject you teach.

Anything is possible in the Mind's "I." From "There's No Place Like Home," The Book / Los Angeles. Levon Parian, *Untitled.*

Preparation

★ Read the Exercise.

★ Set aside 15 to 30 minutes. Pick a quiet place to practice the steps.

★ Use your experience to anticipate areas of class strengths and difficulties; adjust the lesson accordingly.

Materials

guided imagery script (Exercise step 2); a variety of art media (paper, paints, felt-tip pens, and materials for dioramas)

Exercise

(1) Do cleansing and centering breaths to focus class attention (see page 5).

(2) Read the following guided imagery script in a slow, expressive voice while students listen with closed eyes:

a. *Allow yourself to relax as completely as you can, from head to toe. As you breathe deeply, let go of all the tension in your body until you are very, very comfortable. At the same time stay completely alert so you can put all of your attention into an important task—one of the most exciting you can ever do—opening the eyes, ears, and senses of imagination. With inner senses you have the power to experience anything at all, in great detail, no matter how large or small, how real or imaginary. You can remember and re-experience something that happened yesterday, such as a delicious apple you enjoyed. Or you can anticipate something that might happen tomorrow, such as going to a movie. With your mind's eye you can even imagine things that might never happen at all, such planning your own hundredth birthday party.*

b. *Some people see things very clearly using imagination; some people see things fuzzily. Others can hear or feel with their imagination. Let your imagination flow naturally, finding its own course as you listen. Let the part of you that watches just tag along for the ride. Try to open up as many inner senses as possible so you can fully experience all the details. But remember, you are in charge of your experience. If you are uncomfortable or do not want to do something, that is up to you.*

c. *Here we go. Begin by imagining yourself hopping onto a cloud. See its fluffiness. Test out the feeling of weightlessness as you float on the cloud. If you would like, try tasting it to see if the cloud has a flavor. Do some jumps or somersaults if you want to be adventurous. In your imagination, let yourself run and jump and yell. After playing on the cloud for awhile, and only if you feel comfortable and safe, sit in the middle of it, fasten your seat belt, and get ready to drift away. If you do not feel like taking this ride, go to a different place in your mind's eye and join us when you are ready.*

d. *As the cloud rises slowly, it transports you up and up, high above the land. Look at the tiny trees, houses, and roads far below you. Feel the sun on your face and the wind through your hair. It is a wonderful ride. You are being carried toward a special place. The place is special because it is the most beautiful place you can imagine. Let it be a place you have never seen before—one that exists only in the depths of your imagination. Your cloud is ever so slowly arriving now, descending into this place of incredible beauty.*

e. *What is there to explore and discover about this place? Is it in a natural landscape or a city? Is the place indoors or outdoors? What makes it so breathtaking? What kinds of objects or living things are in it? Are there other people or animals? Pay attention to every single detail, from the very smallest to the very largest. (Pause.) Explore every corner. Examine the colors. Notice the weather and the temperature. What sounds can you hear? Are there any smells?*

f. *Although we cannot travel to beautiful places any time we want in real life, we can always visit them in the world of our imagination. We can use our experience to take an inner vacation and feel refreshed or enriched any time we want. We can use places such as this to inspire us to creative expression. Let yourself enjoy your inner place of beauty right now. See, touch, smell, and hear everything you can. (Pause.) When you are ready, hop back on the cloud, return to the classroom, and open your eyes.*

(3) Instruct students to create a poem, letter, fairy tale, painting, picture, or any other art form that best captures and communicates their place of beauty. Encourage them to take their time to decide what creative form their inspiration will take. Artwork does not always spring fully formed from imagination. It needs time to germinate. Help students locate the materials they need. Encourage them to trust their inner sense of what to do, answering questions only when necessary.

(4) Ask students to share one aspect of their experience. They may want to reveal their creations, use words to bring alive their place of beauty, or describe how the guided imagery impacted them.

Discussion

◆ How was this guided imagery experience for you?

◆ Did you tend to see, hear, or sense in some other way the details in your imagination? Was your imagery clear or fuzzy?

◆ Where were you in the scene—in the middle, on the side, completely outside it?

◆ Did your inspiration to create come easily for you, or was the creation process a struggle? Explain.

◆ Was your work of art what you experienced in your mind's eye or ear, or did it take on a life of its own?

◆ How do inner senses of imagination differ from outer senses?

◆ What effects do books, radio, television, and film have on imagination? Which of these media engage the mind's eye? Which do not?

◆ Is guided imagery a useful tool for inspiring creativity? Why or why not?

◆ How can we use more guided imagery in our classroom?

◆ How can we keep the eyes, ears, and other senses of imagination active throughout our lives?

Researchers, such as Dr. Patricia Greenfield at the University of California at Los Angeles, have found that television is less likely to stimulate children's imagination than books or radio. In this cartoon, television brings together people of many different cultures, but at the same time may homogenize ideas at the expense of true cultural diversity.

Extensions

4a. Storybook Fantasy Choose a fairy tale or short story to read to the class. Pick one with many descriptive visual details to stimulate student imagination. Read the story while students close their eyes and listen. Instruct them to engage all their inner senses to vividly imagine the details. Afterward, have students draw their favorite scene from the story. Hang drawings in the order they appear in the story. Review important aspects of the story by moving through the sequence of drawings. Focus on story details as they are pictured in the drawings. Ask students which details of drawings were given in the story. Ask which were supplied by student embellishments. Hang pictures in a completely different sequence to see what new story the order suggests.

4b. Alien Worlds Here is some guided imagery to stimulate a flight of fantasy: "Imagine yourself transported by a beam of light to a very strange and alien planet, different from earth or any place you have ever seen or read about before. Notice all the details you possibly can. Is there life? If so, what form does it take? Is the culture advanced? What is the atmosphere like? What colors are around? What does it feel like there? What does it smell like?" Include other questions to prompt the imagination for details. Afterward, ask students to draw something from the planet they visited. Or ask them to design a science project or experiment that involves some feature of planet's surface or interior composition.

4c. Dream Journals Have students create Dream Journals by drawing and writing about daydreams, fantasies, nighttime dreams, and other images from their imaginations. They may add to journals on a regular basis throughout the year. Have students use entries to inspire thoughts, poems, fiction and science fiction writing, or illustrations for creative writing assignments. Or they may act them out in dramas. The class can read Maurice Sendak's *In the Night Kitchen* for inspiration.

4d. Fantastic Voyage (Or "Honey, I Shrunk Myself") Use guided imagery for visualizing human or plant biology. Begin by asking students to imagine themselves shrinking smaller and smaller until they are microscopic size. They are to enter the body of a plant or person through a pore, the mouth, the ear, or another opening. Read or make up vivid descriptions of anatomy to send students on an inner voyage. *The Magic Schoolbus: Inside the Human Body,* by Joanna Cole, is a good reference. Send the class climbing over organs, swimming in the circulatory system, or riding on a red blood cell through the respiratory system. Ask students to draw aspects of their experience afterward. Make sure they include themselves in drawings!

4e. The Aha! Experience Have students work in groups to do library research on scientists who have made important discoveries through the inner eyes of imagination. Examples include Jonas Salk, who invented the polio vaccine after taking an imaginary voyage through the bloodstream; Albert Einstein, who discovered the theory of relativity after he imagined himself riding on a beam of light; and Friedrich Kekulé, who discovered the chemical structure of the benzene ring following his daydream of a snake dancing around and swallowing its own tail.

4f. Time Machine Here is some imagery to bring alive any history lesson: "In your mind's eye get out of your chair, walk out of the classroom, and go to the playing field outside of our school. Somewhere in the field you will find an odd-looking machine, unlike any you have ever seen before. As you approach it, notice the knobs and pipes sticking out of it. There is a curtain in the front you can open to get inside. Look for the control panel. You are in a time machine that can take you to anywhere, to any era, past or future. Right now, let us set the dials for the date _____ and the place _____." Pick out a small detail for students to use as a vantage point. For example, students can experience the topography and culture of the early American frontier as a spoke on a wagon wheel, or as a feather in the headdress of an Indian chief. Then read or make up vivid descriptions of important events or historical places while the class visualizes with eyes closed. Afterward, ask students to draw or write about their experiences. Compare drawings with photographs or art from the period.

4g. Identity Scrambler Use a version of Time Machine imagery (see 4f) to enhance student empathy for people in current events or history. Ask students to enter the Identity Scrambler which, if you wish, could be a section of the time machine. Tell students to use the control panel to program the name of the person they will be and where and when in history they will go. Once students have adopted their new identities and transported themselves, read or make up passages concerning this person using the second person (the "you" form) while students listen, tuning in all their senses as if directly participating. Have them write about their experiences in first person (using the "I" form). Use a variation of this Extension to deepen understanding and empathy for what it is like to be a different race, sex, or culture.

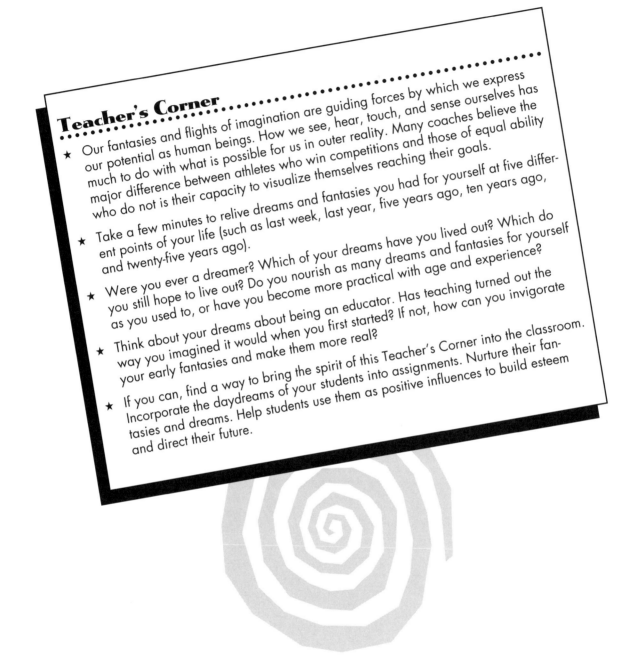

Teacher's Corner

★ Our fantasies and flights of imagination are guiding forces by which we express our potential as human beings. How we see, hear, touch, and sense ourselves has much to do with what is possible for us in outer reality. Many coaches believe the major difference between athletes who win competitions and those of equal ability who do not is their capacity to visualize themselves reaching their goals.

★ Take a few minutes to relive dreams and fantasies you had for yourself at five different points of your life (such as last week, last year, five years ago, ten years ago, and twenty-five years ago).

★ Were you ever a dreamer? Which of your dreams have you lived out? Which do you still hope to live out? Do you nourish as many dreams and fantasies for yourself as you used to, or have you become more practical with age and experience?

★ Think about your dreams about being an educator. Has teaching turned out the way you imagined it would when you first started? If not, how can you invigorate your early fantasies and make them more real?

★ If you can, find a way to bring the spirit of this Teacher's Corner into the classroom. Incorporate the daydreams of your students into assignments. Nurture their fantasies and dreams. Help students use them as positive influences to build esteem and direct their future.

WHEN YOU LOOK, DO YOU SEE?
LESSON 5

Good observation skills involve breaking away from the narrow focus of tunnel vision; it is easy to complain of a bad memory when we have not paid attention to what was going on in the first place. The ability to take in seemingly unimportant and hidden details is central to both learning and the creative process. In art, the ability to notice and incorporate small details brings productions alive. Frequently in science the slight glitch from the expected becomes the key to an experiment. Many of the most important creative discoveries were born of happenstance combined with the ability to notice and interpret small details. "When You Look, Do You See?" is about observation skills and the importance of paying attention to everything that happens around us, whether part of the lesson plan or not. Use this lesson to increase general alertness and enhance observation skills, including attention to and retention of detail.

Preparation

★ Read the Exercise.

★ Find someone from outside your classroom willing to participate in a staged event at a prearranged time.

★ Ask your assistant to dress as follows:
- *Wear two or three unusual pieces of clothing, such as a scarf, a funny hat, and a T-shirt with an interesting message.*
- *Do not wear a piece of essential clothing; for example, a shoe or sock.*
- *Carry something unusual; for example, a fishbowl or monkey wrench.*

★ On the day of the event, before students arrive, place something unusual, such as a bedroom slipper, somewhere in the classroom. Review the Exercise with your assistant for final preparation.

Materials

an assistant; two unusual objects; one "Observation Skills Questionnaire" per student (page 23); pens or pencils

Exercise

1. Have the assistant enter your classroom at the pre-arranged time, in the middle of a lesson or study period, carrying the unusual object.

2. Listen to the assistant apologize for the interruption, then say something slightly bizarre, such as "I'm on the way to Kalamazoo," before requesting a minute of your time.

3. Play along as the assistant walks up to you, whispers something briefly in your ear, then turns as if to leave.

4. Watch the assistant leave the object he or she brought somewhere in the room, pick up the other object you have planted, and walk out with it.

5. Act as if nothing unusual occurred, and immediately resume your lesson.

6. Sometime later in the day, hand out an "Observation Skills Questionnaire" to each student.

7. Provide 5 to 10 minutes for students to complete the questionnaires.

8. Use responses as the basis for the Discussion.

Discussion

◆ How many students realized something unusual was going on?

◆ Did anyone talk about the event to anybody else?

◆ Was it easy or difficult to remember all the unusual details about what the assistant wore, said, and did?

◆ What stops people from really paying attention to what happens around them?

◆ Often we look without really seeing, and hear without really listening. What do you think the difference is between looking and seeing? Between hearing and listening?

◆ Can you name some times and situations where noticing small details is critically important?

◆ Why do witnesses to unusual events often relate completely different versions of what was seen?

◆ Are we more likely to tune out surrounding detail in places where we spend the most or the least time? Why is that?

◆ How does paying attention and noticing details relate to learning? To the creative process?

◆ How are good observation skills important throughout life?

5b. Making the Familiar Unfamiliar Send students equipped with a note pad to visit a familiar place. Ask them to look around extremely carefully. After 10 minutes have them sketch or note as many aspects and details of their surroundings as they can that they have never noticed before. Have students then either make a piece of art inspired by their observations or write an essay about making the familiar unfamiliar. Study the French impressionism movement of modern art, which was an attempt to see things in new ways by paying great attention to sensory information.

Often we grow so preoccupied with our thoughts and concerns that we blind our senses. As with the young woman in this cartoon, we look without really seeing. To really be responsive to the world around us, we must convince those guards to unlock the doors of perception.

Extensions

5a. Where Am I? Take your students to a room other than your classroom and give them paper and pencils. Ask a series of questions concerning details about your classroom. For example: "How many windows panes are in there? Can you name all the plants in the room? Name three objects with very bright colors. What is the smelliest thing in the room? Name as many things as you can that hang on the walls. What is the softest thing in the room? What is the coldest thing?" Use this Extension in the beginning of the school year to help students get to know the classroom better, later in the year to demonstrate how we pay little attention to places where we spend the most time, or after any class outing to hone observation skills.

Impressionism

Impressionism began in France in the 1860s and 1870s with artists such as Edgar Degas, Auguste Renoir, and Claude Monet. The paintings were truly avant-garde, breaking from tradition—the artists invented new painting methods. The style captured the way things appear to the senses at the instant when light falls fleetingly across a subject. Artists frequently painted the same subject over and over again, under different lighting conditions.

The movement's name derived from an early seascape of Monet's called *Impression: Sunrise*. A contemporary art critic first used the term to criticize Monet, calling his paintings sketchy and less finished than a piece of wallpaper. Due to this lack of acceptance, Monet's early work is quite scarce—not because he did not paint much, but because he was so poor he had to use the same canvases over and over.

Mary Cassatt joined the Impressionists in 1877, claiming that a soft pastel painting by Degas changed her life (he later became her teacher). At a time when it was frowned on as an occupation for women, she was able to pursue her career as an artist because she was independently wealthy. She was instrumental in gaining early acceptance of the Impressionists' painting in the United States through her social contacts with rich private collectors. Although she painted in the style of fellow Impressionists, the subjects for her drawings, prints, and paintings were women and children. Cassatt's painting *The Bath* reflects her debt to her colleagues Degas and Monet.

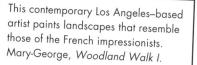

This contemporary Los Angeles–based artist paints landscapes that resemble those of the French impressionists. Mary-George, *Woodland Walk I*.

5c. Candid Camera Have students use cameras to capture spontaneous events or unusual moments and make a photographic essay of such moments. Have a Candid Camera Photography Show in class, for parents or the school, that displays a few of each student's photographs. You and students could also use video equipment. Try putting the video camera on freeze frame. Use the zoom lens. Search for unusual detail.

5d. Making the Familiar Mysterious As a class, read a mystery or watch one on television, film, or video. Discuss the importance of observation skills in solving mysteries. Analyze real clues as well as the false clues meant to distract the reader or viewer. Have students write a mystery story about a familiar place. Be sure they include clues, perhaps false directions along the way, and the solution (unless it remains deliberately unsolved). Students could include a drawing or photograph that contains the solution, or a clue to it, hidden somewhere within a detail of the picture.

5e. What's Wrong with This Picture? Use purposeful misspelling or incorrect answers throughout the day. See how many errors students can catch. Keep a list. For cooperative education, play in groups. If you are doing a social studies or science unit, draw pictures with details that are missing, incorrect, or out of time or sequence. For example, you might show George Washington wearing a digital watch. Using the "What's Going on Here?" sheet (page 24), ask students to find unusual details in the two paintings. Have students draw their own set of pictures, challenging each other to find omissions, errors, and incongruities in detail.

5f. Now You See It, Now You Still Do! Pick a series of three or four photographs from a different era or culture. Use social studies textbooks, magazines, slides, or out-of-date calendars. Photographs should range from relatively simple, with few elements, to more complex and rich in detail. Have students scrutinize one photograph at a time for several minutes, then remove it from sight. Ask four or five questions about each picture, moving from easier and more obvious details to more difficult and obscure ones. Or have students create drawings, character sketches, or short stories that incorporate what they saw. This works well as part of a multicultural lesson. For a real challenge, use two pictures at once. Remove them and then contrast and compare cultures on similar dimensions, such as clothes, coloration, and objects shown. Turn this into a game by assigning students to groups that compete to remember details.

5g. Exploring the Deep See Try the same kind of activity as in 5f using photographs or diagrams related to a current science unit. For example, students could study a diagram of parts of a flower or an engine. Remove the diagram and ask them to draw it from memory. Try a live variation by using plants, leaves, or other things from nature. Have students study and observe these objects, then try to draw or describe them after you have hidden them. Or plant thematic science clues around the room; for example, five different ores or elements. At the end of the day, have the class guess the theme.

5h. A Chancy Event Analyze Louis Pasteur's aphorism, "Chance favors the prepared mind." Study the role of chance, synchronicity, and good observation skills in discovery and invention. Have students report individually, or dramatize in groups, famous instances of unexpected observations leading to major findings. Examples include accidental discoveries of penicillin in 1929 by Alexander Fleming and X rays in 1895 by Wilhelm Roentgen. One good resource is *Great Lives: Invention and Technology* by Milton Lomask.

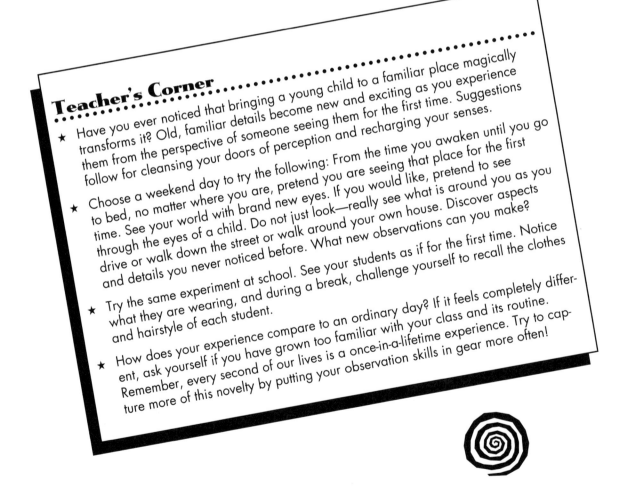

Teacher's Corner

★ Have you ever noticed that bringing a young child to a familiar place magically transforms it? Old, familiar details become new and exciting as you experience them from the perspective of someone seeing them for the first time. Suggestions follow for cleansing your doors of perception and recharging your senses.

★ Choose a weekend day to try the following: From the time you awaken until you go to bed, no matter where you are, pretend you are seeing that place for the first time. See your world with brand new eyes. If you would like, pretend to see through the eyes of a child. Do not just look—really see what is around you as you drive or walk down the street or walk around your own house. Discover aspects and details you never noticed before. What new observations can you make?

★ Try the same experiment at school. See your students as if for the first time. Notice what they are wearing, and during a break, challenge yourself to recall the clothes and hairstyle of each student.

★ How does your experience compare to an ordinary day? If it feels completely different, ask yourself if you have grown too familiar with your class and its routine. Remember, every second of our lives is a once-in-a-lifetime experience. Try to capture more of this novelty by putting your observation skills in gear more often!

Name _____ Date _____

Observation Skills Questionnaire

Something odd happened in the classroom earlier today. Try to remember this event in as much detail as possible when you answer each question below.

1. What time did this event take place?

2. Describe what the person was wearing and then draw it in the space below. Include as many details as possible.

3. Was anything missing from the person's outfit?

4. Draw what the person carried into your room.

5. What did the person say while in your room?

6. Did the person do anything unusual before leaving the classroom?

Name _____ Date _____

What's Going on Here?

Study each of the paintings below. List as many details as possible that appear unusual to you, missing, or out of place. What effect do these details have overall on the painting?

Joan Lehman, *Absent Entrances* (top), *Poupée Palais* (bottom).

PUT YOURSELF ON THE CEILING
LESSON 6

A situation can look very different from different points of view. The ability to see the world from multiple perspectives provides fuel for and sources of inspiration and is an essential ingredient of social intelligence, especially empathy. The process involves seeing experiences through another person's eyes so we can appreciate cultural, racial, personal, and sexual differences. "Put Yourself on the Ceiling" is an exercise in understanding perspective; it links guided imagery with perceptual, spatial, and social skills. Students become better oriented to their surroundings by using imagery to explore them from many vantage points. Use this lesson toward the beginning of the school year to acquaint students with your classroom. Use it throughout the year to explore new environments or to increase sophistication and widen a vantage point for any subject.

Preparation

★ Read the guided imagery script (Exercise step 4).

★ Change the script by adding details that apply to your classroom.

★ Make drawings of the same object from two, three, or even four different perspectives.

Materials

guided imagery script; construction paper; drawing materials, such as colored pencils, markers, crayons, and paints; tape or pins to display drawings

Exercise

1. To help students with the imaginary journey they are about to take, allow them to make a thorough visual inspection of the classroom. Encourage them to walk around the room and carefully look from every angle at their surroundings.

2. After students return to their seats, distribute the drawing materials.

3. Do a few cleansing and centering breaths to focus attention (see page 5).

4. Ask students to close their eyes and listen as you read the guided imagery script that follows. Add detail as you go.

   a. *Sit as comfortably as you can. Let your body feel relaxed, and let go of any tension. Let your mind become focused and clear of distractions. If you notice yourself feeling a little tense or preoccupied, you could try this: collect all of your stress and distracting thoughts. Put them in a basket. Tie the basket to a balloon, and let the balloon float away.* (Pause.) *Now open your inner eyes, ears, and all the other senses of your imagination to get ready for our journey.*

   b. *Picture yourself getting out of your chair, walking to the center of the classroom, and clearing out an area large enough for you to lie down on your back. Look up and really notice what the room looks like from this point of view.* (Pause.) *In your imagination, feel yourself growing smaller and smaller until you are the size of a mouse. As this tiny mouse, explore every corner of the room, crawling under and over the furniture. How do you feel encountering different things in the room? Do you notice anything that you might not if you were your normal size? Spend a couple of minutes exploring the room from this perspective.* (Pause.) *Let yourself get into what it is like to be looking up and around from the point of view of a mouse. Look under all the things you would not be able to if you were your ordinarily size.*

   c. *Now, in your mind's eye, return to the center of the room. Look down at your feet. Perhaps you will find they are growing suction cups on the bottoms that allow you to walk right up the walls, as a fly can. Or if you feel more comfortable staying right side up, you might find springs on your feet and a suction cup landing mechanism on your head. Pick a wall to walk up, or a spot on ceiling to spring up to. However you get there, find the most interesting spot on the ceiling. Remember, you don't have to do this at all if you don't want to. Also remember that imagination is made up of pure fantasy, so we can try new things and still stay safe.*

   d. *Once you have gotten to that special point on the ceiling, try to get comfortable there. Spend some time examining the room from this point of view. Take a couple of minutes to explore.* (Pause.) *Notice all the details you can. What does it look like? Pay attention to everything, no matter how small or unimportant it may seem. How do things look different from when you were exploring through the eyes of a fly? After you have examined the whole room, walk back down the wall and return to the center of the room. Lie down again on your back. Feel the suction cups or springs fall off your feet. Experience yourself growing back to your regular size. Now this transformation is complete, and you are your normal self again. Walk back to your desk and sit down, knowing that even though you are yourself again, you are really an expanded you, carrying inside you new points of view that help to enrich your life. When you are ready, open your eyes.*

(5) Have students either use two different pieces of paper or divide one piece into halves to make two drawings.

(6) Have students pick something in the room to draw from two points of view: one from the perspective of a mouse on the floor looking up and one from the perspective of a fly on the ceiling looking down. Let students with difficulty visualizing crawl around on the floor or stand on tables to assist them with their drawings.

(7) Showcase and compare drawings. Notice differences in perspectives.

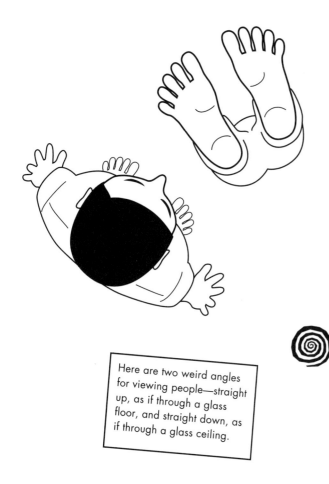

Here are two weird angles for viewing people—straight up, as if through a glass floor, and straight down, as if through a glass ceiling.

Discussion

◆ Can you describe your experiences during this Exercise?

◆ What was it like to be a mouse on the floor?

◆ How was it different to be a fly on the ceiling? Was that scary?

◆ Did you like taking the journey into different eyes, or do you prefer staying in your own point of view?

◆ How does what we see depend upon where we stand and what our point of view is?

◆ How would a tree look different from the perspectives of an ant versus a giant?

◆ What are other examples of the same object or situation looking very different from two contrasting points of view?

◆ Why is it important to be able to see the same thing from many different angles or points of view?

◆ How is it useful to be able to put ourselves in the shoes of other people (an ability called *empathy*)?

◆ What does it take to appreciate people who are culturally different from us?

◆ In what ways is empathy a creative act?

◆ What does creativity have to do with understanding multiple perspectives?

Extensions

6a. Weird Angles Play a game called Weird Angles. Have each student draw a simple or familiar object from an unusual perspective so that it is difficult to tell what it is. For example, when viewed straight on, a comb might look like a row of dots. Have students show their drawings while the class guesses what it is intended to be. You could also carry this out as a photography assignment. Make a Weird Angles Gallery to showcase these unusual perspectives. Try translating this game to words, with each student taking three or four sentences to describe an event or scene from an unusual perspective, such as watching a baseball game from underneath the bleachers. Let others guess what is being described and from what vantage point.

6b. Fan-Fold Pictures Have students make fan-fold pictures with two viewing perspectives. Have them draw and color two 9-by-12-inch pictures depicting two views of the same scene, oriented with the 12-inch side vertical. Possibilities include the same scene viewed in summer and winter or before a war and after. Intense colors work best. Have students lightly draw vertical lines 1 inch apart across the face of both pictures and carefully cut the paper into nine strips. A paper cutter insures sharp, straight edges. Have students orient a piece of 18-by-12-inch construction paper so the 12-inch side is vertical. Show them how to glue their strips side by side, alternating between the pictures, moving from left to right on both. Let the glue dry before having students fan-fold their pictures. Have a Fan-Fold Gallery so others can walk around pictures to see how their perspective changes.

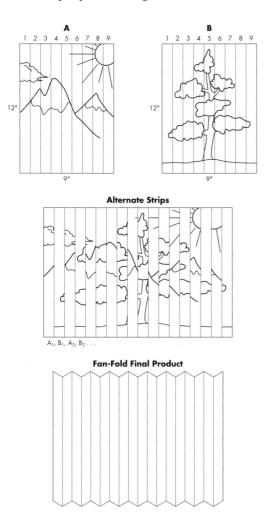

Alternate Strips

A₁, B₁, A₂, B₂ . . .

Fan-Fold Final Product

6c. Same Object, Different Angles Have students create a photographic essay that consists of shooting the same object from different perspectives. Or have students draw the same object from different angles. They might arrange photographs or drawings in a sequence meaningful to the shift in perspective. For inspiration, look at the photo collages of artist David Hockney. Add student creations to your Weird Angles Gallery (see 6a).

6d. Cinderella's Slipper Pick a children's story, such as *Cinderella,* and have students consider it from different points of view; for example, as one of the step sisters, a rat turned into a horse, or the lost slipper. Have each students choose a favorite story and rewrite it from one or more points of view different from the original.

6e. One Trait, Many Takes Have students pick one important characteristic they possess and write an essay describing the trait from their own point of view. Then have them describe the trait through the eyes of two very different perspectives, as in that of a friend, parent, dentist, or stranger. They should pick a characteristic that looks very different to different people. For example, a sense of humor can be fun to have, make a child a hero to a friend, and a trouble-maker to a teacher. If necessary, prepare the class by discussing what traits are and assembling lists of traits.

6f. Sharing Perspectives Place a student in the center of a class circle. One at a time, let other students say "I like (name) because . . ." sharing one positive trait. Students could touch the center person, or someone else with a related perspective, as they present their perspective, thereby making a concrete clustering. Switch the center student and repeat. Take as many sessions as needed for every student to receive feedback. Record and transcribe statements so each student gets a permanent copy. With older or emotionally mature students, pair students, having each share how they imagine their partner to perceive them. This can be a wonderful way for students to discuss uncomfortable feelings with one another. This task can elicit strong emotion, so be sure to create a supportive and safe environment if you try this.

6g. Through Each Other's Eyes Pair students of different cultures, backgrounds, or religions. Have them interview one another to find out about different customs and traditions. Have each student write a short story or essay about some aspect of the culture they have just learned about. Ask them to write from two perspectives: through the eyes of someone in that culture, and through the eyes of a child from a different culture who visits this culture. Students should describe an event or custom and how the experience, reactions, and feelings differed between these two individuals. Use the assignment as a basis for discussing what happens when people of two different cultures come into contact with one another, or as a way for students to get acquainted at the beginning of the school year.

6h. Same Terrain, Different Niches Pick a geographical area that is rich in plant and animal life. Have the class study and describe the area from the perspective of two or more animals (or plants) that occupy different ecological niches. Students may write the descriptions in first person and should include the following: who is friend, who is foe, what there is to eat, and what the shelter looks like. For example, the same small segment of ocean will look very different to marine life that occupy different depths. Diagrams or drawings may accompany descriptions. For a related activity, have students draw different kinds of terrain or animals from radically different viewpoints. It works best to emphasize contrasts, such as high and low, big and small. For example, students could draw the jungle from the point of view of a snake and a bird. For even greater sophistication, study the sensory systems of different animals, such as compound vision in a fly, enhanced sense of smell in a dog, and sonar capabilities of a bat. Then have students describe the same event from the vantage point of two or more animals with different sensory systems. For a touch of humor, use the "It's a Dog-Eat-Dog World" sheet (page 29) to explore what our human world might look like from a dog's perspective.

6i. Paradigm Shifts Study differences in perspective on the earth as science has advanced. For example, people went from viewing the earth as flat to round once they sailed around it. Some astronauts have seen the earth from space. How do students imagine that has influenced their perspective on things? Students could compare views of the earth as seen through the eyes of inhabitants from three different eras; for example, a prehistoric being, who may not have contemplated the edges of the earth; a twelfth-century farmer, who believed the earth was flat; and a twentieth-century astronaut, who viewed the earth from outer space. You could culminate the assignment with a fourth perspective, that of earth and the surrounding universe as viewed from someone imagined in the twenty-third century.

Paradigms

A paradigm is a set of assumptions about our universe and how it is constructed or operates. Paradigms may be based on naive assumptions or the latest scientific theory. In *The Structure of Scientific Revolutions*, Thomas Kuhn argues that our models of the universe often change suddenly when a new piece of scientific evidence shifts our perspective. Some people believe that no paradigm is "truer" than the next—each holds only for a limited perspective or set of facts; each is only a model, useful from within its own framework, with no one model, no matter how good, ever capturing the whole truth.

6j. What a War Pick a war or other major world event and study it from radically different perspectives. For example, in 1990 President Sadam Hussein of Iraq invaded adjacent Kuwait and led his people into war despite slim

chances of success. Students could place themselves in the one following positions: President Hussein, an Israeli child, an Iraqi soldier, an American child whose mother went to war, a Palestinian servant living in Kuwait, or a Kurdish tribesman. Students could collect facts about the event from a social studies or history unit to write about it from each position.

Teacher's Corner..............

★ Read a book written from a perspective radically different from you own, or visit a place extremely unlike your familiar surroundings.

★ Think back to your own perspective as a child. Who was the best teacher you had in elementary school? What did this person do? How did you feel? Now remember the worst teacher you had. Why did you feel as you did? As an educator, what lessons can you learn both from the positive and negative role models in your early experience?

★ Try visualizing two people you admire most. Close your eyes and imagine yourself, one at a time, stepping into the shoes of each. Then visualize each stepping into your role as educator. Take several moments to brainstorm contributions each could make to your classroom. Find ways to use these contributions in your teaching.

★ Close your eyes and visualize two students with whom you get along extremely well. Imagine yourself in the shoes of each. From each of their perspectives, write down how you view the teacher and your relationship with the teacher.

★ Visualize two students with whom you are currently having conflict. Imagine yourself in the shoes of each, writing down qualities of the teacher and how you view problems in the teacher-student relationship.

★ Return now to your own perspective. What new insights can you use from this activity to increase your effectiveness with each problem student and the class?

Name _____ Date _____

It's a Dog-Eat-Dog World

In the cartoons below, J. T. Steiny shows us some examples of what our human world might look like from a dog's point of view. Look at each cartoon carefully and describe on the back of this sheet what makes it so funny. Then draw some examples of your own .

Dog Eat Dog

A

WILL SLEEP ALL DAY FOR FOOD AND SHELTER

B

Tattletail

C

Dog Food

NO ANIMAL TESTING

D

BAXTER

E

SIT

F

SIGN IN AND BE COUNTED
LESSON 7

Our names are fundamentally tied with our identities. Over and over we use our names in the form of signatures to prove our existence, to take credit for original work, or to exchange money, goods, and property. We borrow prestige associated with the words and names of others when we quote them or wear their names on clothes and other products. In "Sign In and Be Counted" students capitalize on the power of their own names by making works of art from signatures. The lesson also touches the significance of labels. You discover the benefits of considering each student in terms of his or her unique learning style as an alternative to labeling. Use this lesson to build pride and esteem and to focus on the power of a name, whether in dictating trends, distinguishing authentic art work from forgeries, or legitimizing contracts, treaties, or laws.

Preparation

★ Read the Exercise variations, and choose an appropriate project for your class. Provide structure and direction for younger students but greater freedom of choice for older or more mature students.

Materials

For Variation 1

large pieces of construction paper; pencils; yardsticks; crayons or felt-tip pens; carbon paper or mirrors (optional); yarn, glue, cloth, and tissue paper (optional embellishments)

For Variation 2

pipe cleaners or clay; for a real challenge, try long balloons or wire (coat hangers) twisted into shape using pliers; cloth, buttons, twigs and leaves, thread or yarn (optional embellishments)

Exercise

Variation 1: Signature Bugs

Signature bugs are two-dimensional creatures made when students sign their name in large, bold script, draw the mirror image of their signature, and artistically embellish the two signatures. Signature bugs are recommended for practicing script or teaching symmetry. They are also a good project for classrooms with limited resources.

1. Have students fold construction paper in half lengthwise.

2. Along one side of the crease, have them write their signatures in large script with heavy dark crayon.

3. Have them refold the paper and rub firmly to transfer a mirror image of the signature across the center crease. Or students can use carbon paper to transfer the image. For more advanced classes, have students try mirrors or free-hand mirror writing to transfer the mirror image of signatures across the center crease.

4. Have students turn the paper vertically and decorate the results to make interesting creatures.

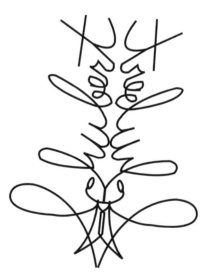

Variation 2: Signature Animals

Signature animals are three-dimensional sculptures made from signatures.

1. Have students use materials of choice to twist, shape, or construct a three-dimensional version of their signatures

2. Let them add legs and other features. They can embellish the animals if desired.

Other Variations

You might have the class try mosaic ashtrays or trivets with tiled names; embroidery or needlepoint; felt name banners; names on pot holders; names sequined or painted onto lunch pails or cans for storing pencils or knickknacks; or stained-glass name patterns.

Discussion

◆ What are ways we use our signatures in everyday life?

◆ Have you ever met someone else with your exact name? How did you feel?

◆ Why are names so important, or are they?

◆ What determines your identity? How important is your name to it?

◆ What are other aspects of an individual's basic identity?

◆ What about labels—how do they relate to names? When are they useful? When are they harmful?

◆ Why do some people forge the signature and work of others?

◆ When is borrowing from other people's work okay? When is it not?

◆ Why do students sometimes forge a sick note from their parents?

◆ Why do we like to wear someone else's name on our clothes; for example, Michael Jordan sneakers, Jordache jeans, and Gucci handbags?

◆ Why do some people like to name drop?

◆ Are you impressed when someone you know knows someone famous?

◆ What are better ways to build our self-esteem than forging, borrowing, or dropping someone else's name?

Our Many Identities

Our identity is our basic sense of who we are and how we define ourselves. Our names form a fundamental part of personal and cultural identity: they speak of our family heritage, yet distinguish us from everybody else. Our roles (teacher, mother or father, student, sister or brother) are an important part of our identities. Some people define themselves primarily by what they do; others by their relationships; others by their state of being. Personal upset and unhappiness can come from shame or confusion surrounding personal, cultural, or sexual identity. Children need support from adults for their unique interests and avenues of creative expression to form solid identities and pride.

Extensions

7a. Designer Clothes Buy or bring in plain T-shirts or jumpsuits. Let students decorate them with signatures or initials that are painted, air-brushed, sequined, embroidered, or stenciled on the material. Or have students cut stencils from heavy-duty freezer wrapper. Iron the stencils onto shirts and apply paint with a sponge, a paintbrush, or an old toothbrush (to splatter the paint). Or have students make a designer label, using their own names, out of cloth or leather. They could remove the label on current clothes, turn it around, sew their name onto it, and sew the label back into the clothes. Have a Designer Clothing Fashion Show where students wear their own designer clothes. A good way to say good-bye at the end of the year is to ask each student to sign every other student's designer T-shirt.

7b. Insignia Stamps Have students make personalized insignia stamps that contain either their initials, logos, or full names. They can make potato stamps by carving the mirror image of initials or names into the smooth surface of a potato. For inked initials, students carve the letters—in reverse—so they rise above the surface. For a more permanent stamp (though a harder task), students can carve the surface of gum erasers. Dip the stamps in ink or tempera paint, then stamp. For eraser stamps, students can ink the letters with felt-tip pens. Students could use insignia stamps instead of signatures on homework assignments or tests. They could decorate lunch bags, book marks, book jackets, or paper cups and napkins at class parties.

7c. Loco Logos Have the class look through magazines and newspapers to collect samples of interesting and creative logos for businesses and companies. Either individually or in small groups, let students analyze what each company communicates through its logo. Have students redesign logos and trademarks for a company of their choice. Ask them to originate a logo or trademark to fit what they imagine themselves to be twenty years from now. For a multicultural twist, encourage students to include symbols and elements specific to their ethnic, racial, sexual, or religious identities. Create a Loco Logos bulletin board. As a class, discuss what students communicate through their designs. Finally, design a class logo.

SO. CALIFORNIA BOAT CLUB

Logo Law

A *logo* is a word, name, symbol, figure, mark, or any combination of these adopted and used by a manufacturer or merchant to mark specific goods or services and distinguish them from others. It may also be a brand name or trademark. Any originator of a trademark can use the symbol ™ to indicate ownership to the public without registration. A trademark is considered officially registered only if the U.S. Patent and Trademark Office issues a federal registration, at which point the symbol ® may be used. This logo from the Southern California Boat Club is used on all club stationary, newsletters, and T-shirts. Courtesy Buz Tarlow, Southern California Boat Club.

7d. Growing into Your Name Have students use window boxes to make a pebble or plant garden that somehow involves their names or initials. They could arrange colored pebbles or shells in the shape of names. Or, more ambitiously, students could try to grow grass or other plants using a name template to guide planting of seeds.

Here is an alternative to planting seeds in the shape of names—planting seeds that grow into plants that sign their own names!

7e. Mirror, Mirror on the Wall Have students use a mirror to draw or paint a self-portrait. Or they can make a collage using a photocopy machine to enlarge photographs of themselves, shrink them, make multiple copies, and so on. Have students incorporate signatures into the work as creative design element. For example, they can repeat their names in patterns or hide them within the work as a puzzle for others to find. Here is another related activity: Have students select things that represent them—such as the jewelry, watch, sunglasses, and keys they have with them—arrange them on a photocopier (taking care not to scratch the glass), and make a photocopy. Study self-portraits of artists, such as Albrecht Dürer, Rembrandt van Rijn, Judith Leyster, Vincent Van Gogh, Norman Rockwell, and M. C. Escher. How does each reflect upon the artist's self-concept? Have students look for artist signatures, comparing different artists and different works of art. Ask them to look at where they are placed, how they differ between artists, and what the signature tells about the artist. Distribute "One Artist, Many Styles" (page 35) to highlight dramatic variation in style and signature within a single artist. If possible, make a field trip to a museum to study portraits, signatures, and stylistic variation in other artists.

7f. Hanging Up the Class Boost student esteem by seeking creative ways to display their creative productions. For example, talk to local restaurants about putting up a bulletin board devoted to student work from the school. You would be surprised how many restaurant owners agree to this—it is good for business. Also try the local city hall, the supermarket, airport, and nursing homes in the area. Make sure students sign their artwork. If possible, take the class on an outing to visit these places.

7g. Discovering Eponyms An *eponym* is a person for whom something is named. The following people invented something sufficiently unique that their discoveries bear their names. Send students on an intellectual scavenger hunt to discover what these people accomplished. You may wish to form groups or ask students to work in pairs. They can find all the answers in a well-stocked library.

Amelia Jenks Bloomer	*Edward A. Murphy*
Anders Celsius	*C. Northcote Parkinson*
Rudolf Diesel	*Henry F. Phillips*
Earl of Derby	*Charles F. Richter*
Gabriel D. Fahrenheit	*Antoine Sax*
Dr. Henry J. Heimlich	*Edward Stanley*
Dr. Fernand Lamaze	*Levi Strauss*
Jules Leotard	*Earl Tupper*
John L. Macadam	

You might also add the fictional Mrs. Malaprop from Richard Sheridan's play *The Rivals,* from which we get the word *malapropism;* and the real-life Rev. William Spooner, whose *spoonerisms* involve transposition of the sounds in different words. Your students may appreciate his "Son, it is kisstomary to cuss the bride." Challenge them to create their own spoonerisms. Brainstorm as many eponyms as possible that are part of our everyday life, such as Kleenex and Frisbee.

7h. Oughta Be a Name With the class, or in cooperative groups, have students brainstorm the following: How many holidays and cities in the United States or other countries can they think of that are named after famous people? Ask the same about your town or city—are there streets and buildings named after prominent members of your community? Ask students if they were in charge at city hall, who in the community would they choose to name a park after. Ask which part of the town or city could be named after each student and why.

7i. Your John Hancock Right Here Study important treaties and signings that changed the course of history. Examples include the signing of the Constitution by Ben Franklin and others; the signing of the Magna Carta by King John and his knights; and the signing of the American Declaration of Independence by John Hancock, whose name is an eponym for *signature.*

7j. Let's Shake on It Have students interview family, friends, and professionals about types of contracts they have signed or come across. Take a field trip or invite contract lawyers or notaries to your class to discuss the nature of their work and show some samples of contracts. With appropriate students, design a contract that spells out an agreement for an individualized unit of study. Be sure to include what is to be accomplished, by what date, consequences the agreement is not held up, and rewards if it is. When you and your student agree on the terms, finalize the contract with dated signatures. This technique is especially useful with Attention Deficit Disorder students.

Sign on the Line

A contract is a written agreement between two people to do something or to refrain from doing something. Marriage, terms of employment, and record deals are just a few of the times when contracts are regularly negotiated. The signatures of both parties are crucial to a legal contract. Contract lawyers devote their careers to drawing up contracts in line with current law. Notaries witness the signing of contracts, a procedure necessary for making some contracts legally binding.

Teacher's Corner

★ A popular children's chant says, "Sticks and stones can break my bones, but names can never hurt me." In the classroom, however, names sometimes can cause damage when we consider how labels can diminish teacher expectations, hurt student self-concept, and create self-fulfilling prophesy.

★ We both expect and often receive more from students labeled "gifted" or "talented." We expect and usually receive less from those labeled "Attention Deficit Disordered," "dyslexic," or "slow learner." While these labels can pinpoint problem areas, they fail to capture student strengths. Most of us have seen instances in which ordinary students perform at extra-ordinary levels. We also encounter "slow" students with talent in drawing, sports, playing an instrument, or building models. One ground-breaking book that focuses on the learning abilities of those labeled "dyslexic" is *Making the Words Stand Still* by Donald Lyman.

★ The labeling system used in Western education is based on cultural values that elevate linguistic and logical-mathematical skills above all others. Yet the five other intelligences proposed by Howard Gardner are equally crucial. One way to avoid debilitating labels in the classroom, while still honoring individual differences, is to recognize the importance of intelli-gences that have not traditionally been part of Western education. In his book *Multiple Intelligences in the Classroom*, Thomas Armstrong proposes that we expand the popular notion of learning styles to include each of Gardner's seven intelligences. This means you can engage any one of the intelligences for learning new material. Read the "Learning Style and Multiple Intelligences" sheet (page 36). It is a simplified account of these ideas based on Armstrong's work. In Lesson 14, you will use this sheet to introduce multiple intelligences in the class-room.

★ For now, begin familiarizing yourself with these con-cepts by doing the following: List two or three students in your class and all labels attached to each individ-ual, whether official ("dyslexic," "Attention Deficit Disordered," "gifted," "culturally disadvantaged") or not ("model student," "smart aleck," "class clown").

★ Try to get beyond these labels. Seek a broader pic-ture. For each student identify and list intelligences representing areas of student strengths and those rep-resenting areas of weakness. Over the next month or so, complete this activity for every student in your class. Hang on to your list to later compare it with stu-dent self-assessments using the "Multiple Intelligences Profile" (page 73).

One Artist, Many Styles

Look at these two very different pieces by the same artist. Notice differences in the style of the pieces, and relate them to differences in the artist's signature. On the back of this page, describe your observations.

Bernard Hoyes, *Praising the Most High* (top);
Journey Alone on Shoreside (left).

Learning Style and Multiple Intelligences

Musical learners tune into melody and beat. They learn through song and tapping into an internal sense of rhythm. They frequently like to sing, hum, and make up melodies and are good at recognizing tunes and identifying artists and composers. Many play instruments and collect tapes or CDs. They may be sensitive to and easily distracted by sounds.

Interpersonal learners learn through direct contact and communication with others. They understand people, feelings, and motivations. They often display leadership skills by organizing, mediating, or diffusing conflicts. They are empathetic and appreciate cultural differences. They may be extroverted, well liked by adults, and popular with other students. They tune into social goings on around them, tend to be "street smart," and may be involved in after-school activities.

Intrapersonal learners learn best alone, away from people and group activities. They are self-motivated, initiate independent activities, and work at their own pace. They are strong-willed and stubborn, possessing deep knowledge of and attachment to their own feelings, fantasies, opinions, and intentions. They may keep a diary or be somewhat secretive. They often seem to possess an inner wisdom or intuition. They are content to articulate and dwell in their inner world.

Body-kinesthetic learners process knowledge through sensation. They may be restless and active. They learn best through moving and doing and tend to communicate through gesture, with strong body language and frequent touching. They may possess interest and talent in sports and other activities requiring gross-motor coordination, such as mime, dance, and acting. They may excel at activities requiring fine-motor coordination, such as woodworking, typing, and crafts.

Spatial learners orient well to their surroundings and tend to conceptualize experience in spatial terms. They may be good at navigating, reading, and making maps, charts, and diagrams, and imagining objects in three-dimensional space. Many like to doodle, draw, and daydream. Some are highly attuned and responsive to visual details and media such as photographs, overheads, slides, videos, and movies.

Linguistic learners have highly developed auditory and oratory skills. They learn best verbally through speaking, hearing, or seeing words. They have good memory for names, places, and trivia. They love to play with language and its sounds, and may be interested in debate, writing or reading poetry or prose, playing word games, or telling vivid stories.

Logical-mathematical learners think conceptually and compute well mentally. They learn best by analyzing and reasoning. They enjoy brainstorming and strategy games, such as chess, and logical challenges, such as Rubik's Cube and computer programming. They like to take things apart and devise experiments for figuring out things they do not understand. They often ask abstract or philosophical questions.

UNIT 2

Voices Within:
Vocabularies for Self-Expression

THE ELEVATOR
LESSON 8

We need personal space to grow, both physically and emotionally. We need emotional space to feel supported for expressing ourselves. In "The Elevator" students compare the tension of being crowded with the relief of carving out an area of their own. Students gain respect for the right of all individuals to have personal space. Use the lesson to introduce concepts of *space* and *crowding* as they relate to ideas, emotions, nature, or urban surroundings. Try doing "The Elevator" early and then later in the school year. Notice whether greater familiarity brings more or less comfort to students cramped together.

Preparation

★ Clear desks and chairs away from a large corner of the classroom.

Materials

paper and pens; drawing materials (optional)

Exercise

1. At your signal, have students, one at a time, approach the cleared corner—the "elevator"—silently and politely. Have them crowd into the corner as if trying to squeeze into an elevator.

2. Once the class is inside, have them spend a couple of minutes standing silently. Encourage students to notice how they feel in the cramped quarters.

3. Tell the class to leave the elevator as they entered, one at a time.

4. Have students carve out personal space in the classroom by defining the area they would like all to themselves. Students should notice differences in how they felt being in the elevator vs. having lots of space for themselves.

5. Repeat the procedure with one difference—once inside the elevator, have students talk loudly with their neighbors. In this way, students compete both for physical and speaking space.

6. Tell students to stop the loud talking only after they leave the elevator.

7. Ask students to return to their seats and write a story about a child who does not have enough space. The story should describe the kind of space missing, the consequences of not having enough space, and a creative

Here is one cartoonist's commentary on space and crowding. From *The Road to Hell* © 1992 by Matt Groening. All rights reserved. Reprinted by permission of HarperPerennial, a division of HarperCollins Publishers.

solution. Encourage students to be imaginative about how they conceptualize the notion of space. Possibilities include being elbowed in line, being too shy to reach out, having no privacy at home, having cultural conflict, or having political differences. If desired, have students illustrate stories.

Discussion

◆ What was it like trying to crowd into the small space?

◆ How did that experience compare with finding your own space?

◆ Was it different about going through this exercise silently versus loudly? Did the noisiness make you feel more or less crowded?

◆ What is personal space? Does everybody need some? Why? Does everybody need the same amount? Explain.

◆ What are advantages and disadvantages of sharing a room with brothers or sisters?

◆ How do cultures differ in their use of personal space? What are some examples?

◆ What are consequences of not having enough personal space?

◆ What is different about having personal space versus being alone?

◆ When is being alone a problem? When is it valuable?

◆ Some people think finding contentment and inner peace involves finding space for ourselves just the way we are. What do you think?

◆ How many different kinds of space can you think of?

Make Room for Me!

Personal space is the amount of room we need surrounding our bodies, with complete freedom of movement, to feel comfortable. The amount each individual needs varies, especially from culture to culture. We also need emotional space—the freedom to think and act independently and to make mistakes. Silence and privacy, in small amounts, can help us find our own voices and sources of guidance. How much personal space we need changes with stages of life; for example, adolescents typically need more room than youngsters. Individuals at any age who feel too crowded—whether by brothers and sisters, teachers, parents, or strangers—often become angry, rebellious, or insecure.

◆ What kind of space do we need to express ourselves creatively?

Extensions

8a. Room for Cultural Differences Individually or in cooperative groups, have each student investigate the nature of personal space among people from his or her own cultural background, using videotape or photographic essays if possible. They should draw information from many sources: their own experience; interviews with family members, other relatives, or acquaintances; library research about their culture of origin. Have them consider the following: How far apart do people physically space themselves? Does touching tend to occur during normal conversation? How much room are people given to express their personal opinions, to explore their differences from others, and to express their individuality? Have students, individually or in small groups, present their findings to the class. One creative way to do this is to stage an event, such as a meal, that demonstrates cultural patterns in spacing, both physically and conversationally. Have the rest of the class observe and take notes for later discussion.

8b. Public Spaces Have students work in pairs to take photographs or notes and to write an essay about the way people space themselves in a public place, such as a cafeteria, park, town square, or library. Assign this activity as homework or take a class field trip. Students can visit the same place during different times of day and conditions; for example, when there are many people around versus a few. Are there differences in how people space themselves under different conditions? Do they tend to stick together or space themselves out when they have more room?

8c. Urban Distress Pick two or three very crowded cities to compare, such as New York, Tokyo, and Mexico City. Have student work in cooperative groups to analyze how the architecture in each city differs with respect to its use of space. Discuss the problems associated with overcrowding (poverty, crime, depersonalization, homelessness). Ask how the culture of each city affects the expression and solution of these urban problems. For example, Tokyo employs professional "stuffers" to cram more people into subways during rush hour. Have groups pick one urban issue to focus on, such as poverty, and analyze it in terms of space and crowding. Students can brainstorm solutions by redesigning features of each city, such as architecture, landscaping, transportation, and customs.

8d. This Space Is My Space We could view history in terms of the division and redivision of space among the peoples of the world. Have students compare various forms of government—for example, totalitarian, socialist, communist, and democratic—and examine the amount of personal space each grants to the individual. Or have students examine a period of history in terms space and crowding issues. For example, many Native American tribes did not believe in land ownership, whereas the early American settlers did and wound up taking the land. Have them look at differences in cultures and maps before and after wars and treaties to see how territory was reapportioned. Students can bring issues to life by dramatizing them. You could have students write scripts where individuals represent countries or groups in conflict over territory.

8e. Room to Grow People are not the only living things that need space to grow and thrive. As a class or as homework, have students take a nature walk and take photographs or notes on how the different kinds of flowers, plants, and trees are spaced. They should notice which varieties appear to need more room than others and which are spaced close together. For an experiment, buy several different kinds of grass and flower seeds. Have students plant many seeds in one cup or box and fewer seeds in the next. They can try mixing seed varieties in some containers and sticking to a single type in others. Observe how each variety of seed grows under different conditions of crowding and different neighbors. Discuss *companion planting*, where plants help each the other grow, such as tomatoes and marigolds. With students, design a garden with the ideal "personal" space for each plant.

8f. Spaced Out or Caged In Have students find patterns in the way animals space themselves, such as ants moving to and from an anthill and birds flying or perched on telephone wires. If possible, take a field trip to the zoo and let students pick a cage to observe that contains more than one animal. Have students take photographs and notes. If a field trip is not possible, look at pictures or slides of animals in large groups. Observe the animals' spacing, finding similarities and differences among various species. Ask students if they think animal behavior might differ in captivity from in the wild. Relate issues of space and crowding in the plant and animal world to aspects of ecology, such as ecological niches and competition between species.

Like Birds on a Wire

Ecologists take note of how birds space themselves on telephone lines. As a branch of biology, ecology deals with, among other things, how organisms space themselves in their environment. As a branch of sociology, ecology studies the spacing and interdependence among people and institutions. And as an aspect of politics, ecology is concerned with preserving the natural environment and preventing disasters caused by carelessness or greed.

8g. This Land Is My Land Some types of animals are loners; some live together in prides or herds. Some are nomadic; others are territorial. Lions and bears will fight to protect their space. Cats and dogs will mark space with urine. Hold a class discussion to compare such differences among animals to human beings. Ask how problems of racial relations and gangs reflect issues of territoriality and how these problems are related to limited resources. Introduce the zero-sum game, in which the only way to win is for someone else to lose, as in checkers or Monopoly. Contrast this with a positive-sum activity, a win-win scenario where everybody wins. An example is the Dutch government's decision to build dikes, which resulted in more land available for people. An example of a negative sum, lose-lose scenario is nuclear war, especially Henry Kissinger's strategy of MAD: mutually assured destruction. Ask for other examples and advantages of each scenario.

8h. Molecular Space With the class, study osmosis by watching drops of colored water spread across a paper towel. Open a bottle of perfume or ammonia (check for student allergies first). Wait for students in the back of the room to smell it. After the experiment, discuss diffusion. Ask students how osmosis and diffusion relate to molecules traveling in different states. Molecules need more or less space, depending on what state they are in—liquid, solid, or gas. Ask students what changes in temperature have to do with molecular space and crowding. Have them make diagrams or choreograph movements to illustrate how molecules space themselves differently in different phases.

8i. Lost in Space Have students research issues of space and crowding in outer space. Here are some possible questions: How much

distance typically exists between different objects in space? Are distances between objects getting larger or smaller over the eons? What happens when objects collide in outer space; for example, what causes craters on the moon? What is a shooting star? What happens around a black hole? Have students find creative ways to answer these and related questions. Students can splatter white paint or use neon colors on black paper to portray events in space. Create a Lost in Space bulletin board.

Natural Movement

All elements in nature are found naturally in one or more of four states: liquid, gas, solid, and plasma. The molecules of *liquids* move freely among themselves, but tend not to separate. The molecules of *gases* move freely among themselves and can separate; their spacing and collisions are governed by random forces in the subatomic world. The molecules of *solids* are fixed in a regular or semiregular crystal-like patterns called *lattices*. Plasma is a highly ionized gas and does not fit easily into any of the other three categories. *Osmosis* is the process when a fluid passes through a semipermeable membrane into a solution with a lower concentration. *Diffusion* is the process when molecules of liquid or gas mix with those of gas, as when a vapor disperses in air.

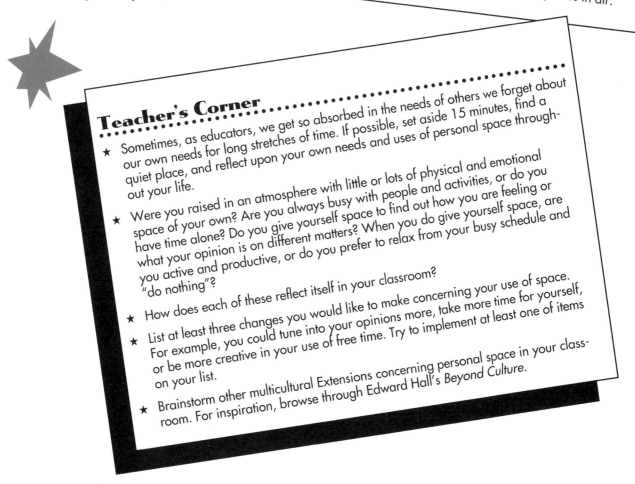

Teacher's Corner . . . .

★ Sometimes, as educators, we get so absorbed in the needs of others we forget about our own needs for long stretches of time. If possible, set aside 15 minutes, find a quiet place, and reflect upon your own needs and uses of personal space throughout your life.

★ Were you raised in an atmosphere with little or lots of physical and emotional space of your own? Are you always busy with people and activities, or do you have time alone? Do you give yourself space to find out how you are feeling or what your opinion is on different matters? When you do give yourself space, are you active and productive, or do you prefer to relax from your busy schedule and "do nothing"?

★ How does each of these reflect itself in your classroom?

★ List at least three changes you would like to make concerning your use of space. For example, you could tune into your opinions more, take more time for yourself, or be more creative in your use of free time. Try to implement at least one of items on your list.

★ Brainstorm other multicultural Extensions concerning personal space in your classroom. For inspiration, browse through Edward Hall's *Beyond Culture*.

LIVING SCULPTURES
LESSON 9

The body has its own intelligence. In a way, our muscles possess many of the same capacities as our minds: awareness, knowledge, wisdom, and a vast repertoire of memories for postures and actions. In "Living Sculptures" students become sensitized kinesthetically. They develop skills of muscle isolation and coordination and use their bodies as learning tools. They practice orienting themselves physically in the room and in relation to one another, and they explore different qualities of movement as they seek original poses and moves. They are creatively challenged to choreograph and perform compositions that communicate their physical discoveries. You discuss the importance of continued practice, discipline, and will power. Use this lesson to introduce body intelligence and to develop a basic vocabulary of movement as a tool for learning.

Preparation

★ Ask students to wear casual, loose-fitting clothing for complete freedom of movement.

★ Clear a large space in the classroom or prepare to move outside.

Materials

chalkboard and chalk; paper and pens; cameras or videotape equipment (optional)

Exercise

1. On the board, brainstorm a list of qualities of movement. Use the following dimensions of movement as a guideline:

   - *Shape: contracted, expanded, round, angular, open, closed, extended*
   - *Speed: fast, slow*

- *Energy: high, low*
- *Texture: smooth, choppy, sharp, floating, flowing, graceful, hard, soft*
- *Direction: forward, backward, sideways, diagonal*
- *Level: high, medium, low*
- *Duration: length of position or sequence*

2. Divide the class into groups of five to eight students. Assign one shape per group: lines, circles, triangles, and squares.

3. Clear a wide area of the classroom or move to a spacious area outside.

4. Give groups approximately 10 minutes to explore ways of using their bodies to make the assigned shape. They should explore in each of the following ways:

   - *Individually, where group members explore their shape alone*
   - *Jointly, in small group sculptures*
   - *In static or still poses*
   - *In moving or dynamic poses*
   - *Using the dimensions of movement listed above*
   - *Using as many parts of the body as possible (such as mouths, eyebrows, elbows, fingers, feet)*
   - *Using negative and positive space*

Positive and Negative Space

Here is a kinesthetic example of negative and positive space. Clasp your hands overhead. The space between your arms is *negative space*—it creates a negative shape. Your arms are *positive space*—they create a positive shape. Both are important in sculpture through the presence of filled (positive) space and empty (negative) space. Both are important in painting through the presence of contrasting colors and shapes that occupy foreground (positive) and background (negative). In this work, the artist has created a face partly from positive and partly from negative space. *Kabuki* by Chuck Bowdlear. Photograph courtesy the artist.

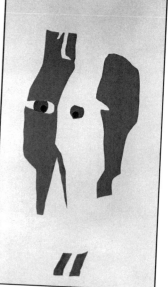

(5) After initial explorations, give groups approximately 10 minutes to choreograph a sequence for demonstrating as many different ways of making their shape as can fit into 3 minutes.

(6) Have groups, one at a time, perform their choreographed sequences for the class.

(7) Have student observers attempt to capture the action by making line drawings. If desired, videotape demonstrations to aid in discussion. Or take photographs of various poses and create a Human Shape bulletin board.

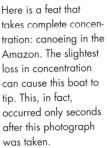

Here is a feat that takes complete concentration: canoeing in the Amazon. The slightest loss in concentration can cause this boat to tip. This, in fact, occurred only seconds after this photograph was taken.

Discussion

◆ How did each group vary the speed, energy, texture, duration, level, and direction of poses and movements?

◆ How was each group creative about using unusual body parts or movements during demonstrations?

◆ Do our bodies have their own kind of intelligence different from the "mental" kind? Explain.

◆ In what ways do we sense, think, and remember with our bodies?

◆ How do will power, practice, repetition, and physical discipline make our bodies "smarter"?

◆ Are there some ways our bodies are smarter than our minds?

◆ When we perform a complex action, such as riding a bicycle, playing hopscotch, and serving a tennis ball, why does it sometimes interfere to talk or even think about what we are doing?

◆ What would it be like if we had to consciously direct every muscle in our bodies and every movement we made?

◆ When does it work better to think first and then do? When does it work better to do first and then think?

◆ When it comes to using body intelligence, what is the difference between having good technique and being creative?

Concentration is essential for rock climbers, too. Consequences of poor concentration can be disastrous. Photograph courtesy Douglas Meyer.

Extensions

9a. The Mirror Divide the class into same-sex pairs who stand facing each other. Make sure each pair has plenty of space. When you give the signal, have one student in the pair start moving slowly. Have the other student mimic the first student's movements perfectly and simultaneously. If done well, it should be difficult to tell who is leading and who is following. Let pairs continue moving in sync until you call "freeze," when all movement instantly stops. Have pairs assume identical positions in space until you read the next set of instructions and signal to start the next round. Use different rounds to explore vocabulary related to various qualities of movement. Be creative! Here are some examples:

- *Pretend you are swimming in mercury.*

- *Explore space left, then right, up very high, then down very low.*

- *Be a private eye secretly following a suspect.*

- *Pretend a sudden wave of uncontrollable energy takes over your body.*

- *Pretend you are walking on peanut butter, with your feet sticking to the floor.*

9b. Living Artwork Have the class make living sculptures to study various pieces of art, perhaps as an adjunct to a history lesson. Choose a painting or sculpture with recognizable figures, such as Auguste Rodin's *Thinker,* Mary Edmonia Lewis's *Forever Free,* Edouard Manet's *Fifer,* or Jan van Eyck's *Arnolfini Wedding.* Ask students to imitate these poses. Use student poses to begin discussing qualities of the artwork, such as composition, texture, feeling tone, and use of negative and positive shapes, as well as aspects of the era, such as subjects of interest, clothes worn, and relationships among people. Poses imitating ancient Greek and Roman statues of athletes can launch discussion into the origin of the Olympic games. If desired, take a photograph of student imitations and display it next to a copy of the original on a Living Artwork bulletin board. For a challenge, have students try the same thing with an abstract piece of art.

9c. Action Poses Have students assume different "living sculpture" poses while the class makes brief sketches. Ten seconds is enough to do stick-figure action poses. Have students broadly examine gesture sketches and human sculptures of famous artists. Discuss different dimensions and qualities of the poses. Ask which poses appear static in nature and which appear to have dynamic movement that is frozen in stone or on the page. Look at Leroy Neiman's paintings of sports figures and animals captured in mid-motion. Take photographs of an action sequence, such as plays in football and baseball. Or use copies of high-speed, serial photographs available in many sports books. Mix them up and have students, either individually or in small groups, place them in correct order. From this sequence, see if students can recreate the original action.

9d. Human Machines Have students study the parts of various simple or complex machines by enacting them. Divide the class into groups of six or seven students. Tell each group to research a machine such as pulleys, cars, or planes. Instruct each student to enact a particular part, combining with group members to create the whole machine. Have the rest of the class guess the machine and identify each part.

9e. Spelling Sculptures Divide the class into several groups. Have each devise its own method for translating letters into body sculptures to spell out words. Have groups form and present vocabulary words to the rest of the class to be correctly identified and then defined. Try a spelling bee using body sculpture. If you are daring, have students spell out messages by lying on the ground in formation to be read from above. If possible take photos and create a Body Bee bulletin board.

9f. Math Sculptures Use student bodies to sculpt math equations. As a class, invent different systems for translating numbers and mathematical symbols into postures and positions, and practice math problems. For students with a specific learning disability in arithmetic, math sculptures provide a concrete method for an otherwise abstract language. Take photos if possible to create a Body Math bulletin board.

9g. Practice Makes Perfect Brainstorm activities, such as sports, dance, and woodworking, that require body intelligence and practice. Have each student focus on one area and find someone accomplished in it. Have students interview this person asking how they got their expertise, who taught them, how many years have they been doing it, how frequently and how long they practice, and whether the discipline is easy or difficult. Have students write reports summarizing their findings and conclusions about developing expertise in their area of choice.

9h. Try, Try Again Ask students to write a short story about a child who is having difficulty finding the discipline to practice something important. They should describe the activity, the problem, and a creative solution to resolve it.

9i. Use It or Lose It Have students research the importance of maintaining good physical fitness to physical and emotional well-being by requesting some information from the President's Council on Physical Fitness. They could then stage a funny skit about the importance of exercise and staying fit. Characters could include Coach Potato, who wants only to watch television, and Lazy Lie-Around, who must be convinced of the need for exercise and mastering a physical discipline. Have students perform the skit for parents or the rest of the school.

Teacher's Corner

★ Over the course of a week, keep a Body Log to record every time you use body intelligence. Record the following for each entry: where you were, what you did, whether it required fine-motor or gross-motor skills (small, highly precise versus large, less precise movements), what you noticed about your body's intelligence, and how you felt during the lesson.

★ At the end of the week, reflect upon the following as you study your Body Log:

• Is your life balanced between activities of the mind and those of the body?

• How often did you draw upon your body's intelligence?

• Do you consider yourself in good physical shape?

• Do you exercise regularly?

• How do you view yourself physically?

• How do you feel about your height, weight, energy, strength, and coordination?

• Do you use your body to express yourself creatively in any way? Remember, activities such as woodworking and embroidery are physical disciplines of a kind.

• If your body could speak to you right now, what desires, complaints, hopes, and fears would it express?

• Have you inherited the physical habits, either good or bad, of your parents?

• Does your image of your body aid or inhibit further exploration of body intelligence?

• Do you regularly use body intelligence in the classroom?

• Are there any ways you would like to draw upon body intelligence more often with your students? You might want to take several minutes to brainstorm some ideas.

★ Try to find creative uses for Body Logs with your students.

ONCE UPON A MIME
LESSON 10

Whether or not we are aware of it, we convey messages through our movements and posture. This is the concept of *body language*. In pantomime, body language is elevated to an art—dramatizing or storytelling using only gesture and movement. In this lesson students use pantomime to learn about the five W's—who, what, where, when, and why—of dramatic structure and action. They develop and practice an action vocabulary of mime to communicate ideas kinesthetically. Use this lesson to study formal story structure while having fun. "Once Upon a Mime" is also a good way to introduce dramatic technique under low pressure.

Preparation

★ At home, over the course of several days to several weeks, videotape or ask students to videotape small television snippets of dramatic and expressive action. Choose segments where you can read the body language and understand the action using visual cues, not sound. If you do not have access to a videocassette recorder, watch a film or television action segment with your class, turning off the sound.

Exercise

(1) With the class, teach or review the five W's that comprise the basic structure of a story, whether oral, written, or dramatized.

Who	*Who is involved; the major roles; the cast of characters*
What	*What is going on; the plot line; the props and costumes*
Where	*Where it is happening; the place of action; the setting*
When	*When the action occurs; time of day; time of year; historical setting*
Why	*Why the action occurs; the intentions of the characters; the underlying meaning*

(2) Show the videotape snippets, one at a time, without sound.

(3) Following each snippet, stop the tape and ask students to imagine what each of the five W's might be.

- *Who do the central characters appear to be?*
- *What might they be doing?*
- *Where could the action be taking place?*
- *What era is it? What time of day is it?*
- *Why is the action happening? What is the underlying meaning and motivation?*

(4) Rerun one or two snippets with sound. Ask student how this alters the picture. Are any of the five W's further clarified by the addition of sound?

(5) Introduce the notion of body language.

Body Language

Body language uses the vocabulary of action: we express ourselves using posture, facial expressions, gestures, and movements. Body language is spoken universally. This is the why we can go to a foreign culture and make ourselves understood, at least about basic needs, without even speaking the language. Kinesthetic learners and class comedians are examples of individuals who rely heavily upon body language.

---

(6) Introduce pantomime and practice it, either as a class or in small groups of six or seven students. Pick and choose activities from the following list to portray each of the five W's. Or try making up your own mime activities for each W.

Pantomime

Pantomime is the art of conveying concepts or stories through body language without using words. A skilled mime like Marcel Marceau creates the illusion of interacting with objects that aren't there. For instance, he can appear trapped in a glass cage. Modern dance companies frequently use pantomime for narrative purposes by isolating tiny muscles, controlling them precisely, and using negative space to create imaginary objects. These dancers need much kinesthetic intelligence and years of practice to refine their technique to this degree. In this photograph, the Los Angeles–based Mums use extreme coordination in their juggling routine.

Who

- Have students mime different animals, letting others guess the animals. Try rounds with and without accompanying sounds.

- Have students mime different occupations.

What

- Let students mine an activity such as driving a car, feeding a baby, planting seeds, or directing traffic. Have others guess the activity.

- Divide students into groups of six or seven to compete with one another. Have them brainstorm as many sports as possible in 5 minutes and then portray the sports through mime, one group at a time. Assign a scorekeeper to record each sport after it is correctly identified by another group member. The group with the most sports listed wins.

Where

- Have students mime an activity that allows others to guess what room they are in.

- Let students choose a place to portray, such as an airport, video arcade, jungle, restaurant, baseball field, or circus. Have them mime the place while others guess where they are.

- Try a round with sound effects alone.

When

- Divide students into groups of three and have them choose an activity easily divided into a three-part sequence. Instruct each group member to mime one part. Have groups present the sequence out of order to the class. Let the class guess the activity and correct order for the sequence. Example: If the activity is doing the dishes, the first student rinses, the second dries, and the third puts the dishes away. Increase the difficulty by increasing the number of steps in the sequence; for example, add eating dinner or clearing the table to the example above.

Why

- Mime, or have a student mime, a simple activity such as bandaging a finger. Give the class 3 minutes to brainstorm all the reasons why you might be doing that activity. Remember, even silly reasons belong in a brainstorming session.

What clues do you use to place these in the correct order? From "There's No Place Like Home," *The Book / Los Angeles*. Levon Parian, *Untitled*.

Discussion

◆ Which do you prefer, telling a story aloud, using words, or miming a story silently, using your body? Why?

◆ In what ways do words enhance a story being told? When do words detract from a story?

◆ What skills does it take to be good at mime?

◆ How do imagination and creativity contribute to our abilities to perform and to understand mime?

◆ Which of the following media are better at portraying mime: film, television, books, cartoon strips, plays, radio? How do these different media portray each of the five W's? Are some media better at portraying each of the five W's than others?

◆ Compare and contrast how each medium above might portray the following:

Who	*A story told from the point of view of a heroine's thoughts*
What	*Action existing at two places at the same time*
Where	*At the center of the earth*
When	*In the future*
Why	*Someone is telling a lie*

◆ What other interesting examples of the five W's can you think of to portray and how might you do so.

Extensions

10a. Who Mime I? Choose five celebrities or figures from a current events or a history unit, such as Bill Clinton, Barbara Walters, Whoopi Goldberg, Napoleon, and Joan of Arc. Write each name on the board. Then, as a class or in small groups, ask one student to mime one of the figures. Have the rest of the class guess which was chosen. Or find or have students draw caricatures of famous people. Political cartoons in the newspaper are a good source. Remove any words, show them on the overhead, and let students guess who is being portrayed. Discuss body language and exaggerated features that provide clues.

10b. What Mime I up To? Repeat Extension 10a using scientific discoveries and inventions. Write a list of five researched inventions or discoveries on the board, such as Ben Franklin's discovery of electricity, the Curies' discovery of X rays, Alexander Graham Bell's invention of the telephone, and Sir Isaac Newton's discovery of the principles of gravity. Have students research the origin of the inventions, and then, individually or in groups, mime a discovery in the making while the class guesses which it is.

10c. Rediscovering Charades Do library research with your students on the arts of a particular period, such as Europe between 1900 and 1915. Then play charades, following the usual rules of the game. Use the names of books, plays, paintings, and works of art from this era. After a work has been mimed and identified, have students discuss the country where the work was produced, the date it was written, and what meaning it might have had. Or try playing vocabulary charades for current vocabulary words and two- or three-word phrases. If feasible, make a class video that explains the rules of charades and includes some examples. Use it for younger students or future classes.

10d. Cartoon Strip Mime Pass out the "Cartoon Strip Mime" sheet (page 51) and have students fill in the words and five W's based on body language of the characters. Next have students make up their own cartoon strip of approximately five panels, drawing the action but leaving out the words—drawing empty balloons above the heads. Have students use scissors to separate each of the panels and then mix them up and exchange with a partner. Have partners place the panels in any order they wish and then fill in the empty balloons with words. After filling in the words, students should glue them to a sheet of paper and give them back to the originator. Have them discuss whether the partner placed them in the same sequence as was originally conceived. Showcase cartoons on a Cartoon Strip Mime bulletin board.

10e. Five W's on Television Have the class select several television shows or movies to watch on a particular evening at home. The following day, either orally or in writing, have students analyze each of the five W's they witnessed. Try playing What If . . .? with the five W's and spontaneously change one or more of them. Imagine and discuss how the beginning, middle, and/or end might have turned out differently. You can play the same game by changing one of the five W's in fairy tales or other stories; for example, "What if the Wizard of Oz were mean rather than kind?" For a real challenge try having students mime or enact alternatives in place of discussing or writing about them.

10f. Story-mime Menu Write on the chalkboard a menu of interesting W's, among which students may pick and choose to structure a story. Have students, either individually or in small groups, mime, dramatize, or write stories that incorporate one or more items from each category. Here is a possibility: one student reads the story while others portray the action through mime. Afterward, other students in the class analyze the story-mime structure for each of the five W's. Below are some possible menu items.

Who	What	Where	When	Why
Monster	Arguing	Desert	Midnight	Because he is from Mars
Ballerina	Sleeping	Skating rink	6 A.M.	Because she is broke
Lost child	Seeking gold	Beach	Summer	Because I said so
Cowboy	Meeting	Store	A.D. 2500	Because they are lost
Liar	Running away	In a train	High noon	Because she is angry
Salesperson	Falling	At a wedding	1500 B.C.	Because it is your birthday
Dinosaur	Buying	North Pole	December	Because things are changing

10g. Madcapping the Five W's Group students into pairs. Give one in each pair a copy of "Madcapping the Five W's" (page 52), in which blanks correspond to the who, what, where, when, and why of the story. The student with the copy elicits responses for each blank, writes the responses, then reads the completed story aloud. This often has hilarious results. If this activity goes well, have each student write his or her own story with blanks for the 5 W's.

10h. The Five W's of Photography Pick an interesting photograph, such as the one by Levon Parian on "The Five W's of Photography" (page 53). Have students examine it closely and then make up five W's for the action and people portrayed. Then have them expand their five W's into a story with a beginning, middle, and end. This is a good way to enhance a multicultural lesson.

10i. The Five W's of Life In some ways, the process of life is like the writing of a novel—except the story is not fiction, it is the reality we experience. Each life story includes the five W's. We are often both the hero and villain of our own stories. Ask the class to write an autobiographical essay that elaborates how the five W's relate to their lives, either as seen currently or imagined for the future. They should include:

- *Who are you? Who else is in your life? Who is no longer in your life?*

- *What are you doing? What has become of you?*

- *Where are you living? Where have you been?*

- *When does the story take place? When do significant life events occur?*

- *Why were you born?*

- *Why did you do the things and make the choices you did?*

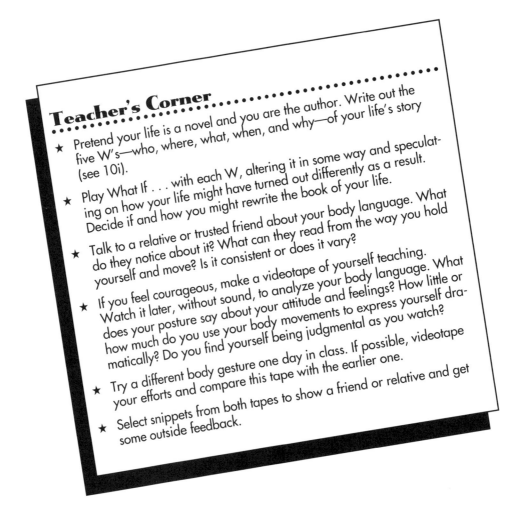

Teacher's Corner

★ Pretend your life is a novel and you are the author. Write out the five W's—who, where, what, when, and why—of your life's story (see 10i).

★ Play What If . . . with each W, altering it in some way and speculating on how your life might have turned out differently as a result. Decide if and how you might rewrite the book of your life.

★ Talk to a relative or trusted friend about your body language. What do they notice about it? What can they read from the way you hold yourself and move? Is it consistent or does it vary?

★ If you feel courageous, make a videotape of yourself teaching. Watch it later, without sound, to analyze your body language. What does your posture say about your attitude and feelings? How little or how much do you use your body movements to express yourself dramatically? Do you find yourself being judgmental as you watch?

★ Try a different body gesture one day in class. If possible, videotape your efforts and compare this tape with the earlier one.

★ Select snippets from both tapes to show a friend or relative and get some outside feedback.

Name _____ Date _____

Cartoon Strip Mime

Cartoons are wonderful tools for exaggerating body language. Look at each cartoon panel below and use cues from body language to fill in the words and answer each of the five W's.

Who are the characters?

When is this?

Where are they?

What is going on in the action?

Why is this happening?

Lesson 10 Once Upon a Mime ● **51**

Name _____ Date _____

Madcapping the Five W's

Choose a partner to complete each of the five W's below. Without letting your partner see the story, ask this person to supply each where, who, when, what, and why to fill in each blank in the order listed. Encourage partners to be imaginative. Write each response below, adjusting answers to make better sense if necessary. After each of the five W's have been filled in, read the story back to your partner or the rest of the class.

Once upon a time, on the edge of _____ [*where;* a place],

_____ [*who;* a person] was talking to _____

[*who;* a second person]. The time was _____ [*when;* a time].

They spoke of _____ [*what;* an activity] as they were

eating _____ [*what;* a thing]. But no matter how long they

spoke, they could not decide on _____ [*what;* an activity].

Why? Because _____

[*why;* a reason]. Finally, they gave up trying to decide, and talked instead about

_____ [*what;* a thing]. This worked out a whole lot better!

Then _____ [*who;* a person] came along wearing _____

[*what;* a thing] on her/his head. "Why are you wearing **that** on your head?" they asked.

"Because _____ [*why;* a reason],"

she/he explained. "When will you take it off?" they asked. "Not until _____

[*when;* a time in the future], but first I must go to _____ [*where;* a

place] to feed my _____ [*what;* an animal]." "We wish you well," they

replied, and they turned back to their conversation.

The Five W's of Photography

Look at the photograph below very carefully. Use your imagination to fill in each of the five W's. Then, on a separate sheet of paper, make up a story that is based your five W's and has a beginning, middle, and end.

From "Angelica," *The Book / Los Angeles.* Levon Parian, *Untitled.*

Who is involved in this scene?

Where is the action occurring?

When is the scene taking place?

What is going on here?

Why is the action occurring?

FEELING TALK
LESSON 11

Recent studies indicate something you may already have suspected: students' abilities to understand themselves and others, or their degree of social—interpersonal and intrapersonal—intelligence, is crucial for academic achievement and success in life. The ability to read feelings in others and ourselves is sometimes called *emotional literacy*. Our emotions are an important springboard for inspiration, and our feelings and thoughts help us interpret and value creative expression in others. "Feeling Talk" helps students recognize the variety, centrality, and universality of human emotions, and sensitizes them to their own emotions and other's feelings. The class explores how emotion is expressed through body language and ways in which feelings are important to self-expression. Use this lesson to enhance self-awareness and to deepen empathy and understanding of others.

Positive Outook

Preparation

★ Collect photographs and magazine pictures that demonstrate many different emotions. Look for images involving interaction between people and/or animals, and that emphasize situations students can readily understand.

Include as many representations of children as possible, and gender and ethnic diversity.

★ Write a different emotion on each of twenty to twenty-five slips of paper, and fold the papers. If desired, involve students in this preparation as part of Step 1 below.

Materials

pictures; chalkboard and chalk; pencil and paper; paper bag containing the folded slips of paper; timer; dictionary; overhead projector (optional); *Happiness Is a Warm Puppy* by Charles Schulz (optional)

Exercise

(1) With the class, brainstorm as many emotions as possible, such as joy, anger, fear, confusion, surprise, rage, love, envy, panic, and pride, and list them on the chalkboard. Send students to the dictionary if there is confusion about word meanings. For example, can they explain the difference between envy and jealousy? Use the photographs (show them on an overhead projector for easy viewing) to add to the list.

(2) Practice sentence completion to identify the range of meanings attached to each emotion, plus the variety of situations that are emotion tinged. Ask students to write two or three sentences for each of the following:

> *Happiness is . . .*
>
> *Frustration is . . .*

Have the class share their answers. If possible, read excerpts from *Happiness Is a Warm Puppy*.

(3) Split the class into pairs or trios. If necessary, rearrange the classroom so teams can act out scenarios and be seen by the rest of the class.

(4) Ask a representative from each group to select a slip from the paper bag.

(5) Give students 5 to 7 minutes to prepare a 2-minute dramatic situation in which the main character or all group members feel and express the feeling written on the slip of paper. Students should prepare dramas either with words or as mimes.

(6) Have groups perform their scenarios, using the timer to keep things moving. Move back and forth between groups using mime and those using words.

7 After each presentation, give the class no more than a minute to guess the emotion and the situation portrayed.

Discussion

◆ Which were the easiest feelings to portray and to guess? Which were the hardest? How do you account for this?

◆ What differences were there when groups could not use words?

◆ What clues do we use to guess feelings or to emphasize body language? What do we learn from facial expressions (mouth, eyebrows, eyes), body postures (slumping, crouching), and ways of moving (running, punching)?

◆ What are some examples of reading friends' or relatives' feelings from their body language or their words?

◆ What are examples of reading the teacher's feelings from body language or words?

◆ Do animals have feelings similar to people? How do you know?

◆ Why do people have emotion? What uses do feelings serve?

◆ In what ways are the feelings of adults similar to those of children? In what ways are they different?

◆ How do feelings fit into various stages of the creative process—inspiration, preparation, production, critique?

Extensions

11a. Emotion Commotion Use the "Emotion Commotion" sheet (page 59) to give students more practice recognizing feelings. Have students identify feelings and possible scenarios giving rise to them by analyzing the cartoon's body language (posture, gesture, facial expression, and such). As a class, compare and contrast student responses. Analyze how features of the cartoons, such as exaggerated expressions and distorted postures, give rise to particular responses. Note cases where feelings depicted by the cartoon differ widely from those evoked in the viewer. What makes the cartoons and student answers funny? Have students draw their own cartoon characters and copy them for another round of Emotion Commotion. Create an Emotion Commotion bulletin board.

11b. Feelingscapes Ask students to find or make artwork that portrays different feelings, such as anger, fear, and love. One possibility is creating landscapes; sharp, jagged mountains could convey anger; a calm, secluded lake conveys serenity. Analyze the features of the artwork in terms of the feelings evoked. Ask if the feelings aroused in the viewer are always the same as those portrayed in the art. Study modern art styles that express feeling, such as expressionism and fauvism. Have students identify feelings portrayed in the paintings, those evoked in the viewer, and features of the artwork that give rise to those impressions.

Expressionism and Fauvism

Although this face is a contemporary piece, it is very much within the style of expressionism. Expressionism is a modern-art style that arose in Europe in the 1880s as a countercurrent to the impressionists. Early expressionists included Vincent van Gogh, Edvard Munch, and Paul Gauguin. They conveyed feelings in a direct way, emphasizing impulsive brush strokes, the strong use of color, and expressive freedom over formal precision. The artists were often unstable and distraught, outcast from society. By contrast, the fauvists, who arose in the early 1900s, turned away from the despair of the expressionists. They tended to express positive feelings, inner joy, and an optimistic view of life. The movement was led by Henri Matisse and included others, such as André Derain, Raoul Dufy, and Georges Rouault. The name *fauve*, which means *wild beast* in French, was given by a derisive critic in response to the wild coloration of the paintings. John Howard, *The Suite*.

Can't houses have feelings too?

11c. Concrete Symbols Have students create concrete symbols to express different feelings; for example, a fist to represent anger and a heart to symbolize love. Have students use the symbols in place of words in a story. For a challenging, in-depth research project, have them discuss or research how the symbols came to represent these feelings.

11d. Feeling Masks Have each student create a mask portraying a particular feeling. Divide the class into groups of four to six students, each with a different "feeling mask." Have students write or improvise a short play with characters based on each mask and the feeling it represents, create costumes to accompany masks, and then perform their plays. After each performance, have the class analyze the feelings being portrayed by each character and scene. For a multicultural twist have students research the use of masks in Japan, Bali, ancient Greece, and Africa. Ask how masks in the Noh theater of Japan compare with their use in ancient Greek theater or in the dances of Bali and many African cultures.

Maskmaking

Here are two simple ways for students to make masks. Perhaps they can come up with other ways.

Paper Bag Masks
In pairs, students take turns putting a paper bag over the partner's head and marking on the bag the positions of the eyes and nose. After taking off the bags, students cut holes for the eyes and nose and then decorate the masks using crayons, markers, and paint; by attaching pieces of cloth, buttons, yarn, or colorful paper; and by crumpling or twisting the paper.

Paper Plate Masks
Paper plate masks can be tied around the head with a string or mounted on a stick. Students can glue the mount between two paper plates and decorate both to make two different characters. Again, students position, mark, and cut out eye holes, then decorate the masks with whatever material you or they collect.

Noh theater is a highly stylized Japanese form of drama that uses masks. Movements are slow and exaggerated; actors use pantomime to improvise gestures and pacing appropriate to each mask. Experts describe a powerful transformation that occurs once the mask is donned, through which the actor becomes one with the mask. Perhaps this helps explain why some African and American Indian tribes ascribe magical characteristics to masked rituals or why masked celebrations such as Mardi Gras can easily get out of control. This piece is clearly along the theme of masks. *Shaman III* by Chuck Bowdlear. Photograph courtesy the artist.

11e. Feelings in Music Bring in a variety of musical selections, each expressing or evoking different emotional states. Selections might include blues, polkas, marches, rock and roll, national anthems, and classical music. Consider composers as diverse as Bach and Sousa. Ask students to listen and discuss feeling tone for each. Include examples from as many cultures as possible. Where appropriate, have students from various ethnic groups bring in samples of their traditional music.

11f. Inflection with Feeling Play a game called Now Feel It This Way to enhance inflection in reading. Make cue cards with feeling words or symbols on them. Select several passages to read, ranging from emotionally charged to emotionally neutral, such as the Declaration of Independence to directions for assembling a toy. To play, have one student pick a card from the deck, look at it, and read the passage using expression and inflection to match the card. Have the class guess the feeling. Let a different student choose another card and reread the passage. Note examples where feeling tone and content differ.

11g. Feelings in Advertising Collect a number of interesting magazine advertisements that use various selling strategies. With the class, analyze feelings portrayed in the advertisements, plus direct and indirect attempts to manipulate emotions in the viewer. Have students brainstorm and create silly alternatives with an opposite purpose in mind. For example, they could change an advertisement depicting a healthy, happy man who smokes a particular brand of cigarette to an unhappy man who is rejected for smoking. What do advertising strategies tell us about human nature; for example, Coca-Cola's slogan "It's the real thing," Newport's "Alive with flavor," or Nike's "Just do it"?

Sometimes it is hard to find a safe harbor in the world of big-bucks advertising.

11h. Same Scene, Different Views Using an overhead projector (if possible) and two or more illustrated editions of a children's classic, such as *Alice in Wonderland* and *The Wizard of Oz,* have students compare and contrast the feeling of drawings or woodcuts illustrating the same moments in the text. Ask the class to discuss their feelings when they look at the illustrations, their sense of whether the artist captured the feeling of the story moments depicted, and to analyze similarities and differences of comparable illustrations.

11i. Feelings in Poetry Pick several poems that convey or evoke strong feeling, such as "Richard Corey" by Edwin Arlington Robinson. Analyze elements of the poems that contribute to its feeling tone. Then ask each student to pick a different feeling tone and rewrite the poem to fit it. Have a poetry reading session where students read their rewritten versions.

11j. Hurt Feelings Ask students to write or find a story about a time when someone's feelings got hurt. They should include what happened to cause the upset, what the feelings were, and how the situation was handled and resolved. Share stories aloud.

11k. Feelings Journal Ask students to keep a Feelings Journal for one week, recording any strong feelings and the situation that prompted the feeling. These are private journals that are not to be turned in or graded. However, the class may want to discuss the experience of recording feelings.

11l. Feelings Role Play With the class, brainstorm common situations in the classroom or everyday life that create strong feelings; for example, being new in a school, getting in trouble, being chosen last in a sporting activity, getting a perfect score on a test, saying good-bye at the end of the school year. This is a good format for empathetically exploring issues related to intolerance, prejudice, racism, and sexism. In pairs or small groups, have students role play different responses to someone in each situation. Ask which responses help the person feel better or help fix the problem and which make the situation worse.

Teacher's Corner

★ Thomas Hatch, a student of Howard Gardner, describes four types of social intelligence related to understanding and working with or around other people's feelings.

Leaders excel at organizing, initiating, coordinating, and maintaining group activities.

Mediators negotiate solutions, prevent social conflicts, and help resolve them.

Therapists are good listeners and analyzers, able to understand and reflect upon the feelings, concerns, and motivations of others.

Friends know how to connect with others, start and nurture relationships, and respond to the feelings and needs of others.

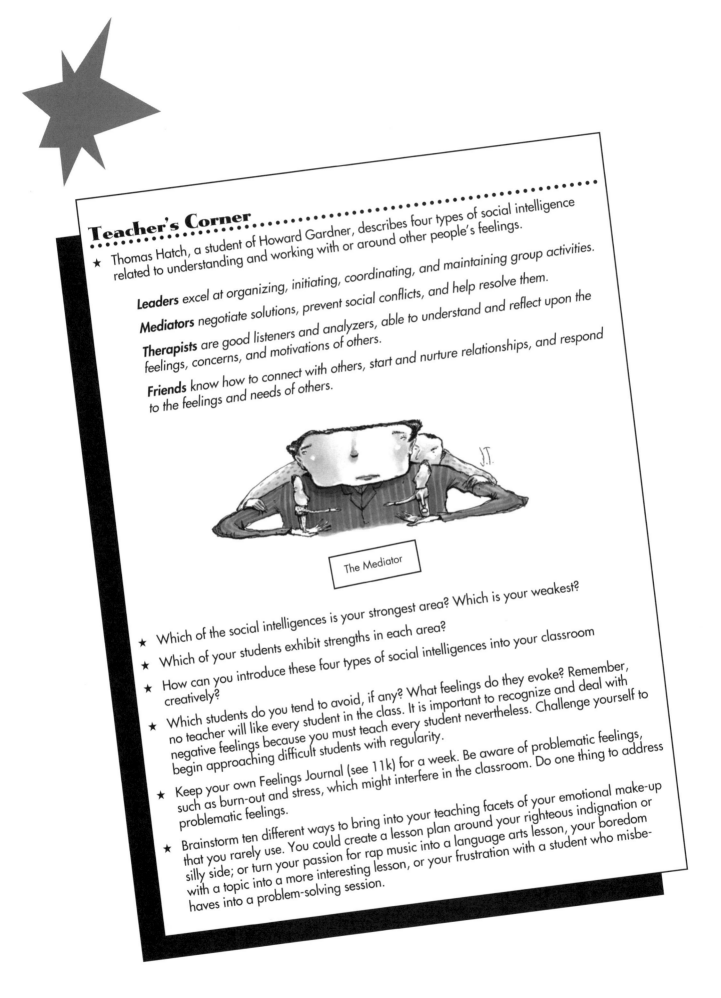

The Mediator

★ Which of the social intelligences is your strongest area? Which is your weakest?

★ Which of your students exhibit strengths in each area?

★ How can you introduce these four types of social intelligences into your classroom creatively?

★ Which students do you tend to avoid, if any? What feelings do they evoke? Remember, no teacher will like every student in the class. It is important to recognize and deal with negative feelings because you must teach every student nevertheless. Challenge yourself to begin approaching difficult students with regularity.

★ Keep your own Feelings Journal (see 11k) for a week. Be aware of problematic feelings, such as burn-out and stress, which might interfere in the classroom. Do one thing to address problematic feelings.

★ Brainstorm ten different ways to bring into your teaching facets of your emotional make-up that you rarely use. You could create a lesson plan around your righteous indignation or silly side; or turn your passion for rap music into a language arts lesson, your boredom with a topic into a more interesting lesson, or your frustration with a student who misbehaves into a problem-solving session.

Name _____ Date _____

Emotion Commotion

Look carefully at each cartoon below, then answer the following questions on the back of this sheet.

1. What feeling or set of feelings could each character be experiencing?
2. What situation might have caused these feelings?
3. What feeling or set of feelings do you, as a viewer, experience as you examine each figure? Be as funny as you would like with your answers.

FOUND SOUND
LESSON 12

Every culture possesses its own brand of music, and every person in the world possesses a musical instinct. This is why we can enjoy and in a sense understand the music we hear, even without formal study. Music is hidden everywhere, from the babbling brook to the babbling infant. "Found Sound" brings an explosion of auditory sensations into the classroom, sensitizing students to the world of sound and helping them to discover its educational applications. Students explore sound-making capabilities of ordinary objects. They are creatively challenged to develop original compositions. The coordination and cooperation skills required resemble activities of conducting and playing in an orchestra. The class examines the difference between noise, pure tone, and music, which helps narrow the gap between art and science. The lesson requires no formal knowledge of or experience in music.

Preparation

★ Collect lots of ordinary items that students can use imaginatively to make different noises. Involve your students by asking them to contribute two or three objects from home.

Materials

sound items, such as tin cans, cheese graters, dried gourds, rubber bands, string, paper, combs, bowls, glasses, rulers, spoons, springs, and metal pipes; chalkboard and chalk; videocassette recorder and video of a children's orchestral concert or Walt Disney's *Fantasia* (optional)

Exercise

1. If appropriate, play the children's concert video or *Fantasia* to demonstrate the operation of an orchestra and its sections, especially for students with limited musical experiences.

2. Place collected objects in a pile and allow each student to select two or three objects.

3. Let students experiment with the sound-making capabilities of their objects for a few minutes. They can bang, tap, scrape, scratch, or otherwise creatively search for obvious and not-so-obvious sounds.

4. Have each student choose one object to demonstrate to the rest of the class the range of sounds he or she discovered.

5. As this demonstration proceeds, keep a running vocabulary list of words on the chalkboard to describe all the sound qualities heard.

6. Divide the class into groups of six or seven students to form Found Sound orchestras.

7. Give orchestras 10 to 15 minutes to create and practice a brief musical composition. Compositions should last 2 to 3 minutes. Each orchestra must have one conductor while the rest play instruments. Compositions should showcase the variety of sounds possible with objects chosen and may include group playing, soloists, scripted playing, or improvisation. As with written compositions, musical compositions should have a beginning, middle, and end, with an introductory theme, its elaboration or refinement, and a resolution.

8. Have orchestras perform compositions for the class. Make sure every composition receives applause and bravos for special appreciation.

"Found Sound" in action. Levon Parian, *Untitled.* Courtesy Carrington McDuffie.

Discussion

◆ What qualities of sound did you hear in the different compositions?

◆ In what ways were the orchestras similar? How did they differ?

◆ Does every object make a sound? Can you think of any that cannot?

◆ Which kinds of sounds are easy to listen to? Which are unpleasant to hear?

◆ Do you think Found Sound orchestras created noise or music? What is the difference between the two?

◆ What sounds around us do we usually screen out without hearing (such as traffic passing and airplanes overhead)?

◆ Name some scary sounds we might hear (car crashes, gunshots).

◆ What are some sounds in everyday life that we could view as music (wind chimes, pinball games)?

◆ Which kinds of music contain sounds that we could view as noise (heavy metal, punk, modern classical)?

◆ Does a tree falling in the forest make a sound if nobody is there to hear it?

◆ An old Chinese *koan* asks, "What is the sound of one hand clapping?" What does this question mean?

Is there a person to be found amidst all this sound?

Extensions

12a. Full-Body Orchestras Allot several minutes for students to experiment individually, discovering as many sounds as they can make with their human body. Use feet, hands, mouths, and such to make clicks, claps, pops, or stamps. Have students showcase different sounds to the rest of the class and then classify sounds by similarities and group themselves into three or four different sections of an orchestra. Each section invents its own music, including a form for recording musical notation. Have the sections select a conductor, combine the sections of the orchestra, and perform the piece. You might want to have students study and compare the different sections of a symphony orchestra (strings, woodwinds, percussion, brass).

12b. Pitching In Introduce the concept of *pitch* by playing high and low notes on an instrument or by singing them. Split the class into pairs to translate high and low pitch into high and low physical levels by bending their knees or standing straight. One student represents the first note heard, the other the second. Students should respond to a two-note sequence by either standing straight or bending their knees, depending upon whether they believe the first note is higher or lower than the second. Start with wide differences in pitch and work toward notes closer together. After mastering this Extension with two notes, rearrange the class into groups of four and try again. Select one Conductor and three Tones. This time, use three different pitches and three height levels—high (fully straight), medium (partly bent), and low (fully squatting). Tones remain silent while the Conductor listens to the sequence of tones and orchestrates their height.

Pitch

Pitch refers to how high or low a tone is, which is determined by the rapidity of the vibration, or the frequency, that produces it. Higher tones have faster vibrations than lower tones. The four major pitch divisions are *soprano* (the highest voices or tones), *alto* (the higher middle voices or tones), *tenor* (the lower middle voices or tones), and *bass* (the lowest voices or tones). In a singing chorus, women often sing the soprano and alto parts while men often sing the tenor and bass parts. Some instruments, such as drums, triangles, and cymbals, are considered unpitched, while others, such as the xylophone, piano, and clarinet, are considered pitched.

12c. The Sound of Music Listen to the music of many cultures, such as Thai, European, Brazilian, Algerian, and Indian. Develop vocabulary words to analyze sound qualities, such as feeling tone, staccato/legato, fast/slow, complex/simple, and melody/harmony. Compare the scales of the same cultures. Are differences in the sound of the music reflected in differences in the scales?

Notes

Staccato refers to a succession of musical notes that are completely disconnected from one another and have a choppy sound. *Legato* refers to a succession of notes that are connected and flow smoothly into one another. *Melody* is a succession of single tones in musical compositions that produces a distinct musical phrase or idea. *Harmony* is a succession of tones blended with a melody, often creating chords that are pleasing to the ear. *Chord* is a combination of three or more different tones sounded simultaneously. *Scale* is a progression of notes ascending or descending in pitch according to fixed intervals, as in the seven-tone diatonic scale: do, re, mi, fa, so, la, ti, do.

12d. Taped Sound Logs You or your students can use a tape recorder to capture interesting, everyday sounds and play them in class. Encourage students to be imaginative about guessing what the sounds might be. Analyze different qualities of each sound. Ask which are very low in pitch (for example, trucks in motion, a heavy object falling). Ask which ones are very high (screeching brakes, fire alarms). Ask how students would spell each sound, and have them use each in a sentence. Listen for and study the Doppler effect: the pitch of an approaching siren or vehicle gets higher, while that of a receding siren or vehicle gets lower. Listen to pieces of music that incorporate ordinary sound, such as Joseph Haydn's "Clock Symphony" and the use of whale sounds in the music of the Paul Winter Consort.

12e. Onomatopoeia Introduce your class to onomatopoeic words, such as *bang* and *pop,* that sound the way they are spelled. Record on the board as students brainstorm onomatopoeic words. Then, make up some new ones, such as *pring* and *flark,* using each descriptively in a sentence. Ask each student to write a short story or a comic strip that uses as many onomatopoeic words as possible and read them aloud in class. Encourage them to use tone, volume, and other sound qualities of the voice so that onomatopoeic words sound as real as possible.

12f. Language Sounds Assign individuals or groups of students to record a wide range of spoken voices; for example, men with low voices, women with high voices, adolescents with squeaky voices, and cartoon voices. Analyze differences in pitch and other sound qualities. Have students record their own voices as well and compare how they sound to themselves with how they sound to others. Next, record declarative statements versus questions and examine differences in pitch and inflection (statements have falling pitch, while questions have rising pitch). Experiment by recording a phrase, such as "You are going to the zoo," as both a question and a statement. Compare the sound patterns of different languages. For example, Spanish syllable length is even, English has more inflection and long and short syllables, French is nasal, Chinese is tonal, German is guttural, and some African languages use clicks and pops as parts of speech.

12g. Radio Daze In class, listen to recordings of old radio shows, paying special attention to sound effects. Have students, in groups of five or six, create their own radio show, complete with sound effects. Three possibilities include creative writing read aloud and embellished with sound effects; a modern-day version of "War of the Worlds" by H. G. Wells (a radio broadcast about aliens taking over earth; it may be available on tape); and student-created newscasts of real events, current or historical, with sound effects in the background. Tape record student radio shows. If the products are professional and informative, broadcast them over the school public address system. If you are really ambitious, approach a local radio station to broadcast student work.

Onomatopoetic Vowels

12h. Hamming It Up Invite a ham radio operator to demonstrate the equipment and how to use it to contact people from all over the world. This is a wonderful way to bring alive a lesson on geography or multicultural differences. For more information write to: American Radio Relay League (ARRL), Educational Activities Department, 225 Main Street, Newington, CT 06111; or call (203) 666-1541. ARRL can put you in contact with ham radio operators in your area, plus send an educational packet about setting up a ham radio in your classroom.

Hamming in the Classroom

Ham radio has many educational tools to offer the classroom, but one especially useful system is AMTOR (Amateur Teleprinting Over Radio). AMTOR lets you converse with other ham radio stations using an operator-supplied personal computer to type and receive messages. Whereas voice contacts carry the excitement of bringing people from around the world into your classroom, AMTOR printouts give students access to written communication long after the contact is over. This enhances comprehension and gives you time to answer questions or plot the location of the operator. You can also print out the contact and send it home to families, which extends the learning environment by allowing them to get involved.

12i. In Sound Health Have students research how sound is used to determine human health and sickness. Invite a physician or veterinarian into your classroom or take a field trip to visit them. Find out what doctors expect to hear when they thump on your back. Have students study how ultrasound is used to diagnose the condition of a fetus. Let them listen through a stethoscope to the sound of breathing or a heart beating. Have them find out what happens when we wheeze, cough, hiccup, or burp. Just before lunch, have students listen to one another's stomachs through a paper towel tube or rolled construction paper. Have them listen again after lunch. Ask if anyone knows what makes our stomachs "growl."

12j. Sounding Out All sound is composed of vibrations moving through air, similar to waves rippling through water when a pebble is thrown into it. As a class, study the physics of sound. Challenge yourself or cooperative groups of students to make visual demonstrations of what vibrations look like and the difference between high and low tones.

Vibration Demo

One way to make vibrations visible is to place a long ruler at the edge of a table, with one-third on the table and two-thirds sticking out. Hold the end on the table firmly and strike the other end so it vibrates rapidly enough to produce a sound. Or place a piece of paper over a drum and show how it vibrates when you strike the surface. To show how differences in pitch are due to differences in frequency of sound waves, place two rubber bands of different thicknesses around a book. One at a time, pluck the rubber bands in the area between the pencils. Listen to the sound produced by each. Make the pitch higher and lower by moving the pencils closer together or farther apart.

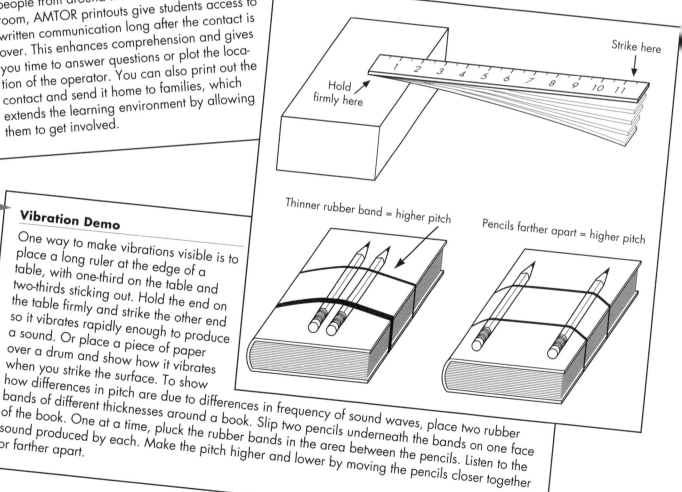

Strike here

Hold firmly here

Thinner rubber band = higher pitch

Pencils farther apart = higher pitch

12k. Good Vibrations Here are some ideas for an advanced unit on the physics of vibration. Have students research sonar waves, sonic booms, and the difference between speeds of sound and light. Study seismic waves as vibrations of the earth's surface, and how an earthquake occurs. Have students define aftershocks. Discover that each object possesses a natural frequency that can be dangerous at times, as when glass cracks by a human voice or a bridge collapses after a gust of wind sets it oscillating. Learn about white noise; have students find and record examples of it. Devise clever experiments to bring each concept alive in the classroom.

White Noise

White noise is a complex sound composed of many different pitches with similar volume spaced so closely together in frequency that the sound ceases to have pitch. Examples include sounds of traffic in the street, a river rushing by, and static on the radio.

Teacher's Corner

★ Take a moment to listen to sounds around you. Do you tend to tune into these sounds or tune them out? How do you use different sounds in the classroom to gauge what is happening? Do you use sounds to address the needs of students who are auditory and musical learners?

★ Be imaginative about using different kinds of sounds in the classroom. Consider integrating these creatively into your curricula. Most local libraries have extensive tape collections.

★ Here is a fun way to self-reflect using sound: Divide a typical week into at least five distinct phases; for example, class time, dinner time, weekends, early morning time, and bowling league. Next, improvise and tape record, if possible, sounds that capture each phase. Have fun—don't worry about being accurate. Then listen to the tape and reflect upon the significance of each sound you have chosen, especially how it reflects your environment and feelings.

★ Go through your phases once again, adding sound effects for an ideal description of each. Can you think of ways to bring your ideal closer to your real?

★ If appropriate, find a creative way to adapt autobiographical Sound Logs (see 12d) into a class assignment.

CAN YOU BEAT THAT!
LESSON 13

Everything, from an opening flower to a beating heart, has its own dance in time. In "Can You Beat That!" the class explores rhythm by keeping time to different meters. Walking to the beat of a metronome or drum, students practice fine- and gross-muscle isolation by moving their arms and bodies to the rhythm in increasingly complex formations. Students practice many levels of coordination with their bodies, the beat, music, and other students. They choreograph their own sequences, which builds confidence. This lesson fuses sound, shape, and direction, and draws upon many of the skills developed in the unit so far. Use this lesson to introduce dance and to examine rhythm across the curriculum—from music, to poetry, to cycles in nature.

Preparation

★ Move to a gym or clear a large area of the classroom.

Materials

drum, metronome, or other instrument to keep beat

Exercise

① Start a regular drum beat. Have students walk precisely to its rhythm, taking one step per beat. They may walk in any direction they wish, being careful not to bump into each other.

② Once everyone is on beat, slow down and speed up the tempo of the rhythm. Prompt students to walk slowly at one extreme and quickly at the other to maintain exactly one step per beat.

③ Arrange the class in one large circle.

④ Again ask students to take one step per beat, walking around in a circle. Use the drum to beat out different meters, accenting the first beat of each phrase as follows:

two beat:	1–2	1–2	1–2
three beat:	1–2–3	1–2–3	1–2–3
four beat:	1–2–3–4	1–2–3–4	1–2–3–4

Have students practice walking and accenting the first beat of two-, three-, and four-beat phrases. They accent the first beat by clapping, stamping, snapping their fingers, or raising an arm, according to what you call out. Switch accenting method without missing a beat. It helps to stop moving between different meters, using the signal "and stop. . . ." Begin again by signaling "and ONE. . . ." As the class gains mastery, return to an unmarked, steady beat, calling out both the meter and the form of accent.

⑤ For an additional challenge, provide movements not only for the accented beat, but also for the others. Possible four-beat sequences include:

CLAP–right arm up–left arm up–both arms out
CLAP–2–3–**CLAP**
1–2–3–jump
1–2–3–reverse direction

⑥ Let students take turns as leaders for changing the sequence. Encourage the class to devise creative movements for the sequences.

⑦ You can get complex and creative with this lesson. If desired, spend several sessions exploring the possibilities. Some examples are listed below.

> *a. Arrange the class into several nested circles, one inside the other. Choreograph different four-beat sequences for each circle. Have the circles move in opposite directions.*

> *b. Split the class into two groups. Use a double-triangle class formation, in which students move in opposite directions along the diagonal. Choreograph different moves for each leg of the triangle; for example skips, gallop, and hops. Try contrasting moves for the groups.*

> *c. Choreograph an eight-beat sequence. Split the class into two groups. Start one group on the first beat, the second group four beats later. Try using longer sequences or more groups. This is similar to a round (as in Row, Row, Row Your Boat), canon, or fugue. Listen to different examples of polyphonic (multivoiced) music and choreograph movements to accompany each voice.*

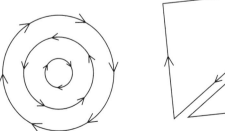

Example A

Example B

Discussion

◆ What did you experience during this lesson?

◆ What was fun about it? What was hard about it?

◆ What is rhythm?

◆ How many different aspects of life can you name that have rhythm?

Rhythm

Rhythm involves a regular recurrence of elements, phases, actions, or functions. In music the rhythm is determined by the pattern of the music's accent or beat. In art or literature, rhythm involves the pacing and repetition of a patterned motif or formal element at regular or irregular intervals. Many, if not most, aspects of our lives involve rhythm—from the beating of our hearts, to our eating and sleeping cycles, to the rhythm of the seasons or tides.

◆ What is syncopation?

Syncopation

Syncopation involves shifting the accent or rhythm by stressing normally unaccented beats. To demonstrate, slowly and regularly speak, "1 . . . 2 . . . 3 . . . 4 . . . ," at first having students clap with your voice on each number. To practice syncopation, have students clap during the silence between each number.

◆ What is dance?

  • *What skills go into being a good dancer?*
  • *What are some types of dance and what are similarities and differences between each type?*

◆ How does this lesson relate to rhythm and dance?

◆ When is dancing a creative activity? When is it not?

◆ How many ways can you think of to use rhythm and dance as tools for learning?

Extensions

13a. Echo in Here Arrange the class in a large circle with everyone kneeling. Present a motion pattern that has four beats and have the class repeat it. The pattern could involve clapping, snapping, tapping the floor or thighs, or crossing arms and tapping shoulders. Repeat the pattern a couple of times, then switch to a new one. Begin simply, then try double time (twice as fast). After some practice, select student leaders to start a pattern. Try to switch leaders without losing a beat. Below are some examples of patterns a leader could use. The class could repeat the pattern without losing a beat.

> **CLAP** . . . clap . . . clap . . . clap
> **CLAP** . . . snap . . . clap . . . snap
> **CLAP** . . . snap . . . clap . . . shoulder
> **SNAP** . . . clap . . . snap . . . shoulders
> **FLOOR** . . . lap . . . snap . . . clap
> **CLAP** . . . lap . . . snap . . . shoulders
> **CLAP** . . . clap . . . clap . . . clap . . . clap . . . clap . . . clap . . . clap (double time)
> **CLAP** . . . snap . . . lap . . . CLAP (accented beat)
> **SNAP** . . . snap . . . (pause) . . . lap (syncopated beat)

13b. You Can Sing That Again Try a singing variation of the above. Have the leader sing and clap any four-beat phrase, which the class echoes. Below is an example.

> **Leader:** Oh, once there was . . .
> **Class:** Oh, once there was . . .
> **Leader:** A very happy boy . . . (echo)
> He had just got . . . (echo)
> A brand new toy . . . (echo)

Encourage students to make up any words, no matter how silly. They can improvise or make up short poems ahead of time, varying words, rhythm, and tune. For a challenge, combine this Extension with 13a, using call-and-response singing combined with movements.

Dance

Dance involves knowledge and control over your body's musculature, the ability to hear and move in relation to music or a beat, the ability to express feelings and images through movement, the ability to orient yourself physically in space, and the ability to coordinate your movements with those of others. Classical ballet is very technical, requiring years of training. It stresses precise control of muscles and coordination with others. Tap dancing, flamenco, and soft-shoe stress rhythm, beat, and sound. Ballroom and folk dancing stress coordination with others. Modern dance emphasizes the ability to evoke feelings and images.

13c. Dancing on Paper Play a piece of live or pre-recorded music. Have students translate qualities, such as tone and duration, into visual art. Have them choose five colors to draw dots, circles, and wavy or jagged lines to represent different qualities of musical sound, rhythm, or beat. Look at the artwork of musicians such as Miles Davis to see other examples of visual music.

In this painting of a jazz musician, we can almost see the frenetic beat. Bernard Hoyes, *New Age Improvisation*.

13d. Music Alive
Videotape and bring samples of music videos to class (or have your students do this). Analyze sound and rhythm qualities of each piece and ways in which the visual images fit the words and music. Have students, in small groups, bring in or make up a song (perhaps relevant to social studies or science). Have groups choreograph the song and perform it. If possible, videotape performances. You could also have students choreograph a dance to music or a poem or make up a poem or a rap and add music or movement to it.

Here is some modern magic—a rock and roll genie. Can you beat that?

13e. Meter in Poetry Have the class explore the relationship between meter and poetry. Review styles of poetry, such as sonnets, limericks, and haiku, which have specific meter requirements. Review the difference between poetry that uses a regular meter and that which does not, such as the work of beatnik poet Allen Ginsberg. Have students practice writing, illustrating, and reciting metered and unmetered poetry related to themes of dance, rhythm, and cycles of nature.

Meter in Poetry

Meter is all about rhythm. In poetry it involves the arrangement of words in rhythmic lines or verses or refers to a particular form of such an arrangement. An example, often used in the sonnets of Shakespeare, Keats, and Shelley, is iambic pentameter: *iambic beat* refers to an unaccented syllable followed by an accented one; *pentameter* means there are five beats (called *feet* in poetry) per line. Sonnets have fourteen lines. The first twelve describe a mood or outline a problem; the last two summarize or conclude the poem. The rhyming pattern is abab cdcd efef gg. Limericks are a form of humorous verse composed of five lines and the rhyming pattern aabba: lines one, two, and five have three feet (or beats); lines three and four have two feet (see page 105). Haiku is a Japanese form of poetry that contains seventeen syllables, divided into three lines of five, seven, and five syllables. It is usually light, delicate, and centered on nature.

13f. Math Meter Combine the study of musical notation with math. For example, you could practice addition and subtraction of fractions by assigning 1/8, 1/4, 1/2, and 1 to eighth notes, quarter notes, half notes, and whole notes respectively. Teach the symbols of musical notation illustrated below. As a next step, include rest notes. Try listening to computer-generated music with the class. Discuss whether computers can be creative.

♪ = Eighth note

♩ = Quarter note

𝅘𝅥 = Half note

o = Whole note

𝄽 = Quarter rest

$\frac{1}{4} + \frac{1}{4} + \frac{1}{2}$ $\frac{1}{4} + \frac{1}{16} + \frac{1}{16} + \frac{1}{4} + \frac{1}{4}$ $\frac{4}{4}$ Each measure adds up to $\frac{4}{4}$.

time signature   measure line

$\frac{1}{8}+\frac{1}{8}+\frac{1}{8}+\frac{1}{8}+\frac{1}{8}+\frac{1}{8}$ $\frac{1}{2} + \frac{1}{4}$ $\frac{1}{2} + \frac{1}{4}$ Each measure adds up to $\frac{3}{4}$.

Meter in Music

In music, *meter* refers to the rhythmic element of musical notation, measured by dividing the piece into parts, or measures, of equal time value. A meter sign, located at the beginning of each musical line, indicates the number of beats per measure and the value of the note per beat. In the example below there are three measures per line. In the top line the meter sign of 4/4 indicates four beats per measure and one quarter note per beat (four quarter notes per measure). In the bottom line the 3/4 meter sign indicates three beats per measure and one quarter note per beat (three quarter notes per measure). Any combination of eighth, quarter, half, or whole notes can make up a given measure. Rest notes indicate silence for a specific duration.

13g. Nature's Got Rhythm Do a unit on rhythms of nature. Have students dance different natural rhythms such as blood circulating in the body, plants growing, phototropism, and birds dancing in courtship. Consider Plato's idea that the movement of the planets is "music of the spheres." Discuss how we can consider the whole ecological system nature's dance. Relate this to James Lovelock's Gaia hypothesis, named after the ancient Greek goddess. This is the view that the earth is one living, breathing, waste-producing organism, who must be carefully nurtured (see Extension 27i, page 169).

The Hindu god Shiva is believed to sustain the world through dance. Shiva often symbolizes the unfolding of time, representing both feared destroyer and adored re-creator.

13h. Everyone's Got Rhythm Like music, dance is a universal art form, existing in every culture throughout history. It is a perfect arena for a multicultural unit. Study dance from different cultures and historical periods. Have students learn and then teach steps of traditional dances from their own ethnic and cultural groups. Look at pictures of costumes together, or have students draw or create ones of their own. Discuss ways in which elements of dance, such as costume, choreography, and music, mirror each culture. Invite guests into the classroom to demonstrate different forms of dance.

An Armenian dance troop. Levon Parian, *Untitled*.

Teacher's Corner

★ Each of our lives has its unique beat, rhythms, and themes. Some of us move quickly through our activities, doing many things; others move more slowly and deliberately. Some of us are morning people who jump out of bed awake and alert; others are nocturnal and become more energetic and active at night. To get more in touch with your unique beat rhythms and themes, divide your life into several distinct phases; for example, childhood, adolescence, early adulthood, and middle adulthood. For each phase select each of the following: a tempo for its beat (fast, slow, regular, irregular); one or more instruments to express it (for example, violins, bagpipes, harmonicas); a kind of music to capture its themes (ballads, marching bands, bluegrass music); and a form of dance to express its rhythms (twists, watusi, waltzes, break dances, jigs).

★ What tempo, instrument, kind of music, and form of dance would you select for your next phase of life?

★ Pick at least one life phase—past, present, or future—and make up a song about it, either by creating your own melody or putting words to a pre-existing melody.

★ Pick at least one life phase and dance it, with or without music.

★ See if you can creatively incorporate aspects of this Teacher's Corner into the classroom; for example, use current vocabulary to make up a class song or use music of a particular era to make up a class dance.

EXPRESSION CITY
LESSON 14

This lesson introduces the notion of multiple intelligences, providing the conceptual framework for all of Creativity Inside Out. Students brainstorm different modes of self-expression, translating an idea from one realm to another, such as poetry to music, music to dance, and dance to spoken language. They explore different symbol systems, some easy to use, some more difficult. Students are encouraged to experiment with unfamiliar systems, putting aside self-consciousness. They learn that they mine the true gems of creativity in the cracks between intelligences—as two or more intelligences blend together. Discussion helps polish these jewels, centering upon the importance of creativity in self-concept and dispelling common myths that restrict creative self-expression.

Preparation

★ Collect photographs of people exercising each of the intelligences; for example, a child playing the piano (musical), a person at a computer terminal (logical-mathematical), a pilot flying (spatial), a person reading (linguistic), a person playing basketball (body-kinesthetic), and a scene of a party (social).

Materials

photographs (described above); construction paper; choice of visual arts materials, such as crayons, paints, and colored pencils; tape or pins for displaying student products; "Learning Style and Multiple Intelligences" sheet (optional; see page 36)

Exercise

1. Use the photographs to introduce students to the theory of multiple intelligences, using the "Learning Style and Multiple Intelligences" sheet as a student sheet or a teacher resource.

What Is Intelligence?

Intelligence is not just about our ability to do a math problem, to score high on an IQ test, or to understand a difficult passage of a book. Along with logical-mathematical and linguistic skills are many other kinds of intelligence, including abilities to orient or visualize things in space (spatial intelligence), to understand ourselves and others (intrapersonal and interpersonal intelligences, or social intelligences), to control and position our muscles and bodies (body or kinesthetic intelligence), and to express ourselves musically (musical intelligence). There may be more kinds of intelligence. Each is a different way of learning, relatively separate from the next. Each has its own vocabulary and set of symbols, its own skills, methods for expression, and for remembering. Every person has a unique blend of talents among the intelligences.

---

2. Arrange the class in circular groups of six or seven, or do the activity with the entire class.

3. Have students brainstorm and act out the many ways people can express themselves. One student might sing a song, another dance, and a third mime using a typewriter. Have students take turns brainstorming modes of self-expression until they run out of ideas. Assign, or allow students to choose, a recorder for each group to keeps a list of modes of self-expression.

4. Have groups translate their list of modes of self-expression to a visual format, such as an Expression City or Multiple Intelligences poster or mural.

5. Showcase, contrast, and compare group products.

Discussion

◆ Why is it important to recognize that each of us possesses many kinds of intelligence and many ways of expressing ourselves?

◆ Does understanding and accepting all aspects of ourselves help us express ourselves more fully? How?

◆ What are some ways our weaknesses can contribute to our strengths; for example, by having persistence or trying extra hard?

◆ Is there a right and wrong for each kind of intelligence? Explain.

◆ Where does creativity come from? How does it develop?

◆ What are some ways we restrict our own creativity unnecessarily?

◆ Is being creative the same thing as having talent in one or more of the intelligences? If not, what is the difference?

◆ How important is technical perfection to any creative act?

◆ Why is it important to consider ourselves creative, no matter what our blend of talents and experience?

◆ How can we make sure creativity always stays a part of our lives?

Extensions

14a. Group Multiples To explore multiple intelligences through creative brainstorming, divide students into groups of three. Have each student represent a different intelligence. Have groups translate a theme into three different modes of expression. For example, the theme could be a vase of flowers, the culture of Afghanistan, or the Stone Age. One student could write a poem, which could stimulate a set of equations by a second student and a dance by the third. Group members should feel free to collaborate on each of the representations.

14b. Math Multiples Translate arithmetic problems into a form that involves one or more unusual intelligence. For example, individually, in pairs, or in small groups, students could glue pebbles to a page (body-kinesthetic), count tones (musical), or use fingers (body-kinesthetic) to count in different bases. You or students could invent word problems (linguistic) that use one or more different intelligences (such as social and spatial). Try having students translate the same arithmetic problem into three different forms.

The most creative acts often grow in the fertile soil between intelligences where two or more domains blend in a unique way. In this cartoon, forms of spatial and body-kinesthetic intelligence appear together.

14c. Literary Intelligence Pick a book or short story to study. Have each student choose a character to analyze. Ask how this character might express himself or herself creatively in one or more of the intelligences. Ask what they might draw, dance, or sing. For example, students could work in small groups to compose dances for the three pigs at various points in the story, such as when they discovered problems with the straw house versus the safety of the brick house. Have the class express other abstract ideas, such as concepts of *friendship* and *freedom,* using as many different intelligences as possible.

14d. Multimedia Feelings Ask students to create multimedia presentations of a feeling using images, words, movement, and music.

14e. Multiple Intelligence Profiles Introduce the connection between the intelligences and learning styles to the class—each intelligence represents another way to learn material. Help students identify which intelligences they use readily and easily during interests, activities, and learning in school, as well as which they have difficulty with. Use the "Multiple Intelligences Profile" sheet (page 73) to help you identify student strengths, weaknesses, and learning styles. Notice if student interests and skills are concentrated in a single domain or spread across many.

14f. Learning Style Speech Brainstorm figures of speech that are slanted toward particular learning styles and intelligences. Throughout the day, have students notice and record figures of speech they use or hear others use related to the intelligences. Try comparing different ways to express understanding or the lack of it. Example could include:

- *Linguistic learners:* "I hear you." "Loud and clear." "Speak for yourself."
- *Logical learners:* "Fair and square." "That make sense." "Prove it to me."

- **Spatial learners:** *"I see." "I get the picture." "I'm lost."*
- **Kinesthetic learners:** *"I have a feel for that." "That doesn't grab me."*
- **Musical learners:** *"Are you tuned in?" "That rings a bell."*
- **Social learners:** *"Just between you and me." "Let's make a deal."*

14g. Multiple Intelligent Tutors

Establish a student tutor training program in which students strong in a particular intelligence are paired with students who are weaker in that intelligence. Pick typical assignments—learning vocabulary, solving a math problem, memorizing facts about a historical period, or comparing and contrasting two characters in a story—and pair each student as both a tutor and a tutee. Make individualized assignments for each pair, formalizing them with contracts if desired (see page 33). Supervise tutor teams regularly.

14h. Multiple Risk

Give students 30 minutes to experiment with an intelligence they rarely or never use. Anticipate the anxiety of trying new modes in which students may not feel knowledgeable or skilled. Discuss the self-consciousness and embarrassment that arises when we try new forms of self-expression. Practice ways of working with these feelings so they will not prevent students from trying new things. One method is to look foolish on purpose. Find tricks to ease experimentation; for example, tearing the paper before drawing or drawing tiny figures in the corner of pages. (If you tear the paper, it's easier to relax and not try to create a masterpiece, since the work is already ruined. Similarly, it can be intimidating to try to make a full-page drawing; "hiding" in a corner can help break the ice.) You might want to make this safer by omitting grades or formal evaluation.

14i. Intelligentsia to the Rescue

Have students write a short story about a child who struggles with a problem in which the solution is the discovery of one of the intelligences.

14j. Intelligent Interviews

As a homework assignment or field trip, have groups of seven students record, write about, or orally present interviews of people who primarily represent one of the seven intelligences; for example, a physicist (logical-mathematical), a psychologist (intrapersonal), a businessperson (interpersonal), a painter (spatial), a musician (musical), a sports figure (body-kinesthetic), and an author (linguistic). Students should include direct quotes, especially related to their intelligence of interest and to how each expert views creativity within this domain.

14k. Multiple Learning Stations

Set up learning stations for each intelligence. You could link each station to the same theme, such as Africa or the Middle Ages. Or each could cover a different theme. Allow students to visit them regularly. Read *Multiple Intelligences in the Classroom* by Thomas Armstrong for more information and ideas.

> Each of us is a full pot exploding with potential.

Teacher's Corner

★ Fill out a "Multiple Intelligence Profile" on yourself. Analyze your strengths and weaknesses and compare them with your general self-concept.

- *Do you generally consider yourself a talented or multitalented person?*
- *With which intelligences are you most creative? Least creative?*

★ Do you consider yourself a creative person? Why or why not?

★ What myths have you entertained about your own creativity?

★ In what ways does your creativity flow smoothly? In what ways do you struggle creatively?

★ How does the absence or presence of creativity in your self-concept affect your teaching and the creative self-concept of your students?

★ If you dare, select four totally unfamiliar modes of self-expression over the next week (such as baking pies, writing poetry, bowling, and song writing). Spend at least 15 minutes experimenting with each.

★ True creativity is usually mined in the cracks between intelligences where a combination of two or more blend in a unique way. Name three ways you could try blending intelligences outside the classroom. Name five ways you could blend more than one intelligence in the classroom.

★ For 5 minutes, brainstorm ways to help your students be more creative using multiple intelligences.

★ There is much room for your originality in using multiple intelligences in the curriculum. Experiment boldly, both personally and professionally.

Name _____ Date _____

Multiple Intelligences Profile

Rank each set of activities with a number from 1 to 7 where 1 is the lowest in total time, preference, or talent and 7 is the highest.

I spend the most time:
_____ Playing an instrument (f)
_____ Drawing or painting (b)
_____ Being with others (d)
_____ Writing poems, stories, or entries for my journal (a)
_____ Working with computers, models, or science projects (c)
_____ Doing things by myself (e)
_____ Exercising or playing sports (g)

I prefer to:
_____ Take objects apart and figure out how they work (c)
_____ Exercise, ride a bike, or be active with my body (g)
_____ Look at comics, art, or movies (b)
_____ Join clubs and social activities (d)
_____ Listen to music (f)
_____ Read a book (a)
_____ Think about myself, my life, and how I handle situations (e)

I am good at:
_____ Recognizing, remembering, humming, or singing tunes (f)
_____ Understanding people, knowing and appreciating people (d)
_____ Talking, writing, or playing with language and words (a)
_____ Looking at things, drawing, using maps (b)
_____ Using my hands or body to make or do things (g)
_____ Constructing things, pulling them apart, or asking "why?" (c)
_____ Being by myself, doing things at my own initiative and pace (e)

I learn best by:
_____ Talking to others (d)
_____ Tuning into rhythm, turning things into a song (f)
_____ Seeing or making a picture, map, or diagram of an idea (b)
_____ Practicing, moving around a lot, and doing things (g)
_____ Taking time to understand things by myself (e)
_____ Listening, reading and writing, or speaking to myself (a)
_____ Analyzing, explaining, and understanding why (c)

Profile
To score, add up the totals for each letter and place them next to the intelligence it represents. The highest number indicates the intelligence in which you have the greatest interest, time, energy, or skill. The lowest number indicates the intelligence in which you have the least interest, time, energy, or skill.

a. Linguistic ___   e. Intrapersonal ___
b. Spatial ___   f. Musical ___
c. Logical-Mathematical ___   g. Body-Kinesthetic ___
d. Interpersonal ___

UNIT 3

The Shape of Things: Explorations of Outer Space

WHAT'S THE POINT?
LESSON 15

The point is the simplest and most fundamental shape. The ability to detect the presence or absence of a point in space and its relative position is a primary skill. "What's the Point?" introduces the most basic of an increasingly complex repertoire of shapes explored in the unit. The class uses dots to explore issues of space and crowding in visual compositions. Students translate their perceptual experiences into words, a first step toward attaining visual literacy skills that enable us to analyze and to communicate in any of the visual media. They are sensitized to issues of space and crowding at the visual level and ways in which they can build complex shapes and colors from simple ones. Extension activities broaden exploration of the point to reveal complexity and order often hidden in the surrounding world.

Preparation

★ Close your eyes briefly and relax. Then open your eyes, as if for the first time. Sensitize yourself all the different kinds of dots, such as dust, sand, freckles, and salt, that you can find in the world around you.

★ Collect pairs of photographs, cartoons, or drawings that display contrasting concepts of space and crowding at the visual level. For example, pair a photograph of a desert scene with one of a rain forest.

★ If you have only one or two hole punchers available, fill small containers with punched dots in various colors and alter the Exercise accordingly. Involve students creatively in this preparation. For example, hole punching could be a reward (or punishment) for fidgety students.

Materials

construction paper in many colors; scissors; pencils and colored markers; hole punchers; glue; pins or tape to display student work

Exercise

① Review with students pairs of photographs or other visual material you've collected. Have students decide which of each pair is more illustrative of space, and which of crowding. Ask them to analyze which features contribute to their impressions; for example, the number of elements, the spacing between them, and the vantage point of the viewer.

② Have each student pick two sheets of construction paper of contrasting colors. The darker sheet should be the same width as and half the length of the lighter one.

③ Have students punch dots from the smaller sheet to display their concept of *space*. Students decide the number of dots to punched, but they should keep in mind that the same number of dots must be used to display concepts of both *space* and *crowding*.

④ Tell students to save each punched-out dot and glue them onto one half of the large sheet of paper, displaying their own concepts of *crowding*.

⑤ Have students glue the half-size representation of *space* onto the unused half of the large sheet.

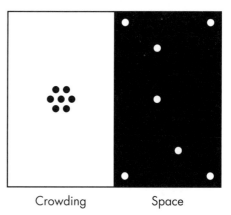

Crowding   Space

⑥ Have students label *space* and *crowding* halves to create a two-paneled piece of artwork known as a *diptych*.

⑦ Showcase student productions side by side.

Discussion

◆ What are similarities and differences in how you and your classmates used dots?

◆ How many different ways did you highlight the concept of *space* (for example, did anyone use dots along edges, in corners only, spaced out across page)?

◆ How did you represent the concept of *crowding* (for example, did anyone put dots in clusters or group them in center)?

- Which were especially unusual strategies to represent these concepts (for example, did anyone glue dots one on top of another)?

- In each composition, how do the two panels relate to one another?

- Does viewing compositions at different distances affect what is seen? If so, how?

- Where in our everyday world can we find collections of points or dots (for example, talcum powder, sugar, poppy seed bread, hour glasses, beaches)?

- In what ways is the point the origin of all shape?

African patterns (for examples, see *Art from Many Hands* by Jo Miles Schuman) or original designs to sketch and transfer a final design onto the aluminum with carbon paper. Working over several layers of newspaper, they hammer out dots one at a time by hitting hard enough to make an impression but not so hard they poke a hole through the metal.

15c. Sand Paintings Study examples of Native American sand paintings. Invite the class to make their own sand paintings by dying sand with various shades of ink. Have students sketch a simple design, either original or based on traditional Indian patterns. They should use separate small sheets of tracing paper to copy and cut out a template for each part of their design intended as a different color. Using the templates, have students glue colored sand onto a background of heavy paper or cardboard.

Here is an example of a diptych. Notice how the elements are similar, but the birds and branches partition space differently in the panels. Joan Lehman, *Blackbirds*.

Extensions

15a. Space Art Collect old toothbrushes. Have students dip them in white paint and then drag their thumb across the bristles while pointing the brush towards a piece of colored paper. This will splatter white dots across the page, providing a starry background for planets, rockets, meteors, satellites, or other objects in space. You could use this activity with an astronomy lesson. You could also have students paint a composition that includes rain drops or snow fall. Have them invent techniques to make the precipitation look realistic.

15b. Counter-Repoussé Nigerian artists have a technique of embossing aluminum plates with dots, called *counter-repoussé,* that you can do with your class (suggested in *KidsArt,* issue 21, 1991). Use thin sheets of aluminum (you can buy this in a hardware store) cut into small rectangles with tin snips. Provide each student with a hammer or large chunk of wood and a large, dull nail or bolt for embossing the metal. Student can use either traditional

Native American sand paintings were often created for spiritual purposes, then the sand dispersed to emphasize the transitory nature of life.

15d. Polka-dotted Komic Kraze Study dots in the blown-up comic art of pop artists such as Andy Warhol and Roy Lichtenstein. Have students examine comics through a magnifying glass and see that they are made from tiny colored dots. Have them mark a square centimeter of a comic strip picture and count the number of dots under a magnifying glass. Ask students to estimate how many dots it would take to cover the entire picture, the top of the table, and the floor of the classroom. To check their accuracy, students could enlarge their square-centimeter section on a copying machine or exchange papers with another student. Students may choose another small section of a comic to enlarge as the basis for a work of art.

15e. What's the Pointillist?
Research pointillism. After viewing examples, have students make pointillist pictures of their own using fine dots made with colored markers or paint. (With paint, it helps to use a firm object such as a stick to achieve dots of uniform size.) Bring color theory into the discussion; for example, show how Georges Seurat created purple by using specks of red and blue. Ask what other secondary colors are perceived through close associations of different primary colors. Have students research or test the difference when colored lights are combined rather than colored paint. In class, examine a color-blind test composed of small dots of different colors. With older or gifted students, study the difference between rods and cones and how the eye perceives color. For a multicultural twist, examine the use of dots in Aboriginal artwork to portray dreamtime.

ric objects, such as a cube, table, and house, using single-point perspective. If your class shows interest and ambition, advance to two-point perspective. Study realism in Renaissance art or in modern American painting, where one- and two-point perspective has been frequently employed.

15g. Connect-the-Dots Math
Have each student make a simple drawing of straight lines, using a hole-punch to punch out key places in the drawing, such as corners and juncture points. (Add an interesting dimension with punchers shaped like stars, hearts, and such.) The punched-out

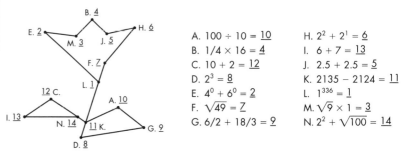

A. $100 \div 10 = \underline{10}$	H. $2^2 + 2^1 = \underline{6}$
B. $1/4 \times 16 = \underline{4}$	I. $6 + 7 = \underline{13}$
C. $10 + 2 = \underline{12}$	J. $2.5 + 2.5 = \underline{5}$
D. $2^3 = \underline{8}$	K. $2135 - 2124 = \underline{11}$
E. $4^0 + 6^0 = \underline{2}$	L. $1^{336} = \underline{1}$
F. $\sqrt{49} = \underline{7}$	M. $\sqrt{9} \times 1 = \underline{3}$
G. $6/2 + 18/3 = \underline{9}$	N. $2^2 + \sqrt{100} = \underline{14}$

drawing serves as a template to draw dots for connect-the-dot pictures. Have students letter the series of dots in any order, then write each letter at the bottom of the page followed by an arithmetic problem. The solution to the problems should indicate the order in which the dots are numbered. Have students exchange papers with a partner who will solve the math problems, connect the dots, and color the drawing. For advanced students, apply the same techniques to algebra using graph paper and dots plotted on the x and y axes. Students could use negative instead of positive numbers, or decimals of increasing values. If possible, copy examples of each student's work for the entire class to complete. Or combine them into a book for other classes.

Pointillism
Pointillism is a style of modern art in which paintings are made from thousands of very small dots of different colors. A single painting could sometimes take more than a year to complete. Georges Seurat, Louis Hayet, Paul Signet, and Albert Dubois-Pillet were pointillist painters.

15f. One- and Two-Point Perspective
Teach your class the drawing technique of one-point perspective. Use the "One- and Two-Point Perspective" sheet (page 80) as a teaching tool. Let students practice drawing simple geomet-

Perspective
Perspective is the use of graphic techniques for representing three-dimensional objects on a two-dimensional surface. One- and two-point perspective involves single or double perspective points drawn on the horizon from which invisible lines radiate. The lines determine the angles of objects drawn, giving them a realistic appearance as they recede into the background. Renaissance and baroque artists, such as Mantegna, El Greco, and Caravaggio, brought these techniques to a new level. Many modern American painters, such as Thomas Eakins, James Whistler, John Sargent, Winslow Homer, Edward Hopper, and Andrew Wyeth, also employed realism.

15h. Bits of Hardware Research how television works. With the class, examine a color television set with a magnifying glass to see how the picture is composed of a series of colored dots. Teach the theory behind the operation of a computer, which has many, many rows of *bits* that are either in "on" or "off" position. Have students play with computer-generated, dot-matrix graphics; print out their pictures; and examine them under a magnifying glass or microscope.

15i. What's the Point of Point? Take 5 minutes of class time to brainstorm all the possible uses for the word *point*. Write a sentence containing each on the chalkboard. Classify each usage according to its part of speech; for example, verb (to point to something), noun (to make a point), and adjective (to hold a pointed debate). Then use your list to review the difference between concrete concepts (to point to something) and abstract concepts (to make a point).

15j. Pointless Pursuits Take 5 minutes in class to brainstorm a list of pointless inventions. Or play a Pointless Pursuits game, involving the art of summarizing pointless information. Have students make up pointless sentences, paragraphs, or stories, which others summarize in a word, sentence, or paragraph, respectively. Mix the pointless originals and the summaries together, and see whether others can correctly match each original with its summary. Try a visual version of Pointless Pursuits, in which a symbol or picture is used to summarize the point of a sentence, paragraph, or story. Try using a pointer as a prop.

It's All Dots

Television images are created when tiny dots of color—red, green, and blue—are excited by an electron beam and radiate light. The eye is fooled into seeing a continuous, moving picture rather than a collection of disconnected dots. Just as red, green, and blue colors can be mixed on a painter's canvas, red, green, and blue dots illuminated at different intensities radiate light of any color. Unlike the artist's palette, white is created when all three colors are illuminated at the same intensity.

Teacher's Corner

★ Over the course of this lesson, we have moved from a concrete Exercise, working with physical dots, to abstract Extensions, which get to the point metaphorically. This Teacher's Corner remains abstract. Write three sentences in response to each question below—from your own point of view.

- *What is the point of focusing on self-expression and creativity anyway?*
- *What is the point of multicultural training to appreciate differences among students?*
- *What is the point of boosting visual literacy skills?*
- *What is the point of emphasizing communication skills?*
- *What is the point of paying attention to student esteem or the lack of it?*

★ Choose two or three of your own sentences from any set above to express in a different style, such as metaphoric, poetic, or as a sales pitch.

★ Pick at least one sentence from above and illustrate it with a drawing or diagram that uses one- or two-point perspective.

★ Try asking, "What's the point?" in class at interesting times during the day—such as a point of high emotional intensity or one of low interest or boredom. This can stimulate critical thinking and help students take responsibility for the importance of what they are doing.

★ Try integrating more pointless pursuits into your classroom to stimulate creative thinking, to have fun, and to keep motivation high.

One- and Two-Point Perspective

In one-point perspective, there is a single vanishing point. Lines of perspective radiate from the point to determine the angle of the objects drawn. The dotted line represents the horizon, drawn at eye level of an observer at the scene.

In two-point perspective, there are two vanishing points from which lines of perspective radiate.

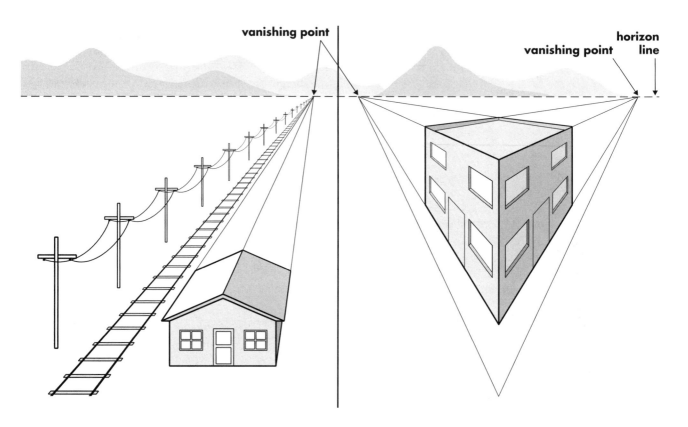

One-Point Perspective

Two-Point Perspective

WHAT A LINE!
LESSON 16

Our lives are crisscrossed with lines of many sorts. Straight, curved, and jagged lines appear as letters on this page. We drop our friends a line through the mail, while comedians drop one-liners on audiences. Power lines, skylines, and clotheslines drape our world. "What a Line!" explores lines, their textures, their qualities, and their uses. Students create sketches, experimenting with straight, jagged, and curved lines. The class discusses representational advantages and disadvantages of different types of lines. Lines are extended into other subject areas, such as time lines, lines of communication, and borderlines.

Preparation

★ Collect an assortment of objects for students to sketch, ranging from simple (a flashlight) to fairly complex (a toy truck). Set up four sketch stations, each containing one object, such as a pencil, or a collection of objects, such as a bowl of fruit. If desired, have students help select the items.

Materials

chalkboard and chalk; straightedges; pencils or pens; drawing paper, 4 small sheets per student; pins or tape to display drawings

Exercise

1. Challenge students to come to the chalkboard and draw as many different kinds of lines as they can and to name each type of line drawn. Be sure students include at least these three types: straight, jagged, and curved lines.

In this drawing, lines alone give the impression of people. Former logo of Zeneta Kertisz-Art courtesy Adrianne Prober.

2. Divide students equally among the four sketch stations, and hand out drawing materials.

3. Allow 7 to 10 minutes for students to sketch the objects in each station, one sheet per station, according to the following formula: First sheet has straight lines only, second sheet has jagged line only, third sheet has curved lines only, and fourth sheet has any combination of lines. Let students choose which kind of line to use for a given sketch station.

4. Create What a Line! bulletin boards for showcasing, comparing, and discussing student drawings. You could hang those of each sketch station next to one another, those of each line type together, or those of each student together.

Variation

Have students cut long strips of colored construction paper or use wide strips of colored ribbons. Have them make visual compositions by gluing strips or ribbon onto a background sheet of paper. They can glue the strips flat to make straight lines, with half-twists to make jagged lines, or glue strips at one end to make curved lines, either by using strips curled with the edge of a scissors or by cutting out coils of paper. They may make compositions with a single line type or with a combination of line types.

Here is a curvy collage made from paper strips. *Wave of Valdez* by Chuck Bowdlear. Photograph courtesy the artist.

Discussion

◆ Did you and your classmates tend toward one kind of line at each sketch station? Why?

◆ Do the same objects drawn with different kinds of lines look very different? Can you describe that difference?

◆ Are some objects easier to draw with one kind of line than another?

◆ Which kinds of lines make the best outlines for still objects? Which kinds of lines work best to convey objects in motion, such as a twirling dancer or the flow of water?

◆ When it comes to line drawings, how would you define *texture*?

◆ Which drawings look very still? Which have a living, moving, or dynamic quality to them?

◆ Apart from sketching, how many different kinds of lines can you think of (such as sewer lines, telephone lines, and lines of communication)?

◆ What purpose does each line serve (such as communicating, transporting, and establishing boundaries)?

◆ Which kinds of lines are invisible? Which can you see?

Art often reflects the mood of the artist.

Extensions

16a. Crosshatching Create sketch stations to study and practice the technique of crosshatching, in which lots of tiny lines are used to create drawings. Or have students try sketching objects or designing pictures using lines in only one direction—horizontal, vertical, or diagonal. Another activity (as suggested in *KidsArt*, issue 10, 1988) is to have students rub a thick layer of white crayon all over a sheet of paper, then paint a coat of India ink over the crayon layer (adding a bit of soap to the paintbrush to help the ink stick). Let the ink dry overnight, then have students use a paper clip to scratch in a line drawing. For a challenge, students can try single-line drawing: drawing an object without lifting their pencils from the page. Bring an Etch-A-Sketch or similar toy to class for a similar challenge. Go to a bookstore or library, take a class field trip to a museum, bring slides or artist's sketchbooks into class, or invite an artist in person. Have students analyze and critique professional line drawings. Discuss texture, shading, and tone qualities achieved by using different kinds of lines. What emotions do different kinds of lines evoke?

16b. Knit One, Weave Two Have students examine a loom to learn how cloth is woven from long lines of thread. Here is a method for making a simple loom.

1. Cut a 10-inch-square piece of heavy cardboard.

2. Make half-inch slits at even intervals across opposite edges of the piece of cardboard. (Decrease or increase the interval for finer or heavier thread respectively.)

3. Tie thread around the slit at one end. Thread it over the cardboard, through the opposite slit, and back across the cardboard to the next slit. These are your warp *threads. Repeat this over-and-under action until you reach the last slit, then tie off the thread.*

Sikhs performing a line meditation. Levon Parian, *Untitled.*

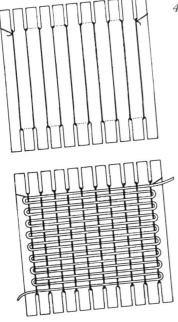

4. Weave the weft threads (the woven threads) over and under the warp threads, looping around and repeating the action until you reach the bottom of your loom.

5. To remove the weaving, cut the warp threads where they wrap around the cardboard. Tie pairs of top and bottom warp threads together. Tie beginning and ending threads to prevent your weaving from unraveling.

From Pamela Elder and Mary Ann Carr, *Worldways: Bringing the World into the Classroom* (Menlo Park, CA: Addison-Wesley Publishing Company, 1987).

Study and compare weaving patterns of cultures from around the world. Have students try to duplicate them on their hand-made looms. Use famous tapestries to study history, such as that from Bayeaux, which dates back to A.D. 1073 and tells the story of William the Conqueror's invasion of England in A.D. 1066.

A modern-day Guatemalan weaver.

16c. Huichol Yarn Pictures Use books, such as *The Popular Arts of Mexico* by Kojin Toneyama, to research *ofrendas,* an art form of the Huichol Indians. Ofrendas, meaning *offerings,* are created from coiled yarn stuck in beeswax. Your class can make its own yarn ofrendas (as recommended in *KidsArt,* issue 23, 1991). Provide each student with a piece of heavy cardboard, pencils, scissors, glue, and plenty of colored yarn. Have them sketch any design they want on the cardboard. If they'd like, they can frame the edges of the cardboard with a yarn border. They create the design by covering one small area at a time with a thin layer of glue, then filling in the area with closely packed yarn twisted back and forth or in a spiral. They must be careful not to get glue on side of the yarn that will show. Students can glue a piece of yarn in the back of the cardboard to hang the art in a class Ofrendas Gallery.

Lines are everywhere you look. Bernard Hoyes, *Hymn in the Night.*

16d. Drop Me a Line Letters and writing are patterns of lines. Try giving younger students the following order of the alphabet. Can they identify the pattern?

A		EF		HI		KLMN		T		VWXYZ
	BCD				G		J		OPQRS	U

Answer: The letters in the top row have only straight lines; the bottom row includes curved lines. Make spelling games out of finding words with letters that are either straight, curved, or jagged. Older or gifted students can research, contrast, and compare the use of lines in letters from alphabets of different cultures. They can also study hieroglyphic symbols from ancient Egypt, making up their own messages and adding symbols for needed letters not present. Or they can study and practice calligraphy.

16e. Border Lines Every city, state, country, and continent is enclosed by boundary lines. Some border lines are smooth and straight, such as that between the North American states of Nevada and Utah. Others curve, such as the eastern coast of Africa. Still others are jagged, such as the northwestern coast of Norway. Study geography by identifying different qualities of line and having students do a visual search for states, countries, and so on that fit those qualities. Try the reverse as well, where you or students trace or copy a portion of a border line and others try to identify where it is. Here is a puzzle for the class: What is the fewest number of colors it takes to fill in a particular map so that countries of the same color do not touch (they may share a point, but not a line)?

Here is one idea of a line graph.

16f. Time Lines Study a unit in history by making lots of different kinds of time lines with your class. Study major events by constructing a One-Way Time Line. Divide a line into three sections: antecedents, the event itself, and consequences. Another possibility is to start with an event and do a reverse time line, where you move from the present to the past, tracing the relevant events. Or try studying the history of scientific discovery by drawing pictures of major inventions and discoveries and hanging them by the appropriate date. Invent your own kind of time line. Use clotheslines draped across your room to hang important date or event markers.

16g. Wired In How many different uses can you and your students think of for wire in the classroom? You could have a local electrician or hardware store donate wire for student sculptures. Students could use small segments of chicken wire mesh for lacing in leather strips, material scraps, cattail reeds, straw, dried flowers, and other interesting objects. You could brainstorm ways for using *wire* in a sentence; for example, "Bob wired him some money," "The election was wired," and "She looked wired after the test." Which part of speech did *wire* occupy in each sentence; for example, the sentences above used *wired* as a verb, past participle, and adjective. How many uses can you and your students think of for *thread, rope, toothpicks,* and *spaghetti?*

16h. Line Up for More Use the "Line Up for More" sheet (page 86) as an exercise in divergent thinking.

16i. Line Graphs Line graphs are useful for tracing the frequency or level of a measure over time. Many different instruments use line graphs: seismographs for detecting earth tremors, polygraphs ("lie detectors") for detecting physical changes in the body, and cardiographs for examining how the heart is functioning. Have the class examine line graphs relevant to current studies. Invent creative assignments that involve line graphs. For example, over the course of a week students could draft the ups and downs of the American stock market, or measure increases and decreases in the value of the American dollar against a foreign currency.

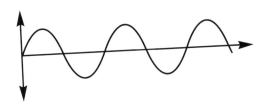

The sine wave is a basic wave shape in nature, describing the motion of sound waves in air and currents in water. Here is a divergent thinking task: How many other types of waves can your students think of?

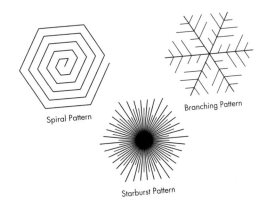

Spiral Pattern

Branching Pattern

Starburst Pattern

Natural Patterns

Many patterns occur again and again in nature. Look around you for examples of spiral, starburst, and branching patterns. The spiral can be found in pine cones, shells, sunflowers, and pineapples. Starburst patterns can be see in asters and fireworks. And branching patterns occur naturally in streams, lightening, and in our own circulatory systems: it is ideal for carrying nutrients to all parts of the body.

Syllogisms

A *syllogism*, an argument from Aristotle and ancient Greece, contains two premise statements and a conclusion. The conclusion is either valid or invalid. A valid conclusion is supported by its premises, as in "All women are Homo sapiens; all Homo sapiens are mammals; therefore, all women are mammals." An invalid conclusion is not properly supported by its premises, such as "All popcorn is made from corn; all corn grows in fields; therefore, all popcorn grows in fields." Can your students describe the error of logic in the second example?

16j. Lines of Reason The study of logic involves lines of reason. Teach your class a form of logic known as the *syllogism*. Ask them to invent silly syllogisms, both valid and invalid. Have students read their creations aloud in class. Others decide whether each is valid or invalid. Have students identify breakdowns in lines of reason.

Teacher's Corner

★ Take a few minutes to consider the many kinds of lines in your life (bank lines, power lines). Make a list that includes lines that are visible and those that are not.

★ Go through the list one item at a time, imagining what your life would be like without each. Which are most important to you? Which would you miss the most? Which would you rather do without?

★ Do you ordinarily stop to consider how complex and delicate the web is that interconnects us to other people and society?

★ Did you consider your own lines of reason? Do you tend to think in straight lines with logic, or with wavy lines of emotion or intuition?

★ What about your lines of communication? How many different ways do you communicate with others?

★ Can you name six ways you could improve your lines of communication? Can you name four ways you could improve lines of communication with your students?

What lines of communication must be open to accomplish this trick? Levon Parian, *Untitled*.

Line Up for More

See how many different kinds of patterns you can make using lines to connect all the dots in each set of dots. Hint: You can find many patterns by starting at the center dot and working your way out.

ROUND WE GO
LESSON 17

Take two ends of a line, curve them, connect them, and a circle is born. The difference between a line and a circle is a line is an open shape, with no inside or outside, and a circle is closed shape. The circle is the simplest closed shape on a plane. "Round We Go" explores the circle and related shapes, such as half circles and ovals. Students make creative compositions out of circles. They learn the difference between figurative and abstract art. By analyzing one another's work, they broaden their visual vocabulary to include concepts such as *apart, touching, behind, in front, enclosed,* and *overlapping.* Use "Round We Go" to sensitize students to circles around them, to expand divergent thinking skills, and to explore curves of many sorts, from pie graphs to bellybuttons.

Preparation

★ Collect slides or photos of figurative and abstract art (see Step 1). If possible, find examples that include circles.

★ Collect a number of objects (coins, cans, bottles, cups) with flat, round bottoms of different sizes for tracing circles onto paper. Feel free to select another method for drawing circles, such as using compasses or string tied to a pencil.

Materials

construction paper in many colors; pencils; scissors; glue; straightedges; examples of figurative and abstract art; slide projector or opaque projector (optional); materials for drawing circles of different sizes; pins or tape for displaying diagrams

Exercise

1 Teach the difference between figurative and abstract art. Have a slide show or show examples from books, using an opaque projector. A third option is to assign students independent research plus written or oral reports to be delivered to the class.

Figurative vs. Abstract

Figurative art depicts recognizable objects in the world around us, such as people and landscapes. This kind of art is as old as humankind, with pictures of people and animals found on caves walls that date back to the Paleolithic age. By contrast, abstract art concentrates on unrecognizable objects and formal properties of line, color, and geometric shape. In these two serigraphs you can see many simple shapes and some common elements. Yet the print on the top is clearly a bird and so is figurative, whereas the one on the bottom is entirely abstract. Abstract designs have been popular throughout history for decorating such objects as rugs and pots. At the beginning of the twentieth century, a new abstract style merged, initially including artist Pet Mondrian, Wassily Kandinsky, and Georgia O' Keeffe, and later, in the 1950s, Willem de Kooning and Jackson Pollock. Although often considered a highly intellectual trend that arose in rebellion to established forces, some consider the abstract style a spiritual search for invisible forces and a new order. *Sad Kosovo Bird* and *Shadows VI,* (serigraphs) by Chuck Bowdlear. Photograph courtesy the artist.

2 Have each student choose two or more sheets of construction paper of highly contrasting colors. They will use one as a background and the others for cutting out circles.

3 Have students use a straightedge and pencil to divide their background sheet in half vertically or horizontally. Have students label one side *figurative* and the other *abstract.*

4 Have students draw and cut out two sets of identical circles of various colors and sizes, one for a figurative composition, the other for an abstract composition. Students can cut two equal circles by folding the sheets in half before cutting. The number, size, and color of the circles needed will depend on student's choice of subject matter for the figurative side. They should first sketch ideas to be sure how many and what size circles they will need.

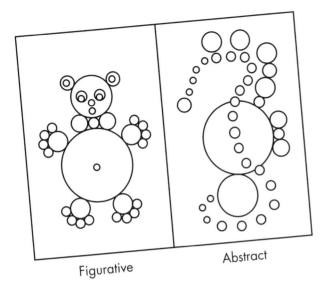

Figurative   Abstract

(5) Have students glue the final layout in place.

(6) Showcase student Circle Compositions in a Round We Go! bulletin board.

Discussion

◆ What is the difference in feeling tone between the two halves of various compositions?

◆ Which compositions make use of crowded space? Which make use of spaciousness?

◆ Which areas of compositions demonstrate the concept of *apart* (each circle occupies its own space without touching)?

◆ Which compositions demonstrate the concept of *touching* (two or more circles share one point of intersection)?

◆ Which compositions demonstrate the concept of *overlap* (part of one circle is hidden by another)? Where there is overlap, which circles are clearly behind others? Which are clearly in front of others?

◆ Which compositions demonstrate the concept of *enclosed* (one circle is entirely inside of another)?

◆ What objects would be very difficult to depict with circles?

◆ Which half did you prefer making, the figurative or the abstract? Why?

◆ Which side do you prefer looking at? Why?

Extensions

17a. Circles Galore! Do a visual brainstorming exercise that taps into divergent thinking. Copy three to five "Circles Galore!" sheets (page 92) per student. Have students, in 7 minutes and using as many sheets as necessary, draw as many different items out of the circles as they can. Hang them side by side on a Circles Galore! bulletin board and look for items commonly drawn, as well as those more unusual.

17b. Mexican Sun Faces Circular sun faces made from pottery are common throughout Mexico, especially on garden walls. Have students research traditional sun faces in books, such as *The Popular Arts of Mexico* by Tojin Toneyama. They may make their own sun faces from dough (as suggested in *KidsArt,* issue 23, 1991). Make the dough by mixing two parts flour with one part salt and enough water to make it a thick consistency. Knead it until it is easy to shape. Have students start with a thick, disk-shaped chuck of dough. They pinch the edges to form the sun's rays, then carve into the dough or attach other rolled pieces of dough with water to form facial features. Bake the sun faces in a 300-degree oven for 2 to 3 hours. Student can decorate the cooled sun faces with tempera or acrylic paints, finish them with a layer of acrylic varnish, and attach a loop of yarn or string to the back to hang them.

A Mexican sun face.

17c. Bucky Balls Use circles to make a model of Buckminster Fuller's beautiful vector equilibrium sphere. (This activity is based on an activity in *Bucky for Beginners: Synergetic Geometry* by Mary Laycock, Hayward, CA: Activity Resources Company, 1984.)

Making Bucky Balls

Students cut out four identical paper circles and fold each into halves and then thirds, so there are six equal pie-piece divisions when the circle is laid flat. They turn each circle into a bow tie by pulling together two opposite folds and fastening them with a bobby pin. They will need to carefully crease some of the original folds in the opposite direction to make a perfect bow-tie shape. They mark the inside corners of each bow tie with A, B, C, and D, as shown, then connect A of one bow tie to B of another and pin that fold, repeating four times to connect all the bow ties. Then they connect C of one bow tie with D of the next. When this is repeated four times, the model is complete. Students can decorate their Bucky balls with colored paper or by coloring circles or pie-piece divisions.

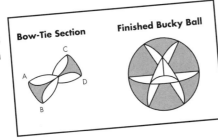

Bow-Tie Section   **Finished Bucky Ball**

17d. Circles of Calculation Study how compasses work and learn to use one. Teach your students, and let them practice by determining the direction of nearby circular landmarks, such as fish ponds and skating rinks. Send students on a scavenger hunt to locate circles in the environment. Students should make maps, bring back samples, and make diagrams on "Circles Galore!" sheets (page 92), including object descriptions, sketches, and circular calculations appropriate to the level of the class; for example, diameters, circumferences, and areas.

17e. Anatomy of a Circle Our bodies are covered and filled with circular shapes. With the class, brainstorm as much circular anatomy as possible. Macro-level examples include nostrils, bellybuttons, irises, pupils, moles, warts, freckles, and open mouths. Micro-level examples include body cells, nucleuses, nucleoli, and vacuoles. Many seeds and microscopic animals, such as spores and diatoms, are spherical. One reason circles are so common in biology is that the sphere is the most efficient shape, containing the maximum volume to surface area ratio (meaning, for example, better heat retention). Using a magnifying glass or microscope, have your class examine slime, mold, and dust from ponds, rotted food, or crawl spaces. Students can draw what they see

on "Circles Galore!" sheets (page 92). They could also find, draw, and show examples of radial symmetry.

Natural Symmetry

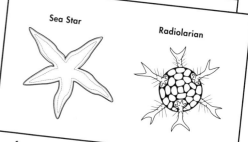

Sea Star   **Radiolarian**

In zoology, symmetry refers to the arrangement of an animal's body in relation to its central axes. The most common forms of symmetry are bilateral and radial. Bilateral symmetry exists when two similar sides flank a central plane along the principal axis of the body. Bilateral symmetry appears in human beings and other actively locomoting animals. Radial symmetry exists when several radii with similar structures extend from a principal axis passing through the mouth of the animal. Radial symmetry appears in sea stars, radiolarians, and other animals that locomote relatively infrequently. Some of these animals, such as the diatom, are able to spin, bob, and float in the ocean, regardless of their up-down orientation. Others, such as some spores, have such small masses that they can spin, float, and drift in air currents regardless of gravity.

17f. Swallow This One
Use the "What Makes the World Go Round" sheet (page 93) to study circular mythology from Tibet. The Wheel of Sangara (or Becoming) portrays a rooster swallowing the tail of a pig that is swallowing the tail of a snake, which is joined back round by the mouth to the rooster. Have students speculate on the Tibetan world view through discussion, oral presentations, poetry, or story writing. Invite them to select animals and originate their own Wheel of Becoming. Have students complete assignments first through drawing then writing their own myths to explain what makes the world go around.

17g. Going Full Circle As a class, brainstorm ways in which circles and spheres appear in technology, astronomy, and physics. Study how sundials work and find out what makes a clock tick. Use the "Cog-itate on This" sheet (page 94) to study the use of wheels and gears in simple machines, such as rope pulleys and two-meshed gear wheels. Have advanced students create other examples of machines with gear wheels.

17h. Full of Hot Air Bring in a package of balloons. Have each student, on a sheet of scratch paper, compose a poem about roundness, then use a ball-point or felt-tip pen to transfer the poem to an inflated balloon, writing around and around the surface. Once poems are completed, balloons are deflated, collected, and saved for a special purpose such as a Round Table meeting—which you can hold to present circular poetry, Wheels of Becoming (see 17f), examples of circular reasoning (see 17I), or samples of circles in nature and technology (see 17g)—or Circle Fair (see 17k).

17i. Circular Reasoning Circular reasoning involves using a conclusion as a premise in a logical argument. Examples include "Unicorns are real because I believe in them" and Groucho Marx's famous line, "I wouldn't belong to any club that would have me as a member." Have students make up statements and jokes that involve circular reasoning. Then have students turn to circular definitions by sending pairs to the dictionary for a Circle Hunt. The object is to seek as many pairs or larger groups of words as possible that are defined in circular fashion; that is, in terms of one another. For example, the 1968 edition of the Random House dictionary defines *gentle* as "kindly or amiable." It defines *kindly* as "gentle or mild, as rules or laws."

17j. Magic Circle Form a Magic Circle at the beginning of the day to enhance self-esteem and boost social intelligence. Have everyone sit in one large circle on the floor. Begin with an incomplete sentence, such as "My favorite thing is . . .," "My biggest worry is . . .," or "My advice to the President is. . . ." You finish the sentence first, then have the next student repeat the sentence fragment and supply his or her own ending. Continue around the circle. To help build an atmosphere of trust and support, begin and end each Magic Circle session with a moment of holding hands.

17k. Circle Fair Many games, sports, and activities, such as Ring-Around-the-Rosey, Drop the Handkerchief, darts, and archery, use circles. Have students, either in small groups or individually, create their own circle activity or game. If desired, centralize activities around a theme, scholastic or otherwise. For example, a plastic dart competition could surround a history unit, with students answering a series of questions to determine how near or far to the bull's eye target they stand. Have a Circle Fair where students sample games and bake or buy round foods, such as muffins, oranges, and casseroles. For a multicultural twist use round games and dishes from other countries, which children purchase at the fair using coins collected from all over the world. Have students contribute round decorations, such as Native American shields (see *KidsArt,* issue 19, 1990) and Mexican sun faces (see 17b).

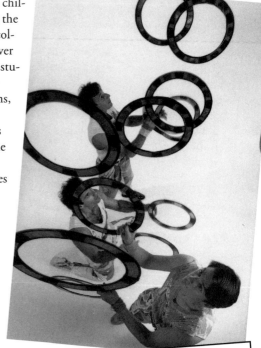

Here are the Mums, a Los Angeles–based juggling and magic act, playing a circle game that takes tremendous skill and concentration—juggling rings. Levon Parian, *Untitled.*

In these modern times, the wheel of fortune turns so quickly that it's easy to get dizzy! Try making up your own variation of the game Wheel of Fortune, suited to your students and classroom activities.

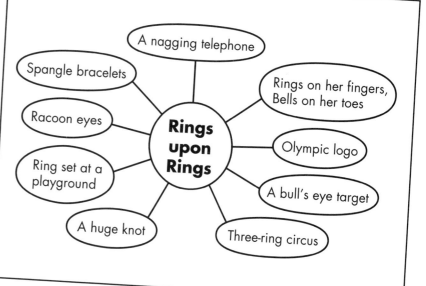

Teacher's Corner . . . .

★ Clustering is an important way to brainstorm ideas visually rather than verbally. One technique is *circular clustering*. Here is how to do it: Start with a word or idea to associate with or a problem to solve. Place it in the middle of the page and enclose it in a circle. Draw a series of lines radiating out from the circle's edge to make associations and brainstorm ideas. Use as many radiating lines as you can in the time you allot yourself.

★ Choose your own word or phrase to practice circular clustering. Take 3 minutes to come up with as many ideas and associations as you can make. Let yourself be silly and whimsical.

★ Teach circular clustering to your students and experiment with your ideas. Try to do at least two circular clusterings a week, one with your students and another for your own personal and creative growth.

Name _____ Date _____

Circles Galore!

Turn each circle below into a different picture. Let your imagination run loose. Try to work quickly, filling in as many "Circle Galore!" sheets as you can in 7 minutes. Or use this sheet to draw what you see through a magnifying glass, under a microscope, or in the environment.

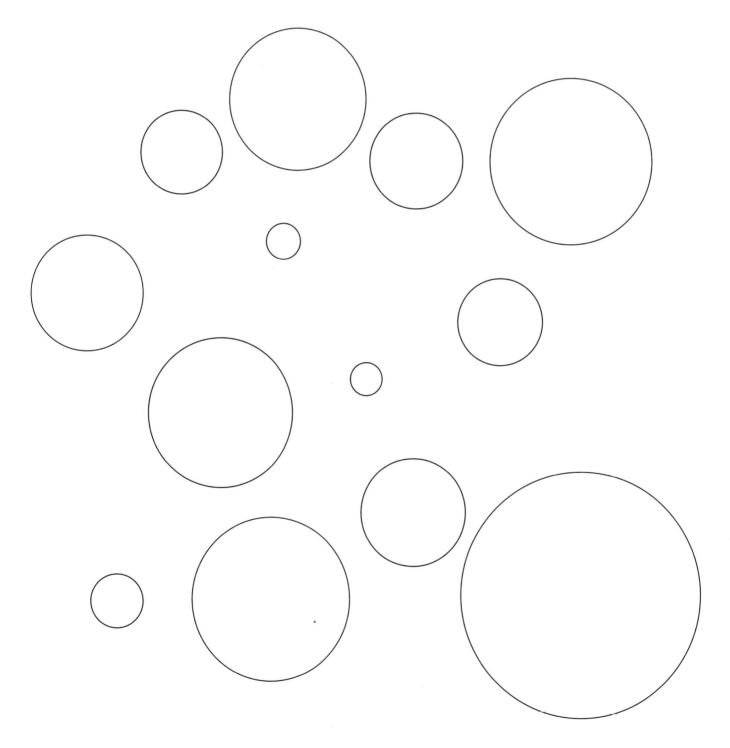

What Makes the World Go Round

In the Tibetan Wheel of Becoming, a pig, a rooster, and a snake symbolize desire, hatred, and stupidity, in that order. They swallow each other's tail to keep the wheel moving. What does this tell you about the Tibetan view of what makes the world go around?

Use the circle below to create your own Wheel of Becoming. Start by selecting the three qualities of life that you think make the world go around. Then, choose three different animals or creatures to symbolize each. Draw them in the circle, swallowing each other's tails. Write a myth that explains how these animals came to their current positions and what makes the world go around according to your Wheel of Becoming.

Name _____ Date _____

Cog-itate on This

Simple machines take advantage of roundness.

Below is a rope pulley. This system transmits force through the use of ropes or chains, along with round pulley wheels and their axles. The mechanical advantage to this system is the ability to move objects of great weight with relatively little force.

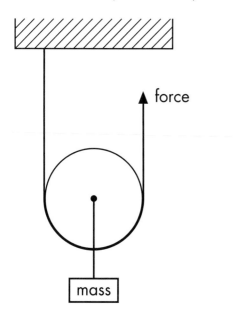

The machine below consists of two meshed-gear wheels. A *gear* is a wheel with projections evenly spaced around it. It is often meshed with a second similar wheel of smaller diameter. Gears are used to send rotational force from one machine element to another.

force

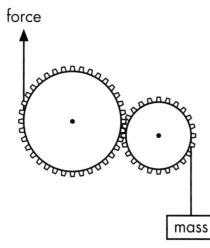

On the back of this sheet, invent and sketch a machine that uses pulleys, gear wheels, a combination of them, or any other round machine elements, such as wheels and axles. Name your machine, describe how it works, and describe uses for it.

TRY ANGLES
LESSON 18

In this lesson the class uses triangles to learn more about visual dynamics in works of art.

Students pay three roles: Creator, Interpreter, and Critic. Each corresponds to a different aspect of the creative process. The Creator finds inspiration for an original work and takes action through production. The Interpreter intuits the meaning of a work and translates it into a different medium, language, or intelligence. The Critic analyzes and communicates about formal and aesthetic features of the work—such as the number, size, position, and shape of design elements—as well as feelings evoked by the piece. By playing all three roles, students practice creative as well as analytic skills and gain flexibility in perspective. They also practice important communication skills related to creative production. Use this lesson to examine triangles and to discover the world of visual dynamics, in which even abstract elements can tell their own story.

Preparation

★ Look through newspapers and magazines for film reviews of movies seen by many of your students.

★ Collect and distribute the materials.

Materials

copies of film reviews, large sheets of colored construction paper; writing paper; straightedges; pencils or pens; scissors; glue; transparent tape; one "Interpreter" sheet (page 100) and one "Critic" sheet (page 101) per student; pins or tape to display artwork

Exercise

1. Analyze the copies of the film reviews to help students distinguish between Creator, Interpreter, and Critic roles. In this case, the film reviewer usually acts as both Interpreter and Critic.

2. Divide the class into groups of three. Each student will be Creator of an original production, Interpreter for a second student's work, and Critic for the third group member's work.

3. Have students choose one color of construction paper as background for triangle art. Have them use their straightedges and pencils to divide the sheet into three equal panels. If desired, students can trim the bottom of the sheet so panels are not too narrow. (With smaller paper, students can tape three identical sheets side by side.)

4. Have students use any number of triangles per panel to create art that tells a visual story from one panel to the next. Have students draw and cut the triangles out of one or more sheets of paper. Students should vary the color, number, position, size, and type of triangle used from panel to panel. The first panel relates the beginning of the visual story, the second panel relates the middle, and the third panel relates the end. Encourage students to use abstract, rather than figurative, style (see pages 87–88). Have students glue their final designs in place. Allow 15 minutes.

5. Have students exchange artwork with a partner. This Interpreter should look carefully at details in each of the panels, noticing the progression of triangles from one panel to the next. Have the Interpreter give the work a title and write a story on the "Interpreter" sheet. The story should have a beginning, middle, and end corresponding to the first, second, and third panels. Have Interpreters tape their completed stories to the bottom of the artwork, halfway between first and second panels. Allow 15 minutes.

6. Have students pass their work to the third group member. This Critic should carefully examine the original triangle art and read the attached story. Have the Critic use "Critic" sheets and lined paper to write a composition analyzing the features of triangles as they vary from panel to panel. The Critic should also comment on the work aesthetically. Have Critics tape completed analyses next to the stories at the bottom of the artwork. Allow 15 minutes.

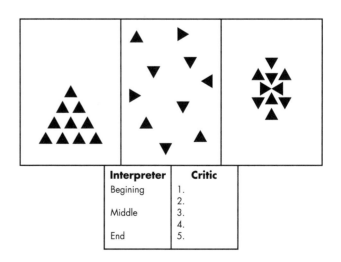

(7) Showcase finished work. Give students ample time to review each group's work before conducting a class discussion.

Aesthetics

Aesthetics are related to our sense of beauty, to our judgments about what we do or do not like, and to what we believe is of value or harm in any piece of art. Aesthetic judgments involve sensation, emotion, and opinion. Each person has a different set of aesthetic standards. Some people prefer simplicity and elegance; others prefer complexity and flourish. Some prefer soothing or beautiful work; others prefer shocking work that may seem harsh but that makes you think. There is no right and wrong when it comes to aesthetics, only differences in opinion.

Discussion

◆ What was your experience trying to create a story using only triangles? Was it easy or hard? Why?

◆ How did you feel about being an Interpreter and trying to read a story into someone else's creation?

◆ Were you surprised at the story attached to your work? Did the story compare to what you had in mind? Did you think the title fit?

◆ How did you react to the Critic's analysis of your triangle composition?

◆ How did you react to the Critic's analysis of the composition with your story on it?

◆ What are aesthetics? How do they come into play when viewing art?

◆ What are visual dynamics? How do they relate to this Exercise?

◆ How do aesthetics and visual dynamics differ in abstract versus figurative compositions?

◆ What are similarities and differences between the three roles: Creator, Interpreter, and Critic?

◆ Which role suits you best? Why?

◆ How do each of these roles fit into our everyday lives?

Visual Dynamics

Visual dynamics concern features of a work of art that make it come alive and convey meaning to a viewer. These include the number of design elements; their size, shape, and color; how and where they are placed; and the relationship between background and foreground elements. Visual dynamics tell a story, even in abstract pieces, that does not depend on figurative qualities. For example, a painting of a horse galloping could look static, while that of a bowl of fruit may hop with activity. When it comes to visual dynamics, what is depicted is much less important than how it is depicted.

Extensions

18a. Try Angles in Art Let the class look through a series of slides or art books. Have them find examples of triangles used in modern abstract art, such as the works of Paul Klee, Piet Mondrian, and Vassily Kandinsky. Have them write accompanying stories and use "Critic" sheets to analyze formal and aesthetic features of the artwork. Have students use triangles to make simple, abstract compositions. This is a good way to review concepts and deepen understanding of visual dynamics. Have student split several blank pages in half and illustrate them with contrasting concepts, such as *tension* versus *equilibrium, movement* versus *stillness, crowding* versus *space,* and *balance* versus *imbalance.* Restrict students to the use of eight same-sized triangles for each half. Showcase and discuss finished products.

18b. Grid and Bear It Copy one "Try Angles" sheet (page 102) per student. Let students use one or more triangular grid to find different polygons and color other complicated patterns.

18c. What's the Angle? Teach the class about different types of triangles: equilateral, isosceles, scalene, and right. Review the angles for each kind. Have students use a blank sheet of paper and ruler to draw fifteen straight lines that intersect throughout the page. They should draw the lines so each type of triangle is represented. Have students exchange pages with a partner to see how many different triangles they can find in one other's work. Have them measure and mark the angles using a protractor and the lengths using a ruler, then calculate the perimeter and area for each. Finally, have students color each triangle according to type; for example, red for right, blue for scalene, and so on.

18d. Pascal's Triangle Have students, working in small groups or individually and according to grade level, ability, and experience, discover patterns in Pascal's triangle. Some patterns that can be found are the sum of the rows; the sum of the diagonals; *figurate* numbers (numbers connected by geometric forms through their arrangement in a polygonal array, such as triangular, square, and pentagonal numbers); the Fibonacci sequence; factorial combinations; and binomial expansion. As a resource guide, use *Visual Patterns in Pascal's Triangle*, by Dale Seymour.

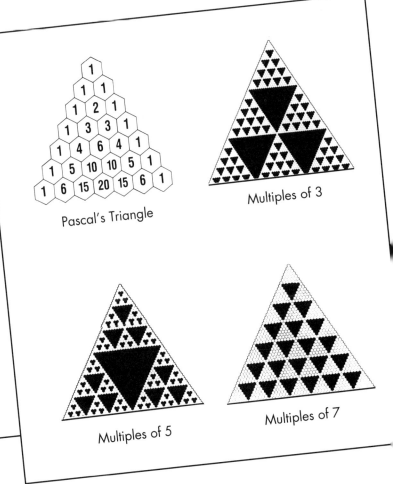

Pascal's Triangle

Multiples of 3

Multiples of 5

Multiples of 7

Pascal's Triangle

Pascal's triangle, named after the seventeenth-century French mathematician Blaise Pascal, was probably known as early as the fourteenth century in China. It consists of a triangular array of numbers, each formed by adding the two numbers in the row immediately above. Pascal's triangle is rich in hidden patterns related to algebra, geometry, probability theory, and other areas of mathematics. The patterns shown here are those that result when multiples of 3, 5, and 7 are filled in.

18e. Triangles at a Distance Discuss the use of triangles for calculating distances or heights. This involves knowledge of the Pythagorean theorem: The square of the hypotenuse of a right triangle equals the sum of the squares of the other two sides. Have students research the use of sextants for ship navigation. Study and compare methods for calculating distances in space with those on the open seas. Ask students to make up deep-sea or outer-space science fiction stories or word problems that require calculation of distances and heights by knowing two sides of a right triangle.

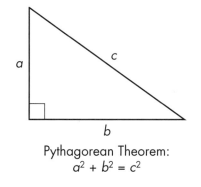

Pythagorean Theorem:
$$a^2 + b^2 = c^2$$

18f. Diamante Poems Teach your class the diamante form of poetry, which looks like a diamond divided horizontally into two triangles. Line 1 = one subject noun, Line 2 = two adjectives related to line 1, Line 3 = three present participles ("-ing" words) related to line 1, Line 4 = four-word phrase making a transition between the idea of line 1 to the idea of line 7, Line 5 = three participles related to line 7, Line 6 = two adjectives related to line 7, Line 7 = one noun, opposite in meaning to line 1. Here is an example:

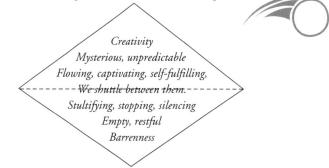

Creativity
Mysterious, unpredictable
Flowing, captivating, self-fulfilling,
We shuttle between them.
Stultifying, stopping, silencing
Empty, restful
Barrenness

Have students try a triangular form for writing a paragraph or news article, going from the main point to the detail. Or they can use the inverse, going from detail to the main point.

18g. Triangles Greek Style On the outside of many ancient Greek temples, above the columns, is a triangular area called the *pediment.* It is often decorated with elaborate sculptural reliefs. Have students research interesting pediments in Greek history. Then they can make their own pediments, either from clay or by drawing a long triangular area on paper and filling it with designs. Encourage students to base their designs on ancient Greek themes, such as a battle with sea monsters, the celebration of spring, the first Olympic games, and horses pulling a chariot (suggested in *KidsArt,* issue 17, 1990). Remind students that the scene must stand tall in the middle and stretch out into the narrow ends of the triangle.

Here is an example of a sculptural relief in rock from Peggy's Cove, Nova Scotia. Notice how the picture is designed to fit into the natural features of the rock.

18h. Triangle in Architecture Have groups research multicultural instances of triangles used in architecture; for example, the Eiffel Tower in Paris, the Transamerica building in San Francisco, the great pyramids of Egypt, and the teepees of Native Americans all use triangular structure. Students should report on other instances and include visuals. Discuss uses, advantages, and disadvantages to triangular structures. For example, one advantage to the A-frame typical of Swiss houses is that it keeps snow off the roof; one disadvantage is that it provides less room inside the building. Ask students to invent and sketch their own architectural designs based primarily on triangles.

Here is one use of triangles in architecture. This ancient Mayan pyramid from Tikal, Guatemala, was built out of stone thousands of years ago.

18i. One on Top; Many on Bottom With your class, brainstorm triangular, hierarchical structures within human social and political organizations, such as the family, organized religion, the school system, and the U. S. government. Discuss how, when, and why this form originated in the shift from hunting and gathering to agriculture. Discuss pros and cons of hierarchical organization. For example, one advantage is that a single leader can quickly mobilize a large organization into action. One disadvantage is that a large organization can be easily immobilized if its leader is isolated or removed. Study examples in history, such as the quick conquest of the Incas by the Spaniards, and President Lincoln's rapid troop mobilization following the incident at Fort Sumter.

Here is another kind of hierarchy—a human pyramid! This can be fun to do, but if you try it with your class, be extremely careful. Use heavier, stronger people on the bottom, and lighter students on top. Photograph courtesy Beverly Hall.

Teacher's Corner

★ Throughout our lives we move back and forth between the three roles of Creator, Interpreter, and Critic. Sometimes we produce work of our own, sometimes we try to understand and translate meaning, and sometimes we analyze and critique someone else's work. Take 5 minutes to brainstorm ways in which you play each role in the classroom.

★ Imagine a triangle with sides of differing lengths, corresponding to the extent to which you play each role. Draw the triangle that best fits your balance between these roles in the classroom. Label the sides. Are you comfortable in all three roles? Is your triangle out of balance? Is the ideal triangle equilateral?

★ In myths and stories from around the world, triangles and the number 3 have always symbolized dynamic processes. This is often why fairy tales grant three wishes and mythological heroes encounter three monsters or tasks. In everyday life, crises are pivotal periods of dynamic change, filled with potential for creative change and danger of negative backsliding. Take 5 minutes to brainstorm and list pivotal points in your life.

★ One way to symbolize crises and pivotal points in life is with a triangle balanced on one tip. The triangle, in a precarious position, must fall in one of two directions. It can fall forward, representing a reach toward new opportunities and new ways of coping. Or the triangle can fall backward, representing a reach toward the safety and comfort of old coping mechanisms, supports, and habits from the past.

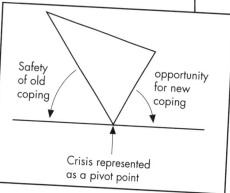

Crisis represented as a pivot point

★ Choose three pivotal points from your list that interest you the most. Symbolize them with triangles that illustrate whether you responded by reaching forward toward the new or backward toward the old. For example, a long triangle side might represent growth. A triangle poised on a narrow tip might represent a more volatile or precarious situation than one balanced on a wide-angled tip. Make up your own system for representing challenges in your life.

★ Are your triangles all the same or do they vary across situations?

★ Are there any ways in which your life is currently at a pivotal point? If so, what can you do to help the triangle fall forward rather than backward?

★ If any feelings or thoughts arise as a result of this Teacher's Corner that you would like to ponder further, try using diamante poetry (see 18f).

Name _____ Date _____

Interpreter

Look carefully at the piece of artwork you want to interpret. Examine all of its features: colors, number of elements, sizes, shapes, and positions on the page. Let these features spark your imagination. Write a story below. The first panel corresponds to the beginning of the story, the second panel to the middle, and the third panel to the end. Use the back of this sheet if you need more space.

Title _____

Beginning

Middle

End

Name _____ Date _____

Critic

Answer each question below on the back of this paper.

1. How do the size and number of elements contribute to the feeling of the artwork?

2. How do the colors contribute to the feeling of the artwork?

3. Look carefully at the position and placement of elements in the artwork. Comment on each of the following features:
   a. Spacing versus crowding
   b. Balance versus imbalance
   c. Feeling of stillness versus feeling of movement

4. How do each of the above elements change from panel to panel?

5. What do you find most appealing, interesting, or likable about this artwork?

6. What do you find least appealing or likable?

7. What is the meaning and importance of this artwork to you?

8. How does the story fit with the artwork?
   a. Which features listed above are reflected in the story?
   b. Were any important features left out of the story?
   c. Which aspects of the story come completely from the imagination of the Interpreter?

Name _____ Date _____

Try Angles

SQUARING OFF
LESSON 19

Although rare in nature, squares and rectangles are common in our human-made environment. Look at most tables, windows, floor plans, books, tiles, and plots of land. In this lesson, students work with square grids to sharpen perceptual acuity. Students will need technical precision to transfer and enlarge patterns from one grid to another, and they will practice artistic skills when they make original designs and fill in details of incomplete designs. "Squaring Off" is an advanced and challenging Exercise, especially when students complete all steps by themselves. Use this lesson to study magic squares and square deals and to integrate arithmetic and technical measurement skills with aesthetic skills.

Preparation

★ Decide whether you or your students will complete Step 1 of the Exercise: involve students to bring more arithmetic and measurement skills into the lesson; do it yourself to save classroom time.

Materials

15-by-15-inch white drawing paper for grids, two per student; scrap paper; straightedges; pencils; colored markers or crayons; graph paper (optional); pins or tape to display grids

Exercise

(1) Give each student two 15-by-15-inch sheets of paper. You or students should use pencils and straightedges to draw twenty-five 3-inch squares on each sheet, five squares per row and column. The dimensions of the grid can vary according to the size of paper available, or you can substitute graph paper.

(2) Divide the class into pairs. Have each student draw an abstract design on one grid, keeping it out of sight from his or her partner. Tell students to use scrap paper to experiment and that designs should extend into every square of the grid. Students may use shapes explored in previous lessons or shapes of their own creation. They may make designs in black and white or color.

(3) Have students choose ten squares of their completed grid to transfer *exactly* as they appear onto the other grid. They may pick vertical, horizontal, or diagonal lines of squares, or randomly choose ten squares throughout the grid.

(4) Have pairs exchange their partially completed grids, making sure they hide original designs.

(5) Have partners look carefully at the filled-in boxes and extend these patterns to complete the rest of the grid. The goal is to create a cohesive design that covers the entire grid, using the exact style and coloration of the original boxes, so an observer cannot tell which boxes came first and which came later.

(6) If desired, students may erase the original pencil grid marks.

(7) Create a Squaring Off bulletin board to showcase and discuss student work. Hang original grids and those completed by partners side by side.

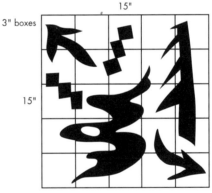

Original grid

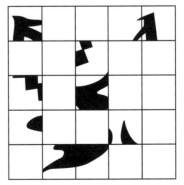

Grid with 10 squares transferred

In this painting, notice how many different ways the artist makes use of squares. Joan Lehman, *The Juggler*.

Variation

Do the Exercise with one difference. Rather than using two same-sized grids, use a smaller grid (for example, with 1- or 2-inch squares) for original designs, and a larger grid (for example, with 3- or 5-inch squares) for the transfer patterns. This requires more sophisticated perceptual, technical, and math skills, especially if students construct their own grids.

Discussion

◆ What did you like about this Exercise? What was hard to do?

◆ In comparing original and partner-completed grid designs, which look very similar to one another? Which look very different?

◆ How do compositions compare in terms of the use of space, balance, symmetry, and sense of stillness or motion?

◆ Can you find the original ten boxes transferred by each student in partner-completed grids?

◆ Did student choices of which boxes to transfer influence resulting designs? How?

◆ Why are squares more useful for this Exercise than circles?

◆ How many other uses for square grids can you think of?

◆ Where are we most likely to find squares in the world around us?

◆ Are squares and rectangles found more often in natural or manufactured objects? Why do you think that is?

Extensions

19a. Filling Out Details Select a photograph relevant to a current multicultural, social studies, or science unit. Use a black paper square or rectangle to block out sections of the photograph. Have students use context clues to determine what is behind the paper. They may respond verbally or by drawing. Move the strip to different locations and repeat the activity. Next, find lots of large, colorful, action photographs. Cut photographs in half horizontally, vertically, or diagonally. Paste each half onto a sheet of blank paper, leaving enough room for students to fill out the missing half with markers, crayons, or paints. This activity is a good esteem builder for students who lack confidence in their artistic skills. With easily frustrated students or those lacking artistic confidence, permit access to the other half of the photograph when they fill out details. Try the same activity using children's drawings rather than photographs. Finally, use photographs of artwork cut in two and have students mimic the style of various artists.

19b. Beyond Gridlock Have small groups research and then design a theme for a class mural. Students should use accurate details based on a current multicultural, social studies, or science unit. Have the class vote on the final design, then grid the artwork with approximately as many squares as there are students in the class. As a class, figure out the dimensions of the final product, and assign each student responsibility for enlarging the design and contributing at least one square. Make sure students coordinate with their four neighbors to ensure the design and colors match up perfectly.

19c. Art Squares Find squares in the figurative artwork of Paul Cézanne, followed by abstract expressionist painters, such as Piet Mondrian and Joseph Albers, and pop artists, such as Victor Vasarely. Study cubism, and analyze and critique the work of cubist artists. Try setting up simple arrangements for students to draw in cubist style.

Cubism

Cubism, a style of art that arose around 1910, is considered a forerunner to abstract expressionism. Cubist artists included Pablo Picasso, Georges Braque, Kasimir Malevich, and Juan Gris. Although still figurative, cubism used mostly geometrical forms. This style sought new ways to depict three-dimensional objects in two-dimensional space without resorting to illusions such as foreshortening, used by Renaissance painters. The result was a very different perspective. Objects appear dissected and their parts recombine from a single viewpoint. Or objects appear painted from a variable and mobile viewpoint, as if the artist had walked around the object, painting it from all angles at once. Some people think the cubists succeeded in bringing the fourth dimension of time to the canvas. It is interesting that the discovery of space-time in art paralleled the discovery of space-time in physics by Einstein.

19d. Class Quilts Find, or have students find, examples of quilts from different countries and eras. Make a class quilt where each student creates and contributes one square. The overall design may or may not be coordinated.

Widow's Diary (quilt) by Chuck Bowdlear. Photograph courtesy the artist.

19e. Box Collages

Have students, individually or in pairs, make box collages in any subject. These work well for science units, such as modeling the planets, or for multicultural studies, such as portraying aspects of another country or culture. Use square or rectangular boxes approximately shoe-box size or slightly larger. Have students paint them a solid color, let them dry, then fill the boxes with elements according to theme. They could use buttons, maps, cardboard, cloth, foil, dried beans or noodles, crepe paper, postcards, or drawings. Students can glue collage elements to the walls or bottom, attach them from the back, or hang from the top of the box. If desired, have another student either write a story based on the box, or analyze its elements and message. Research box collages of American artist Joseph Cornell. Or research the *assemblages* of American sculptor Louise Nevelson. Her creations involve the assembling of preformed objects—natural and manufactured—into artwork. Her sculptures are made from wooden boxes and crates full of children's toys, pieces of wood, and many other items.

19f. Fair and Square

As a class, brainstorm figures of speech that relate to squares, such as "fair and square," "square peg in a round hole," "to even the square," and "sit squarely." Challenge students to use as many of these as possible in writing a story about a land where everything is

square. Another possibility is to have students create a limerick beginning with the line, "There once was a square named Pierre." Have students illustrate their stories or limericks with drawings or paintings.

Limericks

Limericks are a humorous verse with five lines and the rhyming pattern aabba. Lines one, two, and five have three feet (or beats); lines three and four have two feet. Here is an example of a limerick:

There once was a square named Pierre
Who cried that life is not fair.
While circles could roll
His shape took its toll
Now poor Pierre's lost his hair.

19g. Square Off With the class, set up a baseball diamond with portable bases. Measure the distances between bases. For a challenge, find methods to construct a baseball diamond without using standard measurements. Invent your own survey techniques. Check angles to ensure you have a true square. Once your diamond is in place, brainstorm with the class as many arithmetic problems as you can involving the measurements of your diamond and its square features. Once the math is squared away, play baseball!

19h. Square Deal Have students brainstorm different ways of making a square. Use shapes covered in this unit so far—dots, lines (crossed and uncrossed), circles, triangles—as methods for construction. Present students with a square grid of sixty-four dots and challenge them to find as many different squares as possible. Compare how different students approached this square-grid exercise. Did everyone use the outer bounds of the grid as a square? Did anyone use nested or overlapping squares, or did everyone lay them side by side? Did anyone violate the grid space itself, either by drawing lots of small squares or by drawing squares that extended beyond the boundaries of the grid? No matter what the level of development, this activity demonstrates how assumptions can limit creativity. Each of us approaches any task with a set of hidden rules that can limit our perception of solutions. The less we take for granted about a task, the more possibilities we will open, allowing us to break through unnecessary limits.

19i. Magic Squares Introduce your class to magic squares. The numbers in these squares have rows that add up to the same number, no matter whether you compute them horizontally, vertically, or diagonally. Here is one magic square:

4 9 2
3 5 7
8 1 6

Challenge your students to make their own magic squares where, for example, the sides and diagonals total 16. Have them leave some positions blank for other students to fill in correctly. Ask students how many numbers they can leave out, and in what positions, before the magic square has more than one solution.

Here is an old shack from the ghost town of Bodie, California, where we can see how important squares and rectangles are in architecture. They come into play in the overall shape of a building or room, or the parts of a room, such as windows and doors or bricks and tiles. Can you think of creative ways to bring architecture, blueprints, and ratios into your classroom?

19j. Sphinxes and Squares

Propose the riddle of the sphinx to your class and see if anyone guesses the answer or comes up with creative alternatives. Make an assignment that combines the mathematics of squares with creative writing. Have students, in small groups or individually, create a short story about a sphinx who guards a treasure locked in a square vault. The key to its entrance is a riddle involving a mathematical square. The riddle might entail computing the perimeter or area of a square, using square roots, finding square exponents, using magic squares, or escaping from a square labyrinth, as Thesius did in the ancient Greek legend of the Minotaur. Stories should include the nature of the treasure, the riddle, who is trying to get into the vault and why, whether the person answers the riddle correctly, and what happens next. Have students draw the sphinx.

19k. Be Squared

Buy or borrow a copy of *Powers of Ten*, by Philip and Phylis Morrison, which investigates the geometry of scale. The center of the book contains a photograph of people enjoying a picnic. A small segment is squared off and magnified to larger and larger scales in pages following, and reduced to smaller and smaller scales in preceding pages, all by powers of ten. Divide your class into groups and have them create similar books (called, perhaps, *Be Squared*). Have students square off segments of photographs or drawings, then enlarge and shrink the scale by any factor they wish. Make each student responsible for providing a photograph or drawing of one page at one particular level of magnification. This method is useful for studying objects in space as well as large- and small-scale aspects of human or plant biology, such as cell organelle, cell, group of cells, organ, group of organs, and the whole body.

19l. Celebrate the Square

With the class, design a classroom festival called Celebrate the Square. Bring in square crackers, pieces of cheese, sandwiches, and other square food to eat. Use square napkins, place mats, and other square party favors. Learn and practice square dances. Play hopscotch and find other activities that involve squares. Invent and complete crossword puzzles and other word games using squares. Play square board games, such as checkers, chess, backgammon, and Parcheesi, or have students invent their own. Hold a Square Table meeting, in which students recite limericks about squares (see 19f), poems, or short stories. Draw upon student ideas in planning this event.

The Riddle of the Sphinx

The sphinx is an ancient Greek mythological creature with a woman's head, a lion's body, and an eagle's wings. In the story of Oedipus (see *Oedipus Rex*, by Sophocles), the sphinx is a monster who kills travelers unable to answer her riddle, but who kills herself after Oedipus correctly answers it. Here is the riddle, slightly reworded: What walks on four legs at dawn, two legs at noon, and three legs at dusk? The answer is people—they crawl on four legs in infancy, stand on two legs in adulthood, and use a cane in old age. This drawing depicts the Great Sphinx in Egypt, a male statue that guards the entrance of the pyramids at Giza.

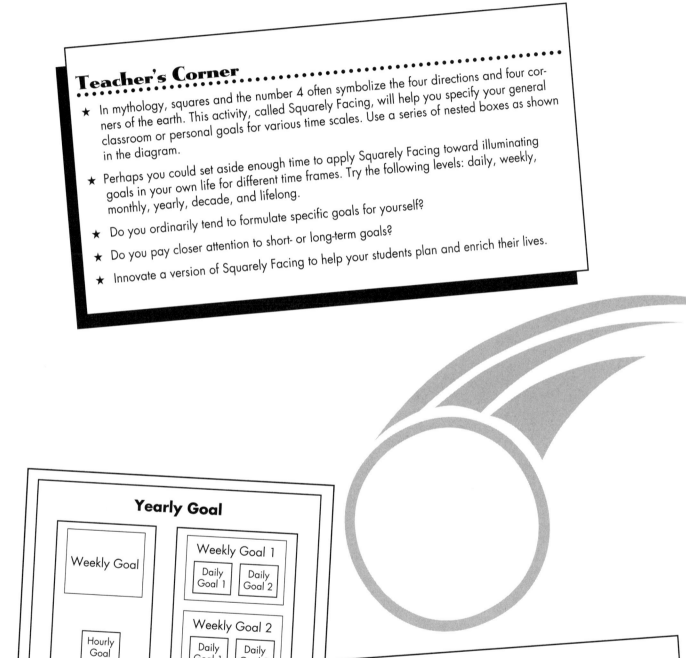

Teacher's Corner

★ In mythology, squares and the number 4 often symbolize the four directions and four corners of the earth. This activity, called Squarely Facing, will help you specify your general classroom or personal goals for various time scales. Use a series of nested boxes as shown in the diagram.

★ Perhaps you could set aside enough time to apply Squarely Facing toward illuminating goals in your own life for different time frames. Try the following levels: daily, weekly, monthly, yearly, decade, and lifelong.

★ Do you ordinarily tend to formulate specific goals for yourself?

★ Do you pay closer attention to short- or long-term goals?

★ Innovate a version of Squarely Facing to help your students plan and enrich their lives.

Yearly Goal

Weekly Goal

Hourly Goal

Monthly Goal 1

Weekly Goal 1
Daily Goal 1
Daily Goal 2

Weekly Goal 2
Daily Goal 1
Daily Goal 2

Monthly Goal 2

Nested Boxes

The largest box represents your main goals for the specified time period; say, a year. Boxes nested within other boxes represent goals for shorter time periods that will eventually lead to the next-larger goals being accomplished—and, through this series of steps, will eventually result in the accomplishment of the largest goal.

3-D DAY
LESSON 20

The world around us consists primarily of three-dimensional objects. This is true even for apparently one- and two-dimensional objects, such as thread or paper. Lessons in this unit so far have dealt with zero-dimensional points, one-dimensional lines, and two-dimensional circles, triangles, and squares. "3-D Day" brings length, width, and height into the classroom. Students construct sculptures and use Creative Logbooks to help them plan, record, reflect, and communicate about the process. Extensions apply sculpture to multicultural and other social studies units, and model-building to science units. Students practice visual literacy and communication skills. Use this lesson to introduce the concept of *dimensionality,* to clarify different phases of the creative process, and to study advanced shapes such as Platonic solids.

Preparation

★ Collect many odds and ends, pieces of junk, and other interesting objects from which students can make three-dimensional constructions.

★ Collect a series of photographs, art books, or slides portraying different kinds of sculpture. Or arrange a field trip to a local museum or sculpture garden for first-hand experience.

Materials

objects such as sticks, string, pebbles, cans, rubber bands, foil, sponges, dried flowers, lichen, leaves, cardboard, nails, hammers, wood scraps, machine parts, broken toy parts, clay, and wire; glue; paper; pens; photographs or slides of sculpture or of work from the museum field trip; materials for creating Creative Logbooks; blank sheets of paper

Exercise

1 Visit a museum or sculpture garden, or show students photographs or slides of sculpture and other three-dimensional artwork, such as assemblages of Louise Nevelson, metal mobiles of Alexander Calder, and sculptures of Henry Moore.

> Consider Michelangelo's famous theory of sculpture: He believed the statue is already in the stone or other material used, and has been there since the beginning of time. It is the sculptor's job to see and release the inner form by scraping away the excess material.

J. Nicholas Borozan, *Torso.* Photograph courtesy Chuck Bowdlear.

Brother Nature's Hand by Chuck Bowdlear. Photograph courtesy the artist.

Are You Sure That's Garbage?

Take several days, weeks, or months to collect odds and ends for this project. Be creative about finding ongoing sources for this and other three-dimensional classroom constructions. Set up a scrap bin in your classroom for daily contributions. Or use 5-gallon ice cream containers clipped together for classroom storage. Search the school trash bin for useful materials, or enlist the cooperation of the school janitor. Check out garage sales, especially at the end of the day. Ask your friends to save useful garbage for you. Contact a local business or industry for help. Local department and variety stores may supply broken items. Decorator stores can give you out-of-date samples. Cabinet and frame shops could donate odds and ends, and billboard companies often have surplus billboard paper. Involve your students and their families in this process if possible. Take your time, and use your imagination. The more interesting your collection of materials, the greater the potential for student projects.

2 Develop a running vocabulary of words for describing features and concepts in the artwork.

This sculpture has a variety of textures, making use of both open and closed space. David Brockmann, *Life*. Photograph courtesy Chuck Bowdlear.

Some Three-Dimensional Concepts

Use of space: Enclosed, open, negative, positive
Dynamics in space: Moving, moveable, static, balanced, unbalanced
Qualities of construction: Textured, bumpy, smooth, delicate, rough, fuzzy, sturdy, symmetrical, asymmetrical, simple, complex

This smooth and polished sculpture is unbalanced and seemingly poised in space, appearing much like its title suggests. J. Nicholas Borozan, *Bird Preparing to Fly*. Photograph courtesy Chuck Bowdlear.

3 Have students choose five or six words from your running vocabulary list and build a three-dimensional assemblage construction to illustrate them. An *assemblage* is a collage that stands on a free base or rises out of the flat surface of a painting. Use cardboard or foam board for a base. Wooden dowels, thin cardboard, or rolled heavy paper can make towers, rooms, and walls, attached with pins, cardboard tabs, or glue. Have students add other collage elements, drawing from your bins or scavenging for their own materials.

4 Have students keep a Creative Logbook describing their process, including project design, critique, and evaluation. They may record original intention, including words and concepts chosen; materials planned; ways for binding separate elements; sketches for possible designs; a process record (including what worked and what did not); and comments and reactions from others.

5 After students complete their projects, arrange a 3-D Showcase.

6 Have students leave several sheets of blank paper with their projects, allowing others to provide feedback. You, students, or visitors should walk around the room to experience the constructions. People are free to respond to anyone else's work with words, drawings, or symbols, and by signing their entries. Students could make a list of vocabulary words for each category (use of space, dynamics, and quality of construction) and later compare it to the artist's original list and intentions. You could also have students write two things they like about each piece and one way it seems creative or unusual. Decide with the class what categories to include in this feedback. Steer away from critical or hurtful responses, and emphasize descriptive ones. Later, have students paste, tape, or staple their feedback sheets into their Creative Logbooks.

7 Have students read their own Creative Logbooks, adding reactions to others' comments and any final thoughts. Students can use their Logbooks again and again to catalogue creative observations about the world and aesthetic reactions.

Discussion

◆ What did you learn from this Exercise?

◆ Did your piece come out as planned, or take on a life of its own as you worked?

◆ What kinds of entries did you make in your Creative Logbook?

◆ What qualities did you discover in one another's work?

◆ Were you surprised at others' comments about your projects? What did you learn from them?

◆ Was it useful to have a Logbook for planning and review?

◆ How would you describe the various stages of the creative process?

What Is the Fourth Dimension?

According to mathematician Rudy Rucker in *The Fourth Dimension: Toward a Geometry of Higher Reality*, no one can point to it, yet the fourth dimension is all around us. It provides fertile ground for speculation by philosophers, mystics, physicists, science fiction writers, and spiritualists. Some say the fourth dimension is time; others say it is mental space or fantasy; still others say it is the direction in which space is curved. There has even been speculation that the fourth dimension leads to other, parallel universes. Rucker believes that at the deepest level, our world should be viewed as "a pattern in infinite-dimensional space, a space in which we and our minds move like fish in water" (p. 3).

The Stages of Creativity

In the 1960s it was popular to analyze the creative process in art and science, breaking it down into various stages. The first stage is inspiration, the source and motivation for the creative idea. The second stage is preparation, which involves planning and gathering materials. The third stage is the production of the artwork or scientific theory. The final stage is evaluation, involving review, critique, analysis, or in the case of scientific projects, verification. Notice that the stages shuttle back and forth between more active and more inactive phases. Also notice how important hands-on work and rationality are to the creative process, but only in certain phases. For example, if we try to judge the value of a project while in the production phase, we can easily inhibit ourselves.

Extensions

20a. Pearls Among Swine Do a unit on the three-dimensional constructions of pop artists. Take a field trip to a junkyard and examine objects such as crushed cars and car parts, discussing their possibilities for sculpture. Have students find an everyday object they consider a true work of art. Students can use their Creative Logbooks to take notes. They could write an essay describing their object and why they chose it. If appropriate, include the concept of *aesthetics* (see box on page 96).

◆ What other uses can you think of for Creative Logbooks?

◆ How does working in three-dimensional space differ from working on a (relatively) two-dimensional surface? For example, how does sculpture differ from painting?

◆ Dance, acting, and performance art use three-dimensional space. What are some other art forms that use three-dimensional space?

◆ Do you prefer working with two-dimensional or three-dimensional materials?

◆ What do you imagine the fourth dimension to be?

Pop Art

Pop art, a kind of anti-art that glorifies everyday objects and commercial art, grew during the 1960s. This trend dates back to 1917, when Marcel Duchamp displayed a urinal under the title *Fountain*. Examples of pop art include Andy Warhol's *Various Boxes*, which displays empty boxes, can, and cartons for manufactured products made by such companies as Heinz, Del Monte, Brillo, and Campbell's; Jasper John's *Savarin Can*, a bronze statue of a coffee can crammed with dirty paint brushes; and Claus Oldenburg's soft sculpture *Floor Cake*, of a giant piece of cake. Here we see binoculars elevated to a higher status in a California building designed by Frank Gehry and a concrete rendition of boot camp from Guatemala.

20b. Famous Statues Use famous statues to study important events, eras, and people in history and other cultures. Have students, individually or in groups, research particular statues, busts, memorials related to events, wars, and cultures under study. Reports should include the item's historical significance and drawings or other visuals. Sculpted human figures provide a good basis for comparing aesthetics of different cultures or eras. For example, compare the perfect proportions of ancient Greek and Roman statues to the distorted ones of modern German expressionists.

Sculpture in Culture

Every sculpture has its own meaning, depending upon the culture, era, and circumstances of its making or destruction. For example, the Kachina doll, shown here, serves an important function in Native American religious ceremonies. In ancient Egypt, carved wooden statues, frequently found in ancient tombs, symbolized servants and slaves meant to follow the dead into the afterworld. In New York, the Statue of Liberty, a gift from the people of France, has come to symbolize democracy and freedom in the United States. The 1991 toppling of the statue of Lenin in Moscow's Red Square highlighted the fall of communism in the Soviet Union. Photograph courtesy Chuck Bowdlear.

20d. Whittle While You Work Have students design and build, if possible, their own statues or other three-dimensional constructions to highlight a current multicultural or history unit. For example, students could model an Native American totem pole, an Inuit carving, or an American eagle. Discuss design choices and symbolism, where to place the piece, and why this site was selected. The class could also make carvings to illustrate an issue, object, or character from a story or make scientific models, such as a simple machine. Use sharp kitchen knives and either large, soft bars of soap, balsa wood, or your own homemade "stone." (If knives in the classroom are a problem, consider doing a classroom demonstration and making the carving extra-credit homework.) Or use papier-mâché, which is especially good for modeling delicate objects. You could also buy modeling books of things to create with scissors and glue.

Make Your Own Carving "Stone"

Combine equal quantities of vermiculite (from a garden store) and dry Portland cement (from a hardware store). Add enough water to get the consistency of porridge. Pour into molds, such as empty milk cartons, and let dry for two or three days at room temperature, depending on the size of the mold. Strip off the container and carve away. Beware of thin areas, which will break off easily. Files work well, as does sandpaper. Paint the finished carving.

20c. Dynamics of Sculpture Use papier-mâché or clay to expand the repertoire of visual-dynamics concepts explored throughout the unit. One possibility is to divide the class into pairs. Have each group use abstract shapes to create a pair of sculptures illustrating contrasting concepts, such as symmetrical versus asymmetrical, open space versus closed space, on-balance versus off-balance, delicate versus clumsy, or static versus dynamic shapes. Can you and your students think of other contrasting concepts to add to the list?

20e. What-If Shapes Play the What If . . . ? game with three-dimensional shapes from the surrounding environment. Be imaginative about asking what would happen if shapes were other than what they are. For example, you could ask, "What if cars had square tires?" "What if houses were spherical instead of square?" or "What if the earth were donut shaped instead of a sphere?" If desired, students can illustrate their responses.

A Recipe for Papier-Mâché

Mix about 4 tablespoons of wheat wallpaper paste with 1 cup of water; stir until creamy. Tear newspaper strips and dip them one at a time into the mixture, wiping off any excess. Place the strips around a form of the object you are making. You can use balloons, chicken wire, or crumpled newspaper for forms. Build up several layers of newspaper to about a quarter-inch thick. After the papier-mâché dries, students can sand, paint, and shellac their work.

20f. America the Beautiful Have students locate examples of sculpture or other three-dimensional artwork in the community, such as fountains, gardens, and elaborate ironwork. Have students, in small groups, brainstorm locations that might be enhanced by the addition of a work of art. Have each group design its own sculpture or three-dimensional piece, making sketches and building a model if feasible. Wherever possible, make projects relevant to local history. When completed, write a class letter to your local town or city government that proposes one or more of the students' ideas.

If you look hard enough, art is all around you. You can find it in nature, as in these tufa formations at Mono Lake.

Challenge students to bring in their favorite paper-making designs and have the class try them. Once confidence is high, ask students to invent their own paper constructions. One possibility: they could design paper Thanksgiving Day ornaments.

20h. Platonic Solids In class, study the five Platonic solids and relate them to real-world objects, such as cubic, tetrahedral, and octahedral molecular structure; icosahedral jungle gyms and geodesic domes of Buckminster Fuller; and dodecahedral seed arrangements, as in the sunflower. Research other examples of the regular polyhedra. Use the "Constructing the Platonic Solids" sheets (pages 114–119) to construct or have students construct these shapes. Students will need a pencil, scissors or craft knife, glue, and a ruler for scoring, Copy the pages onto heavy construction paper, or have students trace or redraw them onto heavy paper or lightweight cardboard (increasing the size of the template if they want to make larger shapes). Or let advanced or gifted students discover their own methods for constructing each solid, either from two-dimensional templates or from straws connected by hairpins. Students may creatively combine and alter their models to make other shapes.

20g. Origami Contest Hold an origami contest, in which students make origami birds, fish, and other shapes by following a precise set of instructions and order for folding paper. Study the Chinese origins of this ancient art. Paper engineering of airplanes fit here as well.

Origami Basics

Origami, the ancient Chinese art of paper folding, was invented over a thousand years ago. Every origami figure begins with a single, square piece of paper that may be folded but not cut or pasted. These are the four fundamental bases of traditional origami: the kite, the fish, the bird, and the frog.

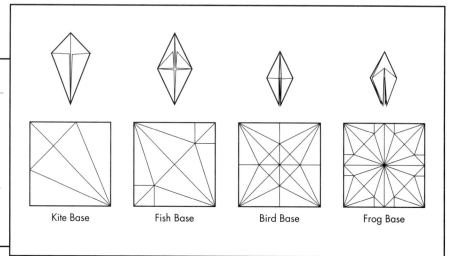

Kite Base Fish Base Bird Base Frog Base

The Platonic Solids

The Platonic solids—hexahedron (cube), tetrahedron, octahedron, icosahedron, and dodecahedron—are named after the Greek philosopher Plato, though he didn't actually discover them. They are the only five *regular* polyhedra, which means all of their sides and angles are identical. Plato believed these solids were the building blocks of the universe and that all other three-dimensional shapes were derived from them. They have fascinated artists and designers for centuries. From Peter Hilton and Jean Pederson, *Build Your Own Polyhedra*, (Menlo Park, CA: Addison-Wesley Publishing Company, 1994).

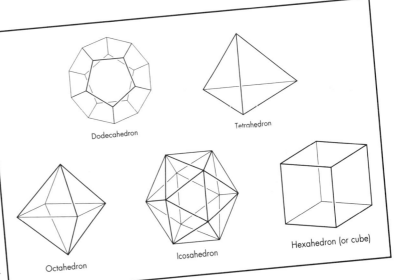

Dodecahedron

Tetrahedron

Octahedron

Icosahedron

Hexahedron (or cube)

20i. 3-D Drawings Create the illusion of depth on a two-dimensional surface (as suggested in *KidsArt,* issue 10, 1988) by having students make 3-D glasses. Copy the "3-D Glasses" sheet (page 120) onto heavy paper. Have students cut out the glasses, bows, holes for the eyes, and slits to insert the bows. They glue or tape a piece of red transparent plastic over one eye slot and blue transparent plastic over the other eye slot. To try out the glasses, have students make a simple line drawing of an object, such as a cube, using a blue pencil, then copy a second identical shape next to the first using a red pencil. Have students view their drawings through the glasses to see the illusion of depth. This Extension leads nicely into the science of how depth perception works.

20j. Flatland Revisited Read *Flatland: A Romance of Many Dimensions,* written by Edwin Abbott in 1884. Abbott, a school teacher, was interested in visually communicating dimensionality. In the book, characters of the 1-D Lineland are points and lines. They live in a limited world. Circles, squares, and other inhabitants of 2-D Flatland have a somewhat larger perspective, although to them the appearance of a sphere from 3-D Sphereland looks magically

similar to a point turning into an expanding, then shrinking, circle.

Make a transparency of the "Lineland and Flatland" sheet (page 121) to foster a discussion about how to represent different dimensions on paper and about how one dimension appears from another dimension. Have the class make its own version of 1-D Lineland, 2-D Flatland, and 3-D Sphereland, creating characters from shapes explored in this and other units. The cartoon strip form works well for this. Divide students in groups and have each student contribute one or more pages that describes and illustrates some aspect of dimensionality. Use the product to teach younger classes about dimensionality. If you are daring, carry this Extension into 4-D Space-Time Land, where three-dimensional objects move through space and time.

Teacher's Corner

★ Use this Teacher's Corner as an opportunity to travel into new dimensions. If you are willing, prepare by taking 2 minutes to list the most important dimensions currently in your life (such as career, family, friends, and particular hobbies). (Here the concept of *dimension* is not used mathematically, but informally as a direction or focus in life).

★ Take another 3 minutes to add to your list as many potential dimensions to living as you can imagine, whether ones you have already considered in the past, might consider in the future, or would never consider (such as gardening, scuba diving, and poetry writing).

★ Set aside an hour or so to experiment with making a sculpture out of clay, papier-mâché, wire, carved wood, foil, or any other material with which you do not ordinarily work. Take 5 to 10 minutes to loosen up by creating the most meaningless piece of work you can. Try focusing on the process rather than the outcome. If you are using clay, consider closing your eyes as you work and enjoying the feel of it.

★ Choose an item from your list of potential life dimensions. Represent it any way you wish through making a sculpture. Try to avoid judging your finished product. Instead, use it both as symbol and inspiration—breaking out of old limitations and moving toward new dimensions in life.

★ Find a way to bring something you learned from this Teacher's Corner into the classroom.

Constructing the Platonic Solids:
Hexahedron (Cube)

Study the picture to figure out how the pattern folds to create the shape. Carefully cut out the pattern on the solid lines. Fold it on the dotted lines, scoring the folds with a ruler. Before applying glue, try the pattern for fit and to see to which side of the tabs glue should be applied. Apply a little bit of glue to the tabs, then fold the pattern.

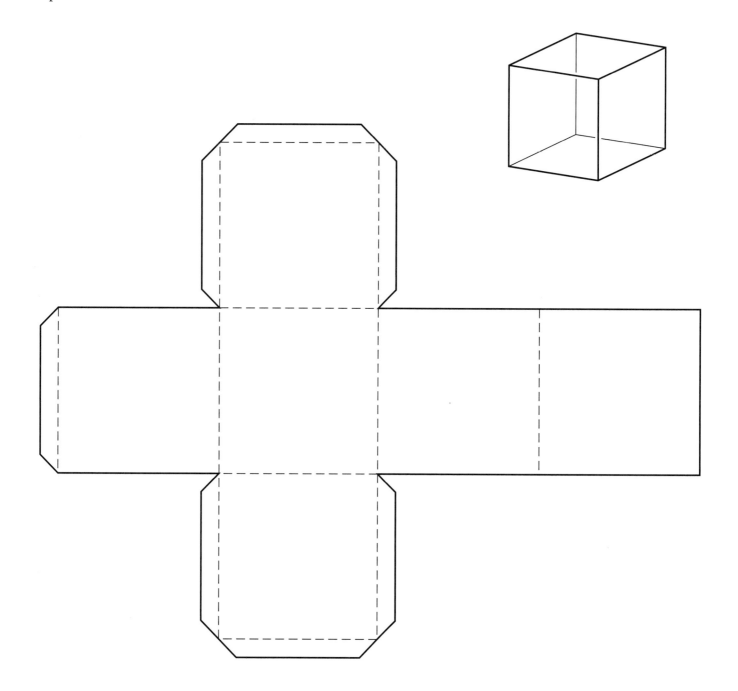

Constructing the Platonic Solids: Tetrahedron

Study the picture to figure out how the pattern folds to create the shape. Carefully cut out the pattern on the solid lines. Fold it on the dotted lines, scoring the folds with a ruler. Before applying glue, try the pattern for fit and to see to which side of the tabs glue should be applied. Apply a little bit of glue to the tabs, then fold the pattern.

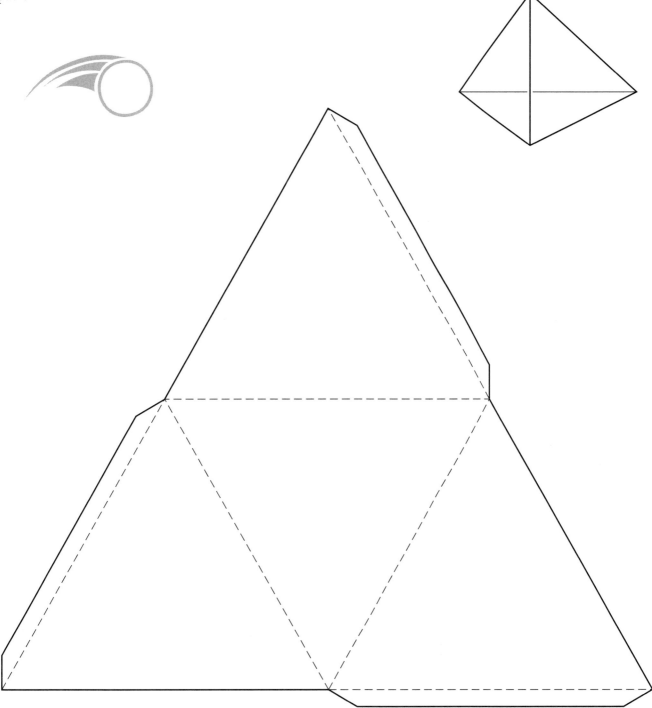

Constructing the Platonic Solids: Octahedron

Study the picture to figure out how the pattern folds to create the shape. Carefully cut out the pattern on the solid lines. Fold it on the dotted lines, scoring the folds with a ruler. Before applying glue, try the pattern for fit and to see to which side of the tabs glue should be applied. Apply a little bit of glue to the tabs, then fold the pattern.

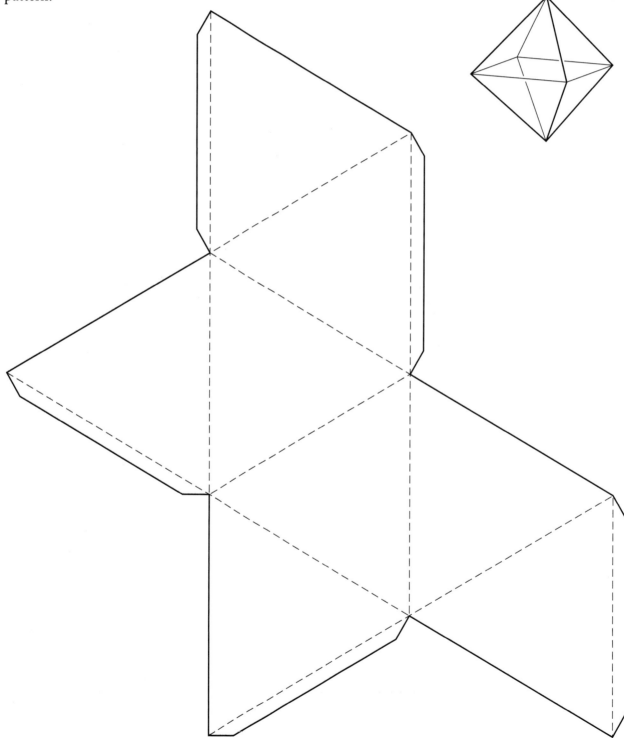

Constructing the Platonic Solids: Icosahedron

Study the picture to figure out how the pattern folds to create the shape. Carefully cut out the pattern on the solid lines. Fold it on the dotted lines, scoring the folds with a ruler. Before applying glue, try the pattern for fit and to see to which side of the tabs glue should be applied. Apply a little bit of glue to the tabs, then fold the pattern.

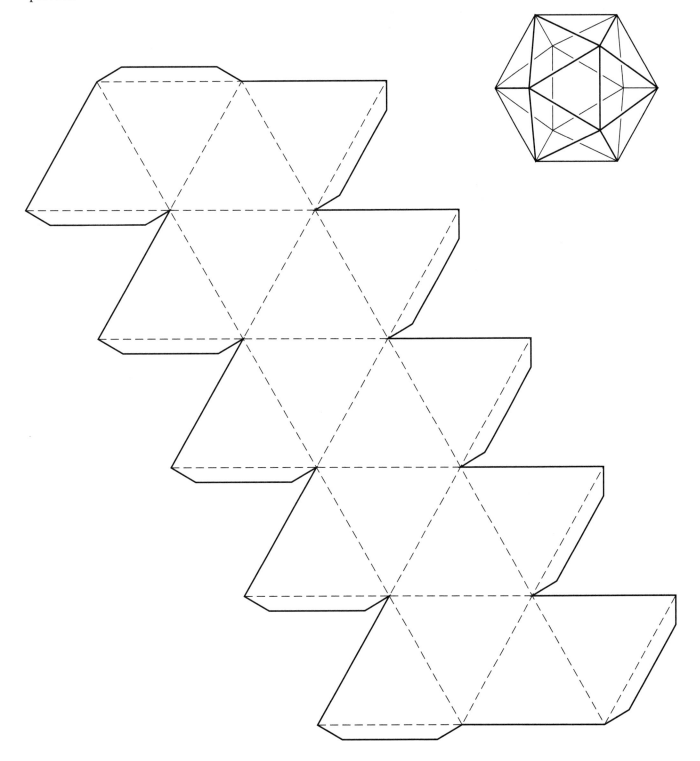

Constructing the Platonic Solids: Dodecahedron

First Half

Study the picture to figure out how the pattern folds to create the shape. Carefully cut out the pattern on the solid lines. Fold it on the dotted lines, scoring the folds with a ruler. Before applying glue, try the pattern for fit and to see to which side of the tabs glue should be applied. Apply a little bit of glue to the tabs, then fold the pattern.

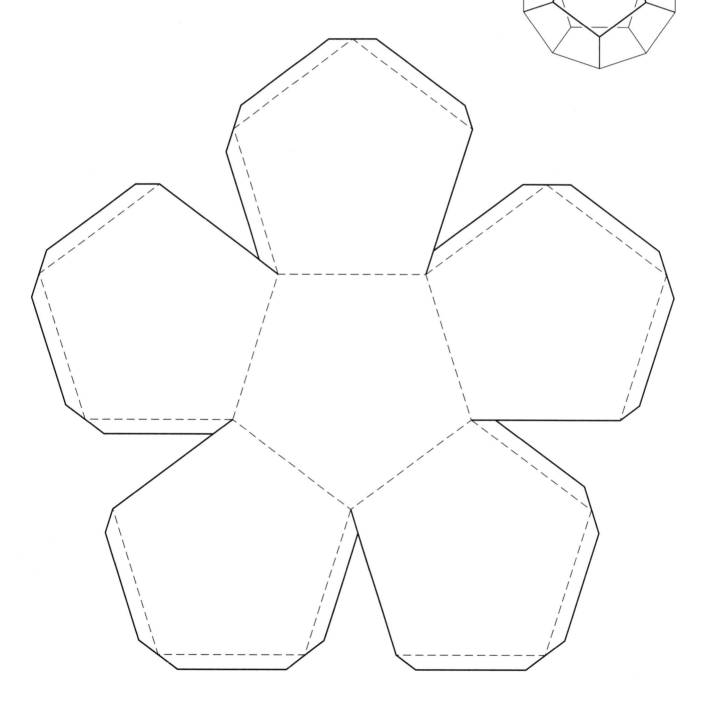

Constructing the Platonic Solids: Dodecahedron

Second Half

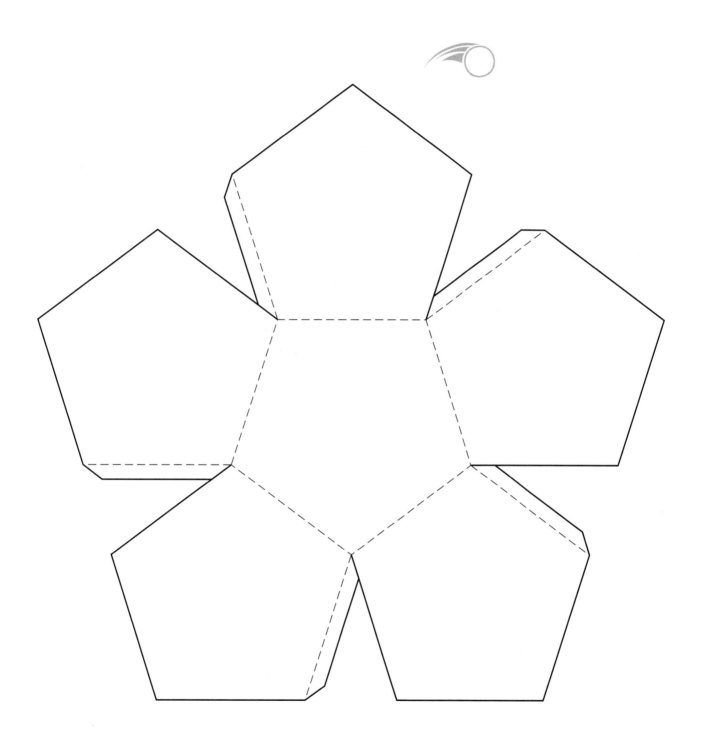

3-D Glasses

Cut out the glasses, the bows, the eye holes, and the slits. Insert the bows into the slits. Glue or tape a piece of red transparent plastic over one eye slot and a piece of blue transparent plastic over the other eye slot.

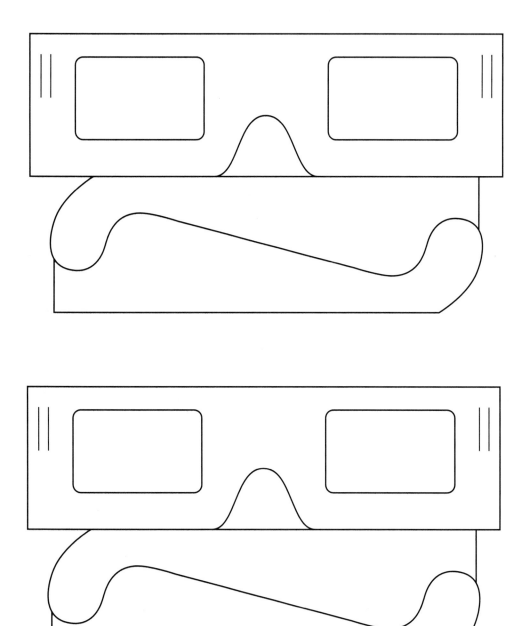

Lineland and Flatland

Here is a square moving through Lineland, being observed by a resident point. What does the point see?

Here is a sphere moving through Flatland, observed by a resident square. What does the square see?

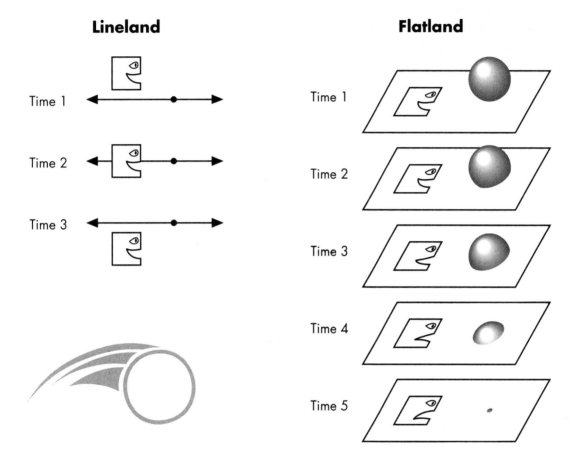

Lineland

Time 1

Time 2

Time 3

Flatland

Time 1

Time 2

Time 3

Time 4

Time 5

GETTING INTO SHAPE
LESSON 21

Although some of the great visual artists have difficulty discussing their work with others, accurate communication of ideas is essential to many aspects of the creative process.

This is especially true when we engage in cooperative ventures, wish to analyze or critique the work of others, or are engaged in scientific research where important findings and discoveries must be interpreted, shared, and reproduced. This unit ends by "getting into shape" on a number of levels. In compositional form, students review the shapes studied so far. Working in pairs, students develop vocabulary and precise listening skills to reproduce shapes and their positions relative to one another. You introduce the class to the concept of *feedback,* which helps us find out how we performed and make adjustments if we were off the mark. Use "Getting Into Shape" to review vocabulary for shapes already known, to create and discover new ones, to sharpen listening skills, and to discuss the importance of precise communication.

Preparation

★ Collect and distribute materials.

Materials

two "Menu of Shapes" sheets per student (page 126); scissors; blank paper; glue or transparent tape (double sided is best); pencils; rulers (optional); building blocks of various shapes and sizes, or Tinker Toys (optional); pins or tape to display compositions

Exercise

(1) Have students cut out some or all of the shapes from a "Menu of Shapes" sheet. Have them arrange and glue or tape the cut-out shapes in a visual composition on another sheet of paper.

(2) Group students into pairs. Designate one person Eyes, the other Hands. Have Eyes use their completed compositions (making sure to keep them out of sight), while Hands use their second "Menu of Shapes" sheet. Have pairs sit back to back, so neither can see the work of the other.

(3) Have Eyes describe which shapes to cut out and exactly how to arrange them in a composition that duplicates their composition. Instruct Hands to listen and follow instructions precisely. The goal is for Eyes to communicate with enough precision that Hands can reproduce the original composition perfectly. This includes choosing the same shapes and placing them correctly relative to one another and to the page. To increase precision, you can give students rulers to measure the objects drawn and spaces between them. In this first round, instruct Hands to listen and follow directions silently, without making comments or asking questions. Allow a maximum of 15 minutes for each round.

(4) Have students compare compositions produced by Eyes and Hands, looking for similarities and differences. Discuss successes and failures in communication in an attempt to improve performance in the next time, when pairs can ask questions.

(5) Have Eyes and Hands switch roles and repeat the Exercise. This time, Hands should make comments and ask questions in an attempt to improve performance.

(6) Hang the work of partners side by side to contrast and compare rounds.

Variation 1
Try the same Exercise in three dimensions using building blocks or Tinker Toys. Hands attempt to build the construction created by Eyes. This variation is easier and will take less time than the original. It may be a good starting point, especially for younger students.

Variation 2
Try a round where students draw simple shape compositions rather than cut shapes out.

Variation 3
For a challenge, do the Exercise using three-dimensional shapes that are drawn (for example, spheres, cubes, bricks, tetrahedrons,

Sometimes a picture *is* worth a thousand words.

cylinders, cones). What makes this variation so much harder than the others?

Discussion

◆ What about this Exercise was difficult? What was easy?

◆ Which role did you prefer, the Eyes or the Hands? Why?

◆ How were precise communication and listening skills essential to this Exercise?

◆ Name other instances when precise communication is essential.

◆ What are cases when precise communication is less important?

◆ Were there large differences when questions were asked versus when they were not?

◆ What is meant by *feedback?* How were questions a way to give and receive feedback?

◆ How did viewing and discussing the outcome after the first round affect your group's performance in the second round?

◆ Would it have been different if the Eyes could watch what the Hands were doing? How?

◆ How many different kinds of feedback can you name?

◆ How does feedback help performance? How can feedback block us from our best performance?

◆ What kinds of feedback are hard to receive? What kinds are easy?

Extensions

21a. Grab Bag of Shapes Here is a kinesthetic Extension to further refine vocabulary for shape and communication skills. Gather paper bags and a variety of small common objects of different shapes and textures, such as spoons, erasers, cotton balls, pencils, and apples. Fill each bag with six to ten items. One bag is sufficient if you do this activity as a class; otherwise gather enough bags and materials to split the class into groups of five or six students. Have a student peek into the bag and choose an object to describe (without removing the item). Hand the bag to a second student. Let the first student describe the object chosen, using words pertaining to its shape and feel—long, round, pointed, thin, squishy. Do not let students name the object or describe its looks, color, or uses. Have the second student attempt to guess the item using feel alone. When the second student makes a guess, have him or her remove the item from the bag. Allow one guess only. Assign one student to keep a running vocabulary list of words used to describe the shape and feel of items.

21b. What Is That Shape? This Extension refines oral language or written skills. Bring in objects of strange or unusual shapes or multicultural origins, such as an Indian turban or an African musical instrument. Hide them, one at a time, in a bag and pass them around the room. Allow students to touch the contents, without peeking or talking. Have student, in groups or individually, brainstorm what the object might be and how it might be used. Encourage free use of fantasy and imagination. You could also use many shapes in a bag or sock as the basis for learning how to estimate large numbers. Dump the contents of the bag to verify estimates. Use this method for a kinesthetic investigation of oceanography by putting different shells and sea shapes in the bag, or of botany by placing fruits and vegetables, twigs, leaves, lichen and other kinds of plants in the bag. Have students feel, describe, study, and, if appropriate, eat them.

21c. What's the Message? Group students into pairs. Have each student make a collage with a message by gluing photographs, magazine advertisements, dried leaves, cloth, buttons, doilies, and other items onto a piece of heavy paper. The collage should communicate something of

Feedback
Feedback literally means to feed the results of a process *back into* its center of control to exert influence. The term originated in electronics, where circuitry is wired so that feedback either opposes or boosts system input. A thermostat uses feedback to maintain a constant temperature; our bodies operate like a thermostat, maintaining our internal environment at 98.6 degrees. In an audio system, if a microphone stands too close to a speaker it can amplify the output, producing feedback often painful to the ears. In social, educational, and professional situations, feedback is an important way to give and receive information about performance, opinions, or feelings. Receiving test results or report cards, being told someone loves you, being coached, or losing a sports competition are all ways we give and receive feedback.

personal or social relevance without words. Protect the design with a layer of acrylic varnish. Have student exchange completed collages with partners. Have each student write a short essay on what the collage message is to them. Have partners exchange and read essays and provide feedback about their intentions for the message. Emphasize that there is no right and wrong here—an unintended message received is as valid as an intended one. This demonstrates how art can communicate on many levels simultaneously.

21d. Shape Scrapbooks

Take a field trip or make a home assignment to start Shape Scrapbooks for logging new and unusual shapes. Students may compile scrapbooks individually or as a class. They should paste in or draw objects and verbally describe them, including how and where a shape was found and any research done on it. Encourage students to be creative with their entries. They could speculate other places and uses for a shape. You could also create an ongoing Shape Scrapbook bulletin board.

21e. Shape Poems

Have students make shape poems—concrete poems written in the shape of the main idea. For example, a poem about a hand would be written in the shape of a hand. Students could perform poetry using shapes in space for dramatic emphasis.

21f. Eyes Leading the Blind

Group students into pairs. Blindfold one of each pair. Those student are Feet; the other students are Eyes. Have Eyes carefully lead Feet around. Feet should try to keep orientation while being led and guess where they are before Eyes remove the blindfold. Discuss the role of feedback in this experiment. Make up different Extensions for each of the following: an Eyes-Ears team, an Ears-Voice team, and an Ears-Hand team. For inspiration, read *The Story of My Life,* by Helen Keller. Discuss the importance of feedback for reaching and teaching individuals with physical disabilities.

21g. Shaping Up Our Lives

Brainstorm and discuss figures of speech involving the word *shape*. Examples include "get into shape," "ship shape," "out of shape," and "shape up or ship out." Discuss how each relates to our health, well-being, or self-esteem. Ask how much we shape ourselves and how much others shape us. Ask if the balance changes as we develop and mature. Have students pretend to be parents who give advice to their own children about how to shape up their lives, perhaps in the form of a letter, a poem, or a short story.

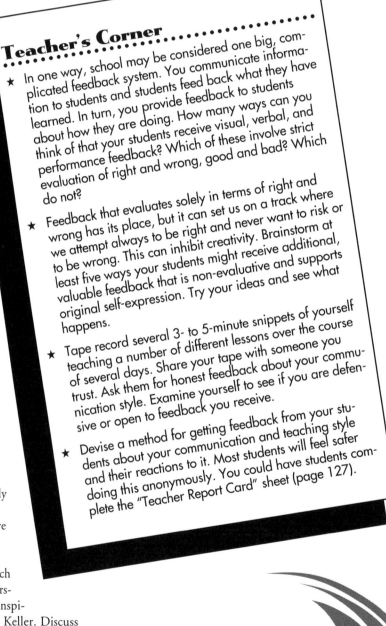

Teacher's Corner

★ In one way, school may be considered one big, complicated feedback system. You communicate information to students and students feed back what they have learned. In turn, you provide feedback to students about how they are doing. How many ways can you think of that your students receive visual, verbal, and performance feedback? Which of these involve strict evaluation of right and wrong, good and bad? Which do not?

★ Feedback that evaluates solely in terms of right and wrong has its place, but it can set us on a track where we attempt always to be right and never want to risk or to be wrong. This can inhibit creativity. Brainstorm at least five ways your students might receive additional, valuable feedback that is non-evaluative and supports original self-expression. Try your ideas and see what happens.

★ Tape record several 3- to 5-minute snippets of yourself teaching a number of different lessons over the course of several days. Share your tape with someone you trust. Ask them for honest feedback about your communication style. Examine yourself to see if you are defensive or open to feedback you receive.

★ Devise a method for getting feedback from your students about your communication and teaching style and their reactions to it. Most students will feel safer doing this anonymously. You could have students complete the "Teacher Report Card" sheet (page 127).

21h. Lines of Communication Have your class play Telephone, a game about lines of communication. Divide the class into three or four long lines of students. Have the head of each line write a message on paper and then whisper it into the ear of the second person in line. Have this person, in turn, whisper the message to the third person, and so on until the end of the line. Have the last person say the message out loud, then compare it to the original recorded message. Try a variation where students research and use famous but unfamiliar quotes from history. Discuss how easily messages get distorted when passed through a long line of people. This is especially true when there is no discussion or feedback. Ask how this applies to the spread of gossip and rumors.

21i. I'm All Ears Group students into pairs. Designate one Voice and the other Ears. Give Voices 5 minutes to describe a problem. When time is up, give Ears a minute or so to summarize and repeat precisely what they heard, with nothing else added. Give Ears an additional minute or so to provide feedback, in the form of reactions, advice, or sharing common experiences. Switch partners and try another round. First in pairs, then as a class, discuss reactions to the two different kinds of feedback—simply being heard versus getting other kinds of responses. Ask if there are situations where we just want to be heard by others. Ask if there are situations where we seek other forms of feedback. Use this format for addressing student problems, developing empathy, or in a peer counseling program that you supervise regularly.

Name _____ Date _____

Menu of Shapes

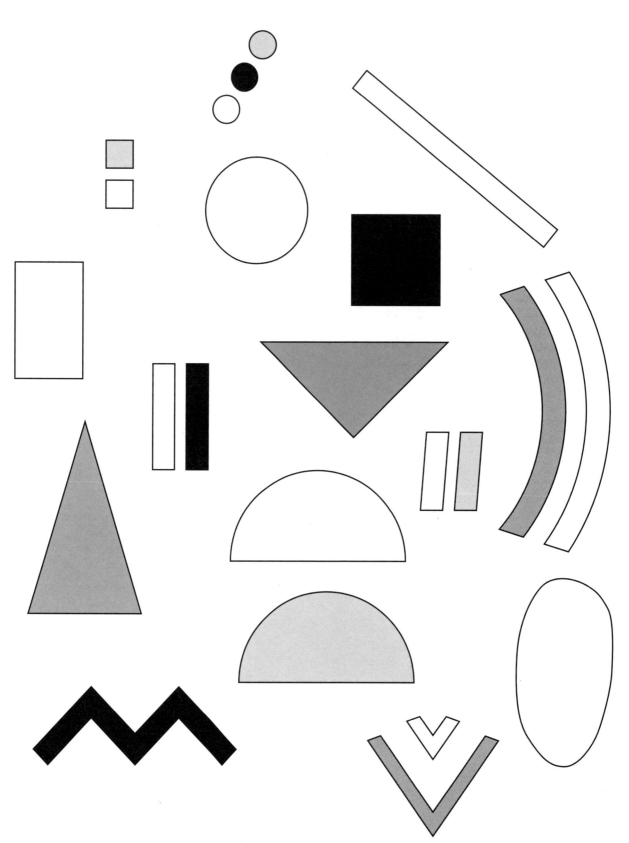

Date _____

Teacher Report Card

Just as students need feedback from teachers to know where they stand, so do teachers. Please answer each question to improve communication in your classroom. Try to stick to descriptions rather than using judgments.

1. Name three ways your teacher communicates to your class well.

2. How does your teacher help you to understand difficult material?

3. What are some things your teacher should do to help you learn difficult material more easily?

4. In your opinion, is there anything your teacher could do to communicate more effectively?

5. Is there anything you have wanted to tell your teacher that has been difficult to communicate?

UNIT 4

PUTTING THE PIECES TOGETHER: QUEST FOR PATTERN

PATTERN DETECTIVE
LESSON 22

Our surroundings consist of layers of overlapping patterns

The least obvious patterns often prove the most interesting. In this lesson students discover these patterns by looking at groups of elements in different ways. This stimulates mental flexibility and encourages divergent thinking. Students learn there is more than one right answer. Detecting patterns is both a challenge and a creative act. Use "Pattern Detective" for any subject, especially if you need to fill short time blocks productively. Because it requires the application and not just acquisition of knowledge, the lesson is an excellent method for demonstrating and applying deep, rather than superficial, understanding of material learned.

Preparation

★ Select three objects randomly.

★ Using pen and paper or a "Pattern-Maker" sheet, take 3 minutes to brainstorm all the ways in which the objects are alike.

★ Using pen and paper or a "Pattern-Breaker" sheet, take 5 minutes to brainstorm how each object differs from the other two.

★ List all the features you used to classify objects.

Materials

chalkboard and chalk; three randomly chosen objects; pens or pencils; one "Pattern-Maker" sheet (page 134) and one "Pattern-Breaker" sheet (page 135) per student

Exercise

(1) Select a student to record ideas on the board.

(2) Select three other students to come to the front of the room and stand side by side.

(3) As a class, brainstorm *pattern-makers:* ways in which the three students are alike. Record the list on the board.

(4) Choose another group of three students to stand side by side.

(5) Brainstorm *pattern-breakers:* ways in which each student differs from the other two, again recording the list. Discourage hurtful or humiliating differences, such as if one flunked math and the other two did not.

(6) Make a list of classification features: dimensions used for detecting similarities and differences. Examples include hair color, physical features, gender, aspects of names, and family histories.

(7) In a second round, place three different objects, instead of students, at the front of the room. Hand out the "Pattern-Maker" and "Pattern-Breaker" sheets, and have students work individually to find pattern-makers and pattern-breakers for the objects. Contrast and compare responses.

Discussion

◆ What is a pattern?

◆ How many different kinds of patterns can you think of?

◆ Which kinds involve creating or making the pattern? Which kinds involve finding or discovering the pattern?

◆ What is your favorite kind of pattern?

◆ Why are patterns so important to us?

◆ What is the first pattern an infant learns to recognize?

◆ How does pattern detection help us survive and stay safe?

Pattern Detective Example

Let's say you selected a pen, a purse, and a penny. A pattern detective could notice that the objects are similar in the following ways: their names begin with the same letter, they are all manufactured, and they all fit in your hand. How does each differ from the others? The penny is money, made of copper, has nothing inside, is round, and is flat. The purse is soft, made of leather, carries many items, and has a strap. The pen is oblong, contains ink, and is made of plastic. The classification features used include name spelling, origin of object, material composition, shape, size, and function.

◆ Is there always more than one pattern in any group of elements?

◆ When analyzing a situation, why is it so easy to think there is only one right solution?

◆ What does pattern detection have to do with creativity?

◆ What are some ways we can extend our range of vision to detect patterns otherwise invisible to us?

The Essence of Pattern

Some people define *creativity* as the ability to perceive or produce new patterns from old elements. *A pattern* is a design composed of a number of elements arranged in a regular, sometimes formal manner. People may create patterns, such as artistic patterns for decorating surfaces, or they may discover patterns, such as scientific patterns that illuminate regularities in nature. Scientific instruments, such as radar, the telescope, microscope, and computer, help extend human pattern-seeking. To some extent, whether a pattern is created or discovered is a philosophical issue. Many artists believe that rather than creating patterns, they discover them, serving as a vehicle or channel for work that exists on another plane (see Michelangelo's perspective on sculpture, page 108). On the other hand, many scientists believe patterns in nature are actually created, not discovered. This is especially true in the subatomic realm of quantum physics, in which measurements taken of a beam of particles can affect the beam itself. It becomes impossible to separate the observed from the observer.

Extensions

22a. Word Patterns Pick three to five words for students to analyze, seeking pattern-makers and pattern-breakers. To tap divergent as well as convergent thinking, use word groups that lend themselves to multiple layers of pattern. For example, you could ask students to find patterns in *late, mate, fate,* and *gate.* Students could notice that the words all rhyme, have four letters, have three letters in common, and have a silent *e.* Another example: What do *record, present, convict,* and *progress* have in common? They all have two syllables, are nouns when accented on the first syllable, and are verbs when accented on the second syllable. Try the same exercise with multiple-word phrases or even complete sentences. Study idioms—regional and other variations in language—by collecting different ways of saying the same thing. Examples include *died, kicked the bucket, passed away, expired,* and *bought the farm.* Ask students what different connotations each has. Relate these specialized words and idioms to euphemisms.

22b. Math Mania Select three to five numbers for students to analyze in search of pattern-makers and pattern-breakers. Try to pick examples rich in multiple layers of pattern. For example, you could ask students to find patterns in 128, 4, 64, and 624. Possible answers include: all are even numbers, powers of two, and divisible by four, and none are prime. Another example: How many different ways can you think of to express the number 8? Keep a list of methods used. Possible answers include: eight, $4 + 4$, $11 - 3$, 2×4, $16 \div 2$, 2 to the third power, : : : : , and 8.00000. The classification methods include words, addition, subtraction, multiplication, division, exponents, concrete representation, and decimals.

22c. Tiling Patterns Tilings make great visual patterns. Use the "Tiling Patterns" sheet (page 136) to find pattern-makers and pattern-breakers and learn about different kinds of tilings. Have students experiment on their own, using graph paper or the "Try Angles" sheet (page 102) as the background. For a multicultural twist, have students research geometric designs that have been used in Islamic art for thousands of years.

22d. Patterns in Style Use the "Patterns in Style" sheet (page 137) and apply pattern-seeking to works of art by artist John Garrett. By finding similarities and differences among a group of six pieces, students must develop a discriminating eye and the vocabulary for expressing subtle distinctions. Once students complete the sheet, compare and contrast student responses, looking for common and unusual grouping patterns. If desired, repeat this Extension by choosing or having students choose several pieces of work by a single artist. You could use slides or an overhead projector. Have students detect and report, either orally or in writing, on pattern-makers and pattern-breakers among the pieces.

22e. What's So Funny? What makes a joke or cartoon funny? Usually it has to do with the violation of our normal expectations. For this reason humor is a pattern-breaker. Use the "What's So Funny?" sheet (page 138) to study and create "concrete" humor, which occurs when a metaphoric concept is depicted literally. Have students bring in examples of cartoons, such as "Far Side" by Gary Larson, and political cartoons. Analyze what makes each funny. Find pattern-makers and pattern-breakers between them. Have joke-telling sessions where each student contributes a joke. Use groups of jokes as the basis for finding pattern-makers and pattern-breakers. Collect student examples of jokes and literal humor for a What's So Funny? bulletin board.

22f. Can You Place This? Use pattern-makers and pattern-breakers to study geography and culture. For example, you could ask how Illinois, South Carolina, Colorado, Oregon, and Maine differ from each other. Possible answers include: only South Carolina is in the South, only Illinois borders the Great Lakes, only Colorado is land-locked, only Oregon is on the Pacific Ocean or the West coast, and only Maine borders Canada or is in the Northeast. Or you could ask how Spain, Brazil, and Guatemala differ from each other. Possible answers include: Brazil is the only country that is not Spanish-speaking, Spain is the only country not in the Americas, and Guatemala is the only country in Central America. You could also use this Extension for cultural studies. For example, each area of Guatemala has distinct weaving patterns. Collect pictures or samples from each area. Do pattern-makers and pattern-breakers with students by seeking similarities and differences among woven designs. George Catlin, the first Caucasian artist to paint Native Americans, portrayed over forty-eight different Indian tribes. Use his artwork to identify pattern-makers and pattern-breakers among the tribes based on face paint, clothing style, poses, and actions.

Wait Lifters

Here is a double pattern-breaker—concrete humor with a homophonic twist.

22g. Flag It Down Because they have so many visual and symbolic levels, flags are wonderful tools for uncovering patterns within patterns. Have students draw or cut out pictures of as many world flags as possible, then group them according to features such as colors, shapes, and symbols. Divide the class into cooperative groups assigned to research ways in which countries represented by different groupings bear political, geographical, historical, or cultural resemblances to one another. Students might work in the other direction as well, using facts about countries to understand their flags. Ask if countries derived from other countries inherit elements of the original country's flag. Have students look at ways the American, Nigerian, and Hawaiian flags retain elements of the British flag.

Tilings

These are examples of tessellations found in Islamic art. A tiling, or tessellation, is a pattern of one or more shapes completely covering the plane without gaps or overlaps. There are three kinds of regular tilings: each corner, or vertex, is surrounded by polygons of identical shape: triangles, parallelograms, or hexagons. There are eight kinds of semiregular tilings: each vertex is surrounded by more than one kind of polygon; for example, hexagons, squares, and triangles. It is possible to have tilings that are uniform throughout, but not laid edge to edge. It is also possible to have uniform tilings—either they have patterns that do not repeat on a regular basis, or that have patterns that transform from one type of polygon to another across the plane through the addition or subtraction of edges, vertices, or faces. Try to find each type of tiling in "Tiling Patterns" (page 136).

22h. Design-a-Country Have students, individually or in pairs, design their own country. They should name it, define its boundaries (one possibility is to separate your county from the rest of the state and country), write a constitution, design a flag, create a stamp, declare a form of government, and write a national anthem. Showcase invented countries and discuss their pattern-making similarities and pattern-breaking differences in terms of student-created and real countries.

22i. How Revolting! As a class, brainstorm as many examples of revolution as you can. Invent different ways to group and regroup instances of revolution according to patterns of similarities and differences. If desired, divide students into groups for follow-up library research. This Extension can range anywhere from 15 minutes to an entire unit.

22j. Classification Schemes Send the class on a scavenger hunt in search of different kinds of flowers, leaves, fruits, and vegetables.

Revolutions

A revolution is a complete, pervasive, often radical change. For many, the word *revolution* first brings to mind a violent political overthrow, such as the Russian and French Revolutions. Yet there have been nonviolent political revolutions, such as that led in India by Mahatma Gandhi. Other kinds of revolutions have nothing to do with political events, such as the industrial, agricultural, or Copernican revolutions, and social revolutions, such as those caused by emancipation of slaves, woman's suffrage, and automation.

Together, classify the collection by different patterns, such as the number of petals or seeds. Or bring in pictures of different kinds of animals. Have students classify the animals according to different patterns, such as four-legged, carnivorous, or egg-laying. Compare classification schemes invented by students with those used in zoology.

22k. Patterns of Survival Do a unit on patterns of camouflage and contrast in the coloring of animals. Have students research which animals are colored or shaped like their environment to hide from predators. Have them research animals that stand out from their environment to protect themselves. Ask which animals change their patterns and colors as needed. Ask how each of the following fit in with the above: chameleons, zebras, venomous snakes, butterflies.

22l. Search for Common Ground Try a new debate format. Pick an issue to debate from opposite points of view, such as whether Christopher Columbus should be credited with discovering America. Each participant takes 5 to 10 minutes to present his or her position on the issue. Act as moderator or pick a third student to do so. Rather than focusing on differences of perspective, the traditional style of a debate, here is the pattern-breaker: The moderator and student observers focus on similarities in perspective, looking for common areas in which both participants agree. Use this format for conflict resolution at any level, whether between students in the classroom or to address global problems in history or current events.

Teacher's Corner

★ Make up your own pattern-makers and pattern-breakers in a subject of your choice. Try them out in class.

★ Try making up an exam consisting only of pattern-makers and pattern-breakers to test knowledge of a subject under study. Evaluate creatively, using several different criteria, such as quantity, quality, and originality of patterns found. Be careful to reward students who find patterns other than ones you originally had in mind.

★ Take time to examine the patterns of your own life. Begin by taking 5 minutes to brainstorm and list as many patterns you can see that concern your life. Then try changing the lens. Take 3 minutes apiece to list the kinds of patterns each of the following might discover when examining your life: a biologist, an anthropologist, an economist, a politician, an artist.

★ How can you use the perspectives above to further enrich your life in and out of the classroom?

Pattern-Maker

Name three to five people, places, or things you wish to compare.

1.

2.

3.

4.

5.

Name all the ways they are similar to one another, no matter how silly or insignificant they seem.

List the features you used to classify similarities.

Pattern-Breaker

Name three to five people, places, or things you wish to contrast.

1.

2.

3.

4.

5.

Name ways each one differs from all others.

List the features you used to classify differences.

Tiling Patterns

Below are samples of many different kinds of tilings. A tiling is a pattern of one or more shapes completely covering the plane without any gaps or overlaps. On a separate sheet of paper, create as many different pattern-makers and pattern-breakers as possible. Create pattern-makers by finding two or more tiling patterns that belong together and describing one or more feature they have in common. Create pattern-breakers by finding a tiling that differs from at least two others and describing the feature it has that the others do not. For a challenge, create pattern-makers and pattern-breakers based on two features.

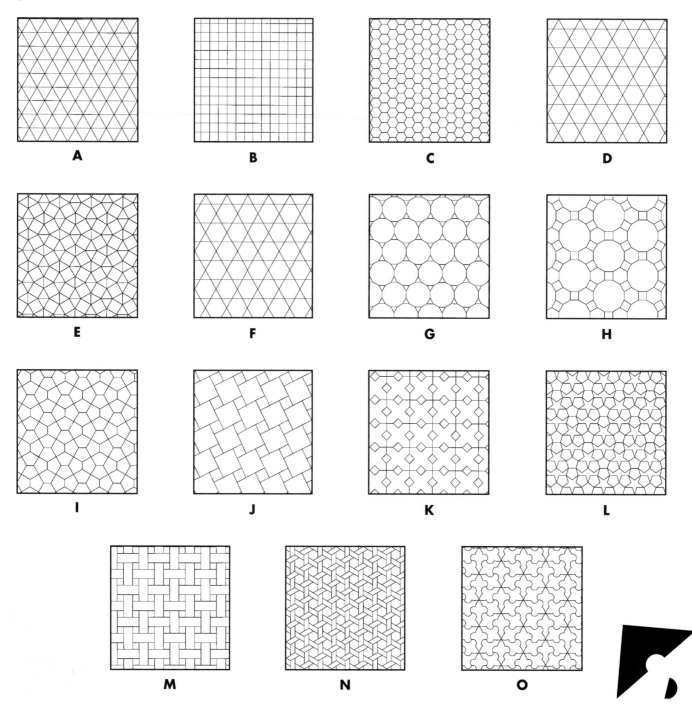

A   B   C   D

E   F   G   H

I   J   K   L

M   N   O

Patterns in Style

On a separate sheet of paper, write out your responses to each of these questions.

1. List all the ways in which each of these four pieces are alike.
2. List at least two ways in which each piece differs from the others.
3. If you had to group these four pieces into two separate groups, how would you choose to group them and why?
4. Find another way to group these pieces and explain your choice.

John Garrett, *Vulcan Vine Basket*

John Garrett, *Poof Basket*

A

B

C

John Garrett, *Spider Basket*

D

John Garrett, *Fiesta Basket*
Photographs courtesy Bill Svendsen

Name _____ Date _____

What's So Funny?

What makes something funny? Often it has to do with a pattern-breaker—an important way in which our expectations are broken. In the cartoons below you will see examples of "concrete" humor, in which a metaphoric concept is drawn literally. After looking at each one, take a few minutes to brainstorm five other metaphoric ideas or phrases that you could draw literally, such as "fast food."

He Sure Is Two-Faced!

Fast Food

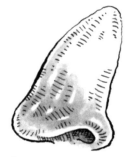

No Body Nose

Fed Up with the City

Stop a Head

Five other metaphoric ideas or phrases that could be drawn literally.

1.

2.

3.

4.

5.

In the space below, choose one or two of your ideas and draw them.

TOPSY-TURVY LAND
LESSON 23

Opposite pairs and reversal patterns are fundamental to existence.

We steer our lives between poles of health and sickness, joy and sorrow, success and failure, and life and death, to mention just a few. This lesson welcomes you and your class to Topsy-Turvy Land, where everything is reversed. What was up is down, what was in is out, hello means good-bye, and happiness makes you cry. "Topsy-Turvy Land" helps bare our hidden assumptions about the world. It enables us to suspend ordinary conditions and open the realm of the extraordinary. Use this lesson to stimulate flights of fancy, to jog students from usual mind sets, and to question the obvious. Everyone will walk away from Topsy-Turvy Land with a broader perspective.

Preparation

★ Gather pairs of photographs that demonstrate opposite qualities. Examples include pretty and ugly, tall and short, good and bad, and up and down.

★ Read the Exercise. Decide whether to give students their choice of final project or assign your preference.

★ Gather materials appropriate to assignments chosen.

★ Think of ways you can reverse your normal appearance to introduce this lesson. Be clever! You could wear a piece of clothing inside out or backward, socks on your hands, or your glasses upside down.

Materials

photographs of opposite qualities; chalkboard and chalk; pens and paper; assorted media (depends upon creative projects assigned or chosen)

Exercise

1 Walk into the classroom backward or on your hands. Wear some aspect of your clothing inside out or upside down. Welcome the class to Topsy-Turvy Land, where everything is the opposite of how it normally is.

2 Using the chalkboard, take 10 minutes to brainstorm as many opposite or complementary pairs as possible. Use the photographs to stimulate student imagination.

3 Make up some examples of Topsy-Turvy propositions; for example:

- *If big were little and little were big, . . .*
- *If up were down and down were up, . . .*
- *If in were out and out were in, . . .*
- *If good were evil and evil were good, . . .*
- *If light things were heavy and heavy things were light, . . .*
- *If strong were weak and weak were strong, . . .*

4 Have students complete a topsy-turvy proposition and express it in a form chosen either by you or the student. An example of a completed topsy-turvy proposition is, "If big were little and little were big, I'd use the world as my marble, and ride on the wings of a butterfly." Possible ways students, individually or in groups, could express the proposition include poems, Haiku, short skits or plays, short stories, mimes, cartoon strips, wall murals, photographic essays, diorama, or songs.

5 Showcase and discuss student work.

Here is what might happen if inside were out and outside were in. Levon Parian, *Untitled.*

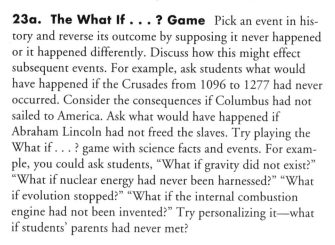

Discussion

◆ What do you think of Topsy-Turvy Land? What do you notice about it?

◆ How is life a constant shuffle or struggle between opposites, such as work and play, good and evil, and disease and health?

◆ Is it possible for one half of a pair of opposites to exist without the other? Can we have good without evil or light without darkness?

◆ What is the Chinese symbol of yin-yang? What does it have to do with opposites?

◆ Would it be fun to play all the time or would you get bored?

◆ Does anyone have a life that always has only good things in it, such as always being happy, healthy, or on the winning team?

◆ How is it possible to experience opposite feelings at the same time, such as love and hate?

◆ Why does it often take losing something before we realize how important that person, thing, or condition is to us?

◆ Which world conditions would you like most to reverse? How might you try?

◆ Which world conditions would you like least to reverse?

Extensions

23a. The What If . . . ? Game Pick an event in history and reverse its outcome by supposing it never happened or it happened differently. Discuss how this might effect subsequent events. For example, ask students what would have happened if the Crusades from 1096 to 1277 had never occurred. Consider the consequences if Columbus had not sailed to America. Ask what would have happened if Abraham Lincoln had not freed the slaves. Try playing the What if . . . ? game with science facts and events. For example, you could ask students, "What if gravity did not exist?" "What if nuclear energy had never been harnessed?" "What if evolution stopped?" "What if the internal combustion engine had not been invented?" Try personalizing it—what if students' parents had never met?

23b. Fractured Fairy Tales Have students make fractured fairy tales by taking a well-known fairy tale theme and reversing expected elements. For example, students could make up a story where kissing a frog turns the princess into one as well. Or how about a tale of Repunzel the bald? Combine the tales of six or seven students into Fractured Fairy Tale books, which students illustrate themselves. Read them to students in younger classes. If the class is ambitious, try to get them published or read over the radio.

23c. Topsy-Turvy Land 'Toons Often humor hinges on unexpected reversals of conditions. Use the "Topsy-Turvy Land 'Toons" sheet for students to experience and analyze the comic reversals of artist J. T. Steiny. Have students make up their own cartoons depicting funny reversals, perhaps linked to a language arts, social studies, or science unit under study. Or take 5 minutes for the class to brainstorm the funniest reversals imaginable.

The yin-yang symbol is the Chinese philosophical and religious symbol for opposites. Yin represents the negative, dark, and feminine side of existence, while yang represents the positive, bright, and masculine side. Both are entwined and believed to influence the destinies of all creatures and things. Neither principle can exist without the other, symbolized by the two interpenetrating shapes. Notice how the seed of each side resides in the middle of the other. According to Chinese philosophy, good cannot completely vanquish evil; right will never eliminate wrong. Both will eternally coexist.

23d. Reversible Art Here is a cornucopia of topsy-turvy drawing techniques, great for enhancing observation skills.

1. *Have students design the front of a drawing or painting on the front of a piece of paper and design the back of the scene on the reverse side. Hang them to make an interesting mobile.*

2. *We tend to draw the outside of objects only. Have students draw the inside of something that is easily dismantled, such as staplers, old clocks, and radios.*

3. *Have students make an exact copy of a simple line drawing or picture that is turned upside down. This helps students to draw what they see, not what they know. It is particularly useful for individuals convinced they cannot draw.*

4. *To achieve figure-ground reversibility, ask students to draw a black object on black construction paper using a white piece of chalk. With this technique, figures can only be established indirectly, by drawing the background. Study prints of M. C. Escher, such as* Sky and Water, Day and Night, *and the* Metamorphosis *series, for interesting examples of figure-ground reversal.*

23e. Opposite Feelings As a class, brainstorm complementary sets of feelings, such as love/hate, happiness/sadness, anxiety/relaxation, fear/excitement, hope/despair, and pride/humility. Ask students to use poetry to write about a pair of feelings. They may use haiku, tanka, chain verse, diamante, or another poetry form.

23f. Palindromes Have students make up funny palindromes, such as "Too hot to hoot" and "St. Pure Erupts." Find palindromic folk and fairy tales that end the way they began. Play the palindromic second movement of Franz Joseph Haydn's "Palindromic Symphony." Create math problems using palindromic numbers such as 232. Make up a palindromic calendar using dates such as the year 2002.

Palindromes

Palindromes are an interesting kind of reversal. A *palindrome* is a word spelled backward the same as it is forward, such as *noon* and *Anna*. Whole sentences may be palindromic, such as "Madam, I'm Adam" and "Able was I, ere I saw Elba." By contrast, *semordnilaps* are words that make a different word when spelled backward. Examples include *gum*, *star*, and *diaper*, which backward spell *mug*, *rats*, and *repaid*.

23g. Semordnilaps Seek semordnilaps for students' and your first, middle, and last names to find nicknames in Topsy-Turvy Land. Individually or as a class, brainstorm other interesting semordnilaps. Challenge students to create a string of words that convey meaning when spelled backward, such as "He lives in it," which backward spells, "Tin is evil, eh?" Semordnilap phrases or sentences are somewhat easier to find. They are a string of words that still possesses meaning with the words reversed, such as "Sue is here" reverses to "Here is Sue." Have students make up their own examples for three-, four-, five-, or even six-word phrases.

Forms of Poetry

Haiku is an unrhymed verse of three lines with five, seven, and five syllables respectively, all with the same thought. Here is an example of haiku:

> *I am strong and weak,*
> *I can stand brave and upright,*
> *But I can bend, too.*

Tanka is similar to haiku, but with five lines of five, seven, five, seven, and seven syllables respectively. In *chain verse*, the last word or phrase of each line forms the beginning of the next. An example of chain verse is "Oh how I feel, I feel so much, so much numbness, numbness to the point where I can't feel a thing." *Diamante* is poetry in the shape of a diamond with seven lines (see page 97).

Here is an appropriately titled semordnilap sculpture of an animal. Removable coat of fur and all, this creature fits perfectly in Topsy-Turvy Land. J. Nicholas Borozan, *Lamina*. Photograph courtesy Gary Silk.

23i. Reversed Literature Take several minutes with the class to brainstorm instances of reversal in literature: the topsy-turvy world of *Alice in Wonderland* and *Through the Looking Glass* by Lewis Carroll, the role reversal in *The Prince and the Pauper* by Mark Twain, and the twisted futuristic vision of *A Hitchhiker's Guide to the Galaxy* by Douglas Adams. Have students, individually, in pairs, or in small groups, author a piece of creative writing or perform a dramatic skit that includes a reversal of some sort.

23j. Oxymorons, Paradoxes, and Irony Ask the class to brainstorm a list of oxymorons in 10 minutes. Have students compose a story that includes five phrases from the list. Define and discuss paradoxes, such as the Liar's and the Barber's. Have students find or make up others. Study irony, as in the story of Oedipus, who vows to get the murderer of his father—ironical, because the murderer turns out to be himself. Read ironic fairy tales or stories, such as *The Gift of the Magi* by O. Henry. With the class, discuss how oxymorons, paradoxes, and irony relate to reversals and opposites. Ask how the concepts relate to sarcasm.

23k. Topsy-Turvy Time Set aside 5 to 10 minutes of weekly or monthly topsy-turvy time. Have students bring in, share, and showcase examples of reversibility in nature, science, and art they have found or made.

23h. Inverted Antonyms Twist student minds by taking opposite pairs and inverting them so they appear to contradict themselves. Some examples:

Underline	<u>No</u> Underline
Straight	Slanted
Small	Big
Solid	**Hollow**
Light	Dark

Have students incorporate one or more inverted opposites into a piece of art or composition. Assign students a trip to a fun house to gaze at themselves in a mirror that inverts the image. Let students look through a pair of prism glasses that inverts the world.

Oxymorons, Paradoxes, and Irony

An *oxymoron* is a figure of speech that appears to contradict itself, such as "cruel kindness," "looking horribly well," and "making haste slowly." A *paradox* is an apparently unsolvable problem that also seems to contradict itself. Here is the Liar's Paradox: "This sentence is a lie." Which is the sentence, true or false? The sentence is true only if it is false, and false only if it is true. Here is the Barber's Paradox: "Who shaves the barber that shaves all the other barbers in the town?" *Irony* is a dramatic technique of indicating, either through character or plot development, an intention or attitude opposite to that which is stated.

Teacher's Corner

Many people think creativity is about finding original answers to difficult questions. Others hold a Topsy-Turvy Land perspective, such as the late Richard Feynman, physics Nobel laureate, and Paul McCready, inventor of human-powered flight. They believed the highest creativity is not in finding clever solutions to already established problems, but in finding interesting new questions and problems to investigate.

★ What are four important new questions you can ask about your life?

★ What are six original questions to ask about the world around you?

★ Can you list seven pressing questions about your teaching or your students?

★ Over the next couple of days, see if simply asking these questions has any effect in your life or classroom.

★ Here are some Topsy-Turvy Land teaching techniques.

- For any subject, reverse the normal sequence of events. Give the answer and have students make up relevant questions. As a class, watch the television show Jeopardy for inspiration. Make a whole test where you supply the answers and students provide the questions. Be sure to encourage multiple-right-answer questions.
- Reverse roles with students for 30 minutes. Let students take turns teaching, make up the tests, and even the grades.
- Handle classroom conflict by having combatants reverse roles with one another. Have each student articulate the conflict as it is seen from the perspective of the other. When students switch back, notice the empathy they have gained. This technique may be especially useful for dealing with a class bully.
- Here is a daring technique. Reverse some classroom rule for approximately 15 minutes. You could say, for example, "Never raise your hand; instead, always interrupt. Say whatever you want, whenever you want." This method shows students why classroom rules are necessary. Following the above experiment, have the class decide whether you should reinstate the original rule as is or modified in some way.

★ Can you think of three Topsy-Turvy Land teaching techniques of your own?

Topsy-Turvy Land 'Toons

Are these dreamers, visionaries, fools, or simply residents of Topsy-Turvy Land? How many Topsy-Turvy Land examples of reversals can you find below? On a separate sheet of paper, create some Topsy-Turvy Land characters of your own.

THE GREAT FRAME-UP!
LESSON 24

By separating patterns from their context, frames enable us to see old objects in new ways.

This ability is crucial to creative thinking and production. By turning particularly interesting examples into abstract drawings, framed patterns serve as launching points for the imagination. In this lesson the class makes frames and uses them to explore features of the environment. Use "The Great Frame-Up!" to demonstrate the difference between foreground and background, to heighten perceptual contrast, to teach the importance of context, and to sharpen the discriminating eye of an artist, scientist, or critic. The central message of this lesson easily extends to other subjects: What we see depends upon the surrounding context. Showcase student artwork to boost pride and feelings of worthiness.

Preparation

★ Decide on a viable method for making frames in your classroom. Choose materials within your budget. If possible, use stiff material so frames are not too flimsy, and involve the whole class in the construction. However, if students are too young to use the tools safely and efficiently, provide ready-made frames. If you do involve students in frame construction, decide whether they are capable of using craft knives and paper cutters. If you have doubts, stick to scissors.

★ Gather materials of choice and prepare at least one frame. Follow directions outlined in Step 1. Make enough frames either for students to use directly, or to use indirectly as models for making their own.

★ Practice using frames by moving them over relatively flat surfaces, both indoors and outdoors, in search of interesting patterns. Try drawing patterns you find. See Step 3.

Materials

thin cardboard (available at professional cleaners) or heavy construction paper; scissors, craft knives and/or paper cutters; straightedges; pencils; pens; note pad paper; four or five "Great Frame-Up!" sheets (page 150) and four or five "Filled Frames" sheets (page 149) per student; clear glass

sheets or windows with interesting views (optional); pins or tape for displaying sheets

Exercise

(1) Make or have students make square frames. Good dimensions for the outer frame are 4 inches by 4 inches with inner cut-out 2.5 inches by 2.5 inches. This size corresponds to "Filled Frames" and "Great Frame-Up!" sheets and is useful for isolating small patterns, such as textures of trees and floors. Feel free to experiment with other sizes and shapes. If you choose other dimensions, have students trace frame outlines on a blank page to create their own "Filled Frame" and "Great Frame-Up!" sheets to record patterns. Measure and draw frame shapes, then cut them out with scissors, paper cutters, or craft knives.

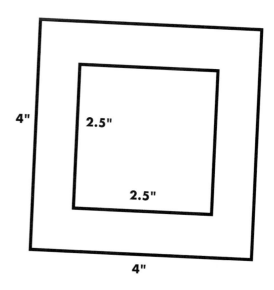

(2) Having students work either individually or in cooperative groups, allow approximately 20 minutes for a field trip to investigate patterns in the environment. Give the class pencils, frames, and plenty of "Filled Frames" or blank sheets for tracing frames and taking notes.

(3) Have students move frames over relatively flat surfaces, such as walls, trees, floors, screens, fences, cloth, and sidewalks. They may use small frames for larger patterns by holding the frame in the air and moving farther away from the object. Have students try this to see how more fits into the frame the further away they move. They may place frames against clear glass or windows for viewing distant patterns.

(4) Have students use "Filled Frames" sheets and pencils to keep a running log of interesting patterns they encounter. They should draw patterns to scale, exactly as seen.

(5) Upon returning to the classroom, have students choose one or more interesting patterns to transfer to "Great Frame-Up!" sheets. Abstract-looking patterns work best. Students may transfer either by drawing or by cutting and pasting. Have students record the source of the original pattern on the back of each.

(6) Collect "Great Frame-Up!" sheets from students. Spread them out in an open area, such as on the floor.

(7) Have each student choose someone else's sheet to examine. They should look carefully at the pattern. Have student write what they think the pattern might be on the last line at the bottom of the page. After responding, they fold their response under so it is not visible and will not interfere with the imagination of the next responder. Emphasize that this is not a test of accuracy. There is no bonus for correctly guessing the original source of any pattern. "The Great Frame-Up!" is intended to be a springboard for creative imagination.

(8) Have students continue choosing and completing "Great Frame-Up!" sheets until all the blank lines are filled in.

(9) Pick a bulletin board for a "Great Frame-Up!" showcase and discussion.

Discussion

◆ Which patterns are regular? Which are irregular?

◆ Which patterns are symmetrical? Which are not?

◆ Which patterns are abstract? Which can you easily identify?

◆ Which patterns stimulated many different guesses? Which patterns stimulated similar guesses? Which patterns stimulated realistic guesses?

◆ Which patterns are good food for creative imagination?

◆ What are the benefits of using a frame to isolate patterns in the environment (for example, making non-obvious patterns more obvious and bringing background patterns into the foreground)?

◆ Can you think of other ways to use frames?

◆ How does this Exercise show that what we see depends on the surrounding context?

◆ Name some other things that seem very different when experienced out of context.

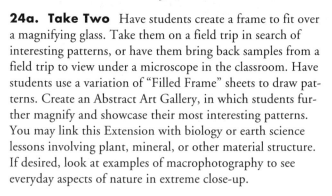

Extensions

24a. Take Two Have students create a frame to fit over a magnifying glass. Take them on a field trip in search of interesting patterns, or have them bring back samples from a field trip to view under a microscope in the classroom. Have students use a variation of "Filled Frame" sheets to draw patterns. Create an Abstract Art Gallery, in which students further magnify and showcase their most interesting patterns. You may link this Extension with biology or earth science lessons involving plant, mineral, or other material structure. If desired, look at examples of macrophotography to see everyday aspects of nature in extreme close-up.

24b. Shifting Frames of Reference Have students select and cut out a small portion of a magazine illustration or photo, place their selection inside a second illustration or photograph, and glue it down. Have them use the contrast between the original photo and its new frame of reference to make a visual point, perhaps with personal or social relevance. If desired, they could also include a word, as in a collage. Showcase student work, creating a Shifting Frames gallery. Compare the interpretations of student viewers with the intentions of student originators.

24c. Homemade Slides Here is an idea from *KidsArt,* issue 16, 1990. Collect old, overexposed slides, one per student. Or shoot a roll of film with the camera pointed toward a clear, blue sky. Provide lots of tiny objects—bits of tissue paper, fabric, cellophane, glitter, and thread, as well as grass, leaves, and feathers. Have students create a miniature, abstract composition by attaching objects to the slide with clear tape or glue applied with a toothpick. They can highlight their art with paint or felt-tip pens. Once the slides dry, make sure everything is secure and nothing protrudes too far, which could jam or damage the slide projector. View the slides one at a time, and discuss how the projection process works and how it changes the appearance of slide compositions.

24d. Film Frames Look at photographs taken by a famous photographer, such as those by Diane Arbus, Man Ray, or Ansel Adams, or use photos by Dorothea Lange to study the 1930s depression. Have students examine how the photographer used the camera to frame the subject. Have each student select an interesting shot to analyze, or select one shot for the entire class to analyze. Have students discuss or write essays describing what they believe was the point of view of the subject or of the photographer toward the subject, using visual details from the photograph to support points made. Ask how students would frame the shot differently to express other points of view.

24e. Same Subject, Different Frames Choose (or have students choose) a news story of interest, and find two different illustrated versions of the same story in newspapers or magazines. Individually or as a class, compare differences in how photographers framed their subjects. Are differences reflected in how the story is covered? You may use this Extension to study current events or those in recent history through library research and review of newspaper or magazine articles appearing at the time. This Extension is a good springboard for discussing bias in the news media.

sequence of action shots. Analyze details of the progression to reconstruct what happened. A final possibility is to make a flipbook by drawing approximately thirty frames with a progression of movement from one to the next. Students can do this easily with stick-figure drawings. Have students stack, staple, and flip the pages for the illusion of movement.

This photograph of the Mums, a Los Angeles–based juggling group, freezes a moment in midair. Levan Parian, *Untitled*.

Here are some other possibilities for film frames.

This photograph captures a moment of frozen nature.

24f. Widening Frames If resources are available, have students use cameras to make photographic essays. If your resources are scarce, try contacting film companies; they often have educational programs that donate cameras. Have students start with a picture of an object or a person up close. Then have them move back to widen their frame of reference and include more information about the surroundings. How do successive shots frame the object differently? You may want to use this Extension to introduce macro photography and choosing the lenses. (Two good resource books for introducing photography in the classroom are *Cameras in the Classroom,* put out by the National Education Association, and *McMahan Guide to Classroom Photography,* by Robert McMahan.) Have students write accompanying text or exchange photographs and analyze the meaning of one another's progression of frames.

24g. Frozen Movement With the class, study how movies and animation work. Examine a short section of film and notice how slightly different images from one frame to the next create the illusion of movement. Capture action in the classroom with a videocamera, then use freeze frame to analyze the action. Alternatively, you or your students could use a camera to take photos in quick succession, framing a

24h. Skeletal Frames Do a unit on nature's solutions for framing and supporting bodies. Include discussion on endoskeletons and exoskeletons and the relative advantages and disadvantages of each. With younger students, use frames to isolate small sections of animals. See if the class can identify animals by fragments alone. Have older or gifted students, individually or in pairs, design a skeletal system to fit a new kind of animal. They should give it a name and describe its unique features. If possible, take a class field trip to a natural history museum to observe skeletal frames up close.

24i. Framed Again! Take a field trip to a framing store or ask a professional framer to come to class to illustrate her or his work. Examine frames in a local museum, or have a slide show focusing on the many creative ways art is framed. If desired, have each student frame a piece of his or her own artwork using large construction paper, cardboard,

or actual wood frames. Be sensitive to an inhibiting effect that frames can sometimes have.

Skeletons

Most animals have either an exoskeleton or an endoskeleton to support their bodies and protect their internal functions. Animals with exoskeletons include arthropods, such as beetles and crabs. Their skeletal shells are hard and on the outside of the body to protect soft organs inside. Animals with endoskeletons include vertebrates, such as birds, reptiles, and beavers. Their skeletal systems exist on the inside of the body, covered by soft tissue on the outside.

These unusual ruins of Native American cliff dwellings are framed out of stone and set into the Arizona mountains.

24j. Architectural Frames In architecture, the frame is the basic structure that supports a building. Provide the class with ice cream sticks, cardboard, wood, or clay to experiment with different ways of framing a structure. Have students find the simplest way of framing a shelter, then invent some more complex ways. Have the class research, discuss, or write about the following: Do different materials invite different kinds of structures? Which kinds of structures would hold best in high wind? Which would be best in a thick jungle? What about a hot desert? For a multicultural twist, investigate the frames of structures belonging to cultures currently under study or represented by ethnic diversity among your students. Ask what kinds of social and environmental conditions these frames were designed to accommodate. Have students build models of shelters they study and place them in dioramas displaying their natural contexts.

Teacher's Corner

★ Here is a new skill called *reframing*. Reframing is a useful technique for shifting perspectives, turning problems into challenges, and sometimes finding solutions. We reframe something when we view the same facts from a different frame of reference. The following is an exercise to practice.

- *Identify your three greatest weaknesses as a teacher.*
- *Creatively reframe each in a more positive light, even into a strength, and brainstorm ways of capitalizing on it in your classroom. For example, you may consider yourself lazy; try reframing it as being reflective. Capitalize on it by reflecting how your students might motivate themselves, and even you.*
- *Now identify what you consider the three greatest problems in your class this year.*
- *Creatively reframe each. Brainstorm ways to capitalize on your frame-of-reference shift.*

★ Teach your class the skill of reframing. Try reframing student problems or conflicts in a more positive light. Did you notice how reframing relates to Topsy-Turvy Land from last lesson?

★ Have you ever framed a piece of your own artwork? Try framing something you create or have already created, such as photographs, drawings, paintings, and collages.

★ Hang your framed piece on the wall and see how you feel. Or give it to someone else as a present.

Filled Frames

Fill in each frame below with abstract patterns you discover in the environment. Be creative in finding interesting and unusual patterns. Draw each pattern exactly as you see it.

Great Frame-Up!

Choose an interesting pattern from your "Filled Frames" sheet to copy into the frame below. Choose a pattern in which the origin cannot be easily recognized. When you are done, let 12 other students use their imagination to write down what the pattern might be. The first student should begin at line 1. He or she should fold the response under so the next person, writing on line 2, cannot see it. Each student will fold the response under until all 12 lines are filled in.

Let your imaginations run free in guessing what this pattern might be.

12. _____

11. _____

10. _____

9. _____

8. _____

7. _____

6. _____

5. _____

4. _____

3. _____

2. _____

1. _____

A BETTER MOUSETRAP
LESSON 25

Sometimes a new product creates both its own need and a market. Many inventors share an unquenchable curiosity about things that surround them. They want to take everything apart, figure out how it works, and see how to improve it. Successful invention has three phases: identifying or inventing a need, or finding a problem with existing conditions; working within available resources to address the problem; and reviewing possible solutions critically to evaluate whether each is reasonable, practical, and cost efficient. "A Better Mousetrap" explores each of these features of invention. Students are empowered to ask questions, seek problems, and find solutions in their everyday world. Use this lesson to stimulate curiosity and to sensitize students to inventions around them. Meanwhile, have fun reinventing the wheel!

Preparation

★ Read the "Inventor's Resource Guide" (page 156). Pick those best suited to your and your students' interests.

★ Send away for relevant information to integrate with this lesson.

Materials

pencils; pens; blank paper; one "Invention and Design Guide" sheet (page 157) and one "Patent Application" sheet (page 158) per pair; resources to build models of inventions (thin cardboard, balsa wood, glue; optional)

Exercise

1. Introduce the lesson with discussion of the quote, "If you design a better mousetrap, the world will beat a path to your door." Ask students what this means and whether it is true.

2. Tell students that in this lesson they will design not a better mousetrap, but a better desk. Split the class into pairs.

3. Hand out "Invention and Design Guide" sheets to the pairs. Give them 20 minutes to complete it.

4. Give pairs 10 minutes to transfer their best solution to the "Patent Application" sheets, which describe student design solutions.

5. Have pairs include separate sheets with drawings or diagrams of design solutions. If possible, have them outline steps for building their solution.

6. If the class has the resources, skills, and time, have pairs build a model of their best solution to see how it works.

7. Ask each pair to showcase problems tackled, products, and best solutions for the class.

> Here is one artist's idea of a new design for a chair. How would you like this one in your classroom?

Discussion

◆ What did you learn from your experience about design and invention?

◆ Is necessity always the mother of invention? How so or why not?

◆ In what ways is invention the mother of necessity?

◆ What have been the most important inventions in history? Why?

◆ Would you like to be an inventor? Why or why not?

◆ What would be most difficult in the profession of inventing? What would be most rewarding?

◆ Which are more important to keep inventors going—"outside" factors such as fame and money, or "inside" ones such as curiosity, fascination, and determination? What makes you think so?

◆ When is it important to invent something totally new versus changing something that already exists?

◆ If you could redesign anything in your life, what would it be?

◆ What inventions might exist in a hundred years that do not exist now?

Creation Motivation

A researcher on the social psychology of creativity, Teresa Amabile, has investigated sources of motivation in creative individuals. She found that extrinsic factors, such as money and other rewards, can actually decrease creative production. Intrinsic factors, such as natural interest and curiosity, stimulate motivation and make the creative process itself inherently rewarding. When it comes to creativity, you can support the intrinsic motivation of your students by reducing emphasis on grades and encouraging their natural interest, curiosity, passion, and persistence.

Extensions

25a. Use It or Lose It Here is a classic divergent-thinking task that is quick, easy, provides a good time-filler, and stimulates fluidity and flexibility of imagination. Ask students how many different uses they can think of for a chosen item, such as a paper clip, ice cream stick, large spring, ice cube, foot-long nail, brick, or bag of popcorn. Give students 10 minutes to brainstorm ideas, either individually or as a class. Remember, ideas that are silly, weird, or impossible are just as welcomed as realistic ideas. Use this task repeatedly throughout the year to loosen up students mentally.

25b. Reinventing the Wheel Here are some things that need to be invented: self-cleaning boots, a more efficient school bag, a portable chair taking up almost no storage space, the perfect space for watching television, a hat that keeps you cool in the heat, and a new kind of transportation across sand. As a class, brainstorm wild and wacky solutions

to these problems. Let students, in groups, select one to follow up on, using adaptations of the "Invention and Design Guide" and "Patent Application" sheets. Hold an Inventor's Fair to showcase designs and inventions.

Could this be an energy-efficient wave of the future: dog-powered transportation? Levon Parian, *Untitled*.

25c. Eberle's Pearls Robert Eberle has come up with a methodology, which he calls SCAMPER, that encourages original and divergent thinking and can be incorporated into any invention assignment. Select a common item, such as a screwdriver, comb, or flashlight, to present this methodology to your class. Students may express ideas in words or pictures. Here is SCAMPER as it might apply to a fork:

> S = **Substitute:** *To have a person or thing act or serve in the place of another. For example, instead of a fork, substitute chopsticks or your fingers.*
>
> C = **Combine:** *To bring together or unite. For example, combine a fork with a spoon and knife for an all-in-one camping set.*
>
> A = **Adapt:** *To adjust for the purpose of suiting a specific condition or purpose. For example, adjust the pitch to make a tuning fork.*
>
> M = **Modify:** *To alter, to change the form or quality, or to magnify or minimize. For example, enlarge the fork to make a pitch fork or shrink it to make a baby's fork.*
>
> P = **Put to other uses:** *To find purposes other than the original. For example, use it to rake the soil of a flower box.*

E = Eliminate: *To remove, omit, or get rid of a quality or need. For example, pulverize all foods and use only a spoon.*

R = Reverse: *To place opposite or contrary; to change the order, purpose, or scheme. For example, use a fork to poison rather than feed people.*

25d. Invent a Need Ask students to brainstorm in 3 minutes ten things needing invention. Have them work individually, or in small groups. Tell the class to be as silly as possible. Have students exchange papers with another individual or group. The second group or person looks at each idea and uses it to piggyback to other possible design problems. Use this as warm-up for a more serious round, or continue by having each student select one silly design problem with which to work. Another idea for a round of practical design begins with groups interviewing family members, friends, other students, or community members for things in their lives in need of invention. Have them inquire about possessions owned or used in daily life that just do not seem to work right or somehow need improving. Have groups select their own design problem on which to follow up and perhaps contribute designs to an Inventor's Fair.

Piggybacking

Piggybacking is an important technique for group brainstorming. It involves using one person's idea as a springboard for other ideas. Because piggybacking is such an effective tool, an idea that initially seemed silly, impractical, or irrelevant can often wind up invaluable.

25e. Six Hats Method Use Edward de Bono's system (*from Masterthinkers II: Six Thinking Hats*) to practice thinking styles related to invention. Make or get colored hats, one set for each group of six students.

> **White** *hat wearers ask for information or offer it to others. They use this information to fill gaps in their knowledge and to define their need for more facts.*
>
> **Red** *hat wearers offer hunches or feelings about ideas without having to give reasons for them.*
>
> **Black** *hat wearers offer logical and often negative judgments about ideas but must give reasons for them.*
>
> **Yellow** *hat wearers offer positive, logical judgment. They look for sensible things about an idea that justify it or help determine how and why it will work.*
>
> **Green** *hat wearers have the freedom to propose wild ideas. No red (intuitive) or black (critical) input is allowed until an idea has had yellow (affirmative) input.*
>
> **Blue** *hat wearers provide control, helping the group to stay on track and to summarize what they have done.*

For older students, divide the class into invention groups of six students. Assign an invention problem—such as a new use for 30 coat hangers or 60 balloons—and have each student choose a hat to wear. Try out different sequences. Here are two possibilities: white, green, yellow, black, red, and blue; and red, yellow, black, green, white, and blue. With younger students, simplify the method by reducing the number of hats and students to three; for example, red, black, and yellow, or green, black, and blue. Give groups between 5 and 15 minutes to brainstorm their joint solution to the invention problem, using the chosen sequence of hats to facilitate the process.

25f. Rube Goldberg Machines Look at examples of Rube Goldberg machines, which use a complex process and series of events for carrying out a simple function. Have students design their own Rube Goldberg machines, either individually or in pairs. They should first pick a simple function or goal for the machine; for example, pouring a glass of water or turning off an alarm clock. Have students describe a complex series of steps eventually leading to this goal, then

draw the sequence or build a working model. Be sure students include an initial trigger for the machine.

25g. Designer Role-Play Have students pick a kind of professional designer—fashion, aerospace engineer, inventor, landscape, building, urban architect, etc.—that interests them. Have them research the work of this professional, which could include interviewing individuals in the community over the telephone or in person. Have students pretend they are that person and present their line of work using pictures, diagrams, and drawings to the rest of the class. Or you could have students research the life of a famous inventor and present reports by role-playing the individual.

25h. Educational Designs Divide the class into groups of five or six. Have each group interview teachers and students in a class two or three years behind them to find out what is being studied. Have them design a toy or game that teaches a relevant lesson. They should make the toy appealing so younger students will want to use it. Have groups build the toy and introduce it to the younger students, then later interview the teacher and students to find out how it was received. If desired, groups can redesign the toy based on information collected. Evaluate student projects according to what and how much they learned, not whether or not the toy works or is popular, to encourage an atmosphere of safety and promote risk-taking.

25i. Your Dream House Ask students to design and draw their ideal house. Make sure they include the following features: style, location, materials, number of floors and rooms, and what is in each room. If possible, have students use blueprints and sketch floor plans. Combine this with a math lesson on fractions or ratios by converting the blueprint to life-size scale. Have students calculate the dimensions of the rooms and floors. Ambitious students could try making a model of their ideal house out of corrugated cardboard.

25j. R2D2 Revisited Have students design the perfect robot. Have them specify what it can do, its features, how it is programmed, its potential problems, and how they might address the problems. Here are two fun ways to design a robot (suggested in *KidsArt,* issue 16, 1990). Carefully cut up tool, toy, and appliance catalogs along the edges of products. Students can glue these parts together on paper to build a robot, including small details such as dials, digital readouts, control panels, and antennae. A similar three-dimensional technique is to have students combine pieces from broken appliances and other collected junk, connecting them with clay, putty, glue, or wire. After this flight of fantasy, students could study the Family of Robot series of video sculptures by artist Nam June Paik. Or they could do library research on robotics and compare their robot to those already created. Ask if students' robots contain features currently possible, or if science has to catch up with their imaginations.

25k. Back to the Future Science fiction writers Alex Raymond and Phil Nowlan were the creators of the first superheroes of comics, Buck Rogers and Flash Gordon, respectively. These comics predicted many real inventions, such as spaceships, monorail trains, and walkie-talkies. Have students review comics from the past and draw their own futuristic comics, centering on inventions to come.

Teacher's Corner

★ If you cannot reinvent the wheel, how about reinventing your classroom? Use the guidelines below or the "Invention and Design Guide" and "Patent Application" sheets to identify and address current needs.

- *Examine the room's current organization very closely.*
- *Take several minutes to identify any and all problems, no matter how trivial.*
- *Pick one or two primary goals. Take 5 minutes to brainstorm options.*
- *Choose criteria to select among options. Criteria could include how disruptive, costly, or efficient the option is.*
- *Choose a solution that fits best.*
- *Try out your solution in the classroom for a day or two to see if it works.*
- *If it does not, go back to the drawing board and design a new organization.*

Remember, the most important sign of success is not whether your idea works, but how much you learned in the process. Redesign your classroom at least two or three times over the course of the school year.

★ Pick something else in your life to redesign. Try out your ideas and evaluate your success.

★ Find ways to creatively employ community resources related to design. For example, visit a factory with your class and study how different products are made.

★ Patents are grants issued by the U.S. government that allow an inventor to exclude all others from making, using, or selling the same invention within the United States or its territories. Ask a local patent lawyer to come to class and describe his or her experience with the patent system.

★ Contact a local inventor to come into the classroom. Use parents, colleagues, or the local Chamber of Commerce as resources to find someone who has a patent or at least has applied for one. Ask the person to bring in his or her invention for Show and Tell. Ask the person the following questions:

- *How was the idea conceived?*
- *What was the actual work of invention like?*
- *What was the patent application process like? What were the frustrations and problems with the system and how were they overcome?*
- *What is the present state of both the patent and the invention?*

★ As a learning experience for the class, go through the process of patenting an original student design or invention. The book General Information Concerning Patents is available at a minimal cost from the Superintendent of Documents, Government Printing Office, Washington, DC 20402. Choose one or more original designs or inventions (for example, at your Inventors Fair) and carry out at least the initial stages of patenting them. Under its Disclosure Document Program, the Patent and Trademark Office accepts and preserves for two years papers describing inventions awaiting the filing of a patent. Specific questions about the process may be directed to the Public Service Center, Patent and Trademark Office, Washington, DC 20231, or call (703) 557-HELP.

Inventor's Resource Guide

Project XL
U.S. Patent and Trademark Office
Washington, DC 20231
(703) 557-1610

Project XL was started as an educational outreach program of the Patent and Trademark Office in 1987 by former Commissioner Donald Quigg. The following publications are available to educators at no cost: *Inventive Thinking Curriculum Project,* which contains classroom activities suitable for elementary and high school; *Inventive Thinking Resource Directory,* a compilation of local, state, and national resources; and *Black Innovators in Technology: Inspiring a New Generation,* a summary of a nine-module course about present-day and historical black leaders in science and technology. Inquire about the Donald J. Quigg Excellence in Education Award, which is granted on a yearly basis in conjunction with Project XL and recognizes the efforts of an individual or group to promote the teaching of inventive thinking skills at all levels of education.

Future Makers Inventor/Mentor Program
Saturday Academy, Oregon Graduate Institute
19600 NW Von Neumann Drive, Beaverton, OR 97006
(503) 690-1190

This program helps teachers of grades 6 through 12 establish an educational partnership with local businesses. Students are provided creative and inventive thinking skills instruction linked with business mentor experiences. Students gain concrete experience with careers in the math/sciences, plus opportunities to apply problem-solving skills in a real-world context.

Foundation for a Creative America
1755 Jefferson Davis Highway, Suite 400, Arlington, VA 22202
(703) 521-0455

This organization cosponsors the Young Inventors' and Creators' Competition, along with Project XL and various other government and corporate sponsors. The yearly contest helps students cultivate creativity skills, express original ideas, and learn more about the patent and copyright systems. To be eligible for participation in this competition, your state must be listed in the program brochure. Foundation for a Creative America also acts to increase public awareness in various ways. It cosponsors museum exhibitions, such as "America Creates: 200 Years of Patents and Copyrights," established in honor of the bicentennial of the first U.S. patent and copyright laws.

Odyssey of the Mind
P.O. Box 27, Glassboro, NJ 08028
(609) 881-1603; Fax (609) 881-3596

Odyssey of the Mind is an annual international creative problem-solving competition among students in kindergarten through high school, designed to foster the development of creative thinking and problem-solving skills among young people. Participants compete in a variety of areas—from building mechanical devices, such as spring-driven cars, to giving their own interpretations of famous poems. The competition is run by the OM Association, Inc., a private, nonprofit corporation.

U.S. Copyright Office
Library of Congress, Washington, DC 20559
(202) 707-9100

The pamphlet *Copyright Basics* describes the copyright system and is available free of cost.

National Inventive Thinking Association
c/o The National Invention Center, Inc.
80 West Bowery, Suite 201, Akron, OH 44308

NITA was founded by a group of educators, business people, and government representatives to disseminate information and ideas and promote inventive thinking in education. It sponsors a newsletter, a network of schools, and a National Creative and Inventive Thinking Skills Conference. Annual memberships are available to individuals and institutions.

Name(s) _____ Date _____

Invention and Design Guide

1. I am (re)inventing _____.

2. Take 5 minutes to describe problems, issues, and concerns, no matter how small they seem.

3. Describe one or two problems you could focus on.

4. What are your desired outcomes and goals for reinventing or inventing?

5. Brainstorm all possible solutions, without judgment or criticism. Use additional sheets and make sketches to help in the process.

6. Below are some questions to help you select a final design solution.
Can you carry out the solution?
Does it accomplish your desired goals?
Is it safe? Will your solution withstand use or break easily?
Is it practical to build? What materials will you require? Are they readily available?
Is it cost efficient? If it is costly, is it worth the extra expense?
Is it as simple as possible, or can you reach it with fewer steps?
What are the benefits of this solution over others?

7. What is your best solution?

Translate your best solution to a "Patent Application" sheet.

Name(s) _____ Date _____

Patent Application

I/we, _____, hereby request
from the Commissioner of Patents that a patent be granted giving the aforesigned
inventors the right to exclude all others from making, using, or selling the (name of
invention/innovation):

which functions in the following manner:

Formal Description
Be specific and clear in describing your invention.

Composition
Name all the materials needed to make your invention.

I/we certify that this invention is an original idea.

_____

_____
          Signature(s)

Office Use Only
Patent Approved _____
Patent Rejected _____
Date _____

(Include diagrams, drawings, or other visuals on a separate sheet.)

WHAT NOW?!
LESSON 26

We often express originality by responding to life's little and big choices and dilemmas. "What Now?!" is intimately tied to the creativity of ordinary life—a type of creativity that does not always result in a product we can see, touch, or keep. Yet by recognizing everyday problem solving as a valid kind of creativity, it becomes easier to include creativity in our self-concept, whether or not we are artistically inclined. This lesson applies guided imagery and creative reasoning to tasks of problem solving and decision making. A step-by-step method empowers students to stop, think, analyze problems, and make creative, rational decisions. By placing them in critical decision points, this lesson helps prepare students for positions of authority and the greater responsibility of adult life. Use "What Now?!" to develop and sharpen problem-solving and critical thinking skills, to heighten empathy, and to brainstorm solutions for personal, interpersonal, community, or global problems. Variations and extensions without guided imagery are useful to teach self-reflection and self-control to students with Attention Deficit Disorder.

Preparation

★ Read the Exercise.

★ Bring a pen or pencil and blank paper or a "Response Mapping" sheet and a "Critical Thinking Skills" sheet to a quiet place.

★ Close your eyes, relax, and visualize the problem scenario from the Exercise.

★ Practice creative brainstorming by imagining what you might feel, think, and do in the problem situation. Let yourself be fanciful, even silly.

★ Open your eyes and use the "Response Mapping" sheet to diagram your combination of feelings, thoughts and possible actions. Add new ones that emerge.

★ Use the "Critical Thinking Skills" sheet to list possible solutions, with advantages and disadvantages to each.

★ Rate alternatives to arrive at one or more best solutions.

★ Use your experience to anticipate class strengths and difficulties. Adjust the lesson accordingly.

Materials

chalkboard and chalk; colored chalk (optional); one "Response Mapping" sheet (page 164) and one "Critical Thinking Skills" sheet (page 165) per student (optional); paper and pencils

Exercise

(1) Use centering and cleansing breaths (see page 5) to focus class attention.

(2) After students close their eyes, use suggestions of relaxation, attentive listening, and full involvement with all the inner senses.

(3) Read the following problem scenario in a slow, steady tone.

One day, a couple of months from now, your mother tells you she wants to visit your aunt. She asks you to stay home and watch your little brother. You would rather play with your friends but agree to be nice. You and your brother decide to make the best of it and play a game of hide and seek. Your brother hides first; you have no trouble finding him because he always hides in the same place, under the kitchen table. Now it is your turn to hide and you decide to try something different. You go down the steps into the basement. You are about to hide behind the furnace when you think you see something moving in the corner of the room.

You go over to investigate. And what do you find? There is a very odd creature, unlike any you have ever seen before. It looks kind of like an animal, but it speaks English. It tells you it is a Corlian, one of many who have lived under the surface of the earth in a highly advanced culture for many thousands of years. The creature tells you it does not feel well and needs some help, but it also says it is scared, because no Corlian has been seen before by human eyes. It begs you to be careful; it is afraid of getting captured, being studied, and having its culture invaded and hurt by scientists or government officials, even those who mean well.

You must decide what to do. Take a moment to see what kinds of reactions you are having. What are all the different feelings you are having? What thoughts or ideas cross your mind? Is there anything you need to find out? What might you consider doing first? Take a moment to review your own reactions, being honest with yourself about everything you are thinking and feeling. Then open your eyes and we will discuss the situation together to figure out a plan of action.

4 On the chalkboard, teach response mapping. Make sure the three different layers are distinct, either by using different colored chalk or by using different kinds of lettering or boxes, as demonstrated below.

a. *Before beginning, make sure students are clear about the difference between feelings, thoughts, and actions (see the "Response Mapping" sheet).*

b. *Ask for all the emotions students had and can imagine having in response to the scenario. Give permission for lots of different feelings, even opposite or contradictory ones. Record each emotion on the chalkboard in the innermost layer of your map.*

c. *Ask for thoughts or ideas that might be connected with each feeling. Diagram thoughts in the middle layer of your map.*

d. *Have students brainstorm possible actions that might follow from thoughts and feelings already recorded. Diagram action responses (including the possibility of no action) in the outermost layer.*

5 Use the chalkboard to teach critical thinking skills.

a. *To start, transfer six to twelve of the most reasonable actions from your Response Map onto another section of the board. Title it Critical Thinking Skills.*

b. *Next to each, list several advantages and disadvantages.*

c. *Have students tell, write, draw, or act out their favored choice and reasons why. The example below is a completed "Critical Thinking Skills" sheet. For students who have not yet learned negative numbers, simplify the rating system by rank-ordering favored actions from 1 to 6.*

d. *Emphasize that for any problem scenario, different people may arrive at different solutions. There is always more than one valid course of action.*

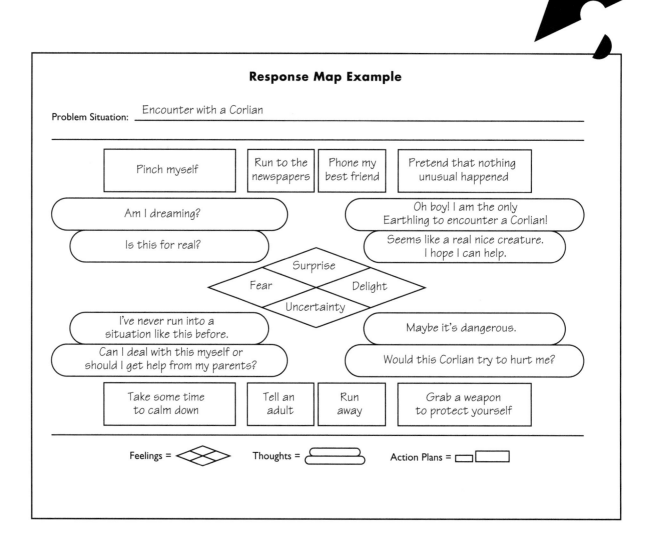

Response Map Example

Problem Situation: Encounter with a Corlian

| Pinch myself | Run to the newspapers | Phone my best friend | Pretend that nothing unusual happened |

Am I dreaming?

Oh boy! I am the only Earthling to encounter a Corlian!

Is this for real?

Seems like a real nice creature. I hope I can help.

Surprise / Fear / Delight / Uncertainty

I've never run into a situation like this before.

Maybe it's dangerous.

Can I deal with this myself or should I get help from my parents?

Would this Corlian try to hurt me?

| Take some time to calm down | Tell an adult | Run away | Grab a weapon to protect yourself |

Feelings = ◇ Thoughts = ⬭ Action Plans = ▭

Critical Thinking Skills Example

Action		± Ratings
1. **Run away**	**Advantages:** I could get out of this mess and not worry about making the wrong decision.	+
	Disadvantages: I would miss the fun of this adventure and finding out what is next.	– – – – **Total:** –3
2. **Grab a weapon**	**Advantages:** I would feel a lot safer and I would be able to attack.	++
	Disadvantages: I could scare the creature or I might provoke its attack.	– – – – **Total:** –2
3. **Phone my best friend**	**Advantages:** I always share everything with my best friend.	+++++
	Disadvantages: I might lose the trust of the Corlian by talking to anybody.	– – – **Total:** +2
4. **Run to the television stations**	**Advantages:** I could get famous for discovering a new creature that would fascinate the public and scientists.	++
	Disadvantages: I could sacrifice the well-being of a potential new friend and its culture.	– – – – – **Total:** –3
5. **Take some time to calm down and think**	**Advantages:** I would not act on first impulse and I'd give myself a chance to find the best solution.	+++++
	Disadvantages: I'd lose a little time and I'd be all alone in figuring out what to do.	– **Total:** +4
6. **Talk to my most trusted adult**	**Advantages:** I would have company deciding and I'd have the wisdom of my friend's experience.	+++++
	Disadvantages: I would not have the glory of acting on my own.	– – **Total:** +3

Discussion

◆ How was this Exercise for you? What were your reactions?

◆ What do you think about the idea that if we just wait long enough, problems will go away by themselves?

◆ What is the danger of taking action immediately, on first impulse?

◆ What is the value in first stopping to think and taking some time to weigh alternatives?

◆ When you face a difficult situation, do you try to figure it out by yourself, or do you like to ask for help? What are advantages and disadvantages of each?

◆ What uses can you think of, either in the classroom or outside of school, for response mapping and critical thinking?

◆ Does it take creativity to solve problems and make decisions in everyday life? Explain.

◆ Why is it so easy to overlook this everyday kind of creativity?

◆ Can something be creative, even if there is no artistic product to show for it? What are other examples?

Extensions

26a. In Another's Shoes Pick a critical dilemma or decision from a short story or novel currently under study; for example, the scene in Mark Twain's *The Adventures of Tom Sawyer* in which Tom has a fence to paint, but does not feel like doing it. Or choose a dilemma of a character in a cartoon strip. Have students put themselves in the character's shoes, using "Response Mapping" and "Critical Thinking Skills" sheets to detail what they might feel, think, and decide to do in the same situation. If desired, have them rewrite or redraw an outcome.

26b. Storybook Decision Ask students to write a story about a kid who faces the most important decision of his or her life. Here are a couple of possibilities, one serious and one more lighthearted: write about a girl whose parents are getting a divorce, and who must be part of the decision of where and with whom she will live; or write about a space alien that contacts a kid named Esteban and invites him to move to its planet; now Esteban must decide what to do. Encourage students to use "Response Mapping" and "Critical Thinking Skills" sheets to prepare for story writing. Make sure stories include what the dilemma is, how the student makes a decision, and what happens as a result.

26c. Action Shots Choose an interesting photograph, such as the one below, that illustrates a dilemma or tells a story. Have students choose one character and use response mapping and critical thinking techniques to identify feelings, thoughts, and possible actions. Done orally with the class, this is a good way to practice identifying the difference between feelings, thoughts, and actions. In multicultural studies, this technique helps students approach emotionally charged issues, such as prejudice and intolerance, with empathy. If desired, students can write an accompanying short story.

What might the child in this picture be feeling, thinking, and planning or hoping to do? From "Angelica," *The Book / Los Angeles*. Levon Parian, *Untitled*.

26d. Tough Decisions Have students place themselves in the role of a leader in history who has faced an important or difficult decision. Examples include Abraham Lincoln's decision to fight the Civil War and Franklin Delano Roosevelt's decision on how and when to become involved in World War II. Have students use response mapping and critical thinking techniques to identify feelings, motivations, goals, and the best strategies to accomplish goals if they were in the position of this leader. They should try to stick with the facts as they were known at the time, not as we know them in hindsight.

26e. To Tell or Not to Tell Here is a guided imagery scenario that portrays a social dilemma commonly faced by students: "You walk into the school bathroom. You find your close friend there using drugs (select between, or use in sequence: smoking marijuana, sniffing cocaine, or injecting heroin). Your friend asks you not to tell anyone and then invites you to join in. What are you feeling and thinking? What are you going to do?" Use response mapping to spell out feelings, thoughts, and possible actions, and critical thinking to decide on a course of action.

26f. Galileo's Shoes Galileo had an idea about the nature of the universe that was revolutionary for his time: he believed the earth revolved around the sun. This was heresy to the church at that time, which viewed the universe as revolving around the earth. Galileo was faced with a difficult dilemma. He could hold onto his beliefs and be excommunicated from the church, or he could recant his beliefs and remain a part of the religious community. Have students research the facts in preparation for placing themselves in Galileo's shoes. Then hand out "Response Mapping" and "Critical Thinking Skills" sheets to help students summarize how they might feel and respond, given the facts.

26g. Spock's Quandary In the last minutes of the movie *Star Trek III: The Search for Spock,* the starship Enterprise is faced with potential disaster—the ship is about to explode. Spock makes a decision to sacrifice his life to save the others, proclaiming, "The needs of the many outweigh the needs of the few—or the one." Watch the movie, or at least this portion as a class, or have students view it at home. Have students place themselves in Spock's position to discuss his dilemma. Hand out "Response Mapping" and "Critical Thinking Skills" sheets to help students decide what course of action they might take. Discuss pros and cons of other instances of self-sacrifice.

26h. To Build or Not to Build Group students into cooperative-learning groups of six. Give them the following ecological scenario: a town has a valuable lake with lots of clean, fresh water. The lake is a place where people love to swim, fish, and have fun. Due to lack of rain, there is a shortage of water this year. The people of the town must decide whether to drain the lake for drinking water. Have each group use "Response Mapping" and "Critical Thinking Skills" sheets to brainstorm possible responses and the best course of action. Hold a debate or have each group write and perform a script that dramatizes their solution. Discuss group differences. Find other ecological problems for which to apply these methods.

26i. Question of Overkill Here is an imaginary scenario for staging a debate concerning the pros and cons of using dangerous weapons: "You are with your worst enemy. You have been feuding for years. You are standing in a room that is knee-deep in gasoline. Each of you has one book of matches. What do you do?" As a class or individually, use response mapping and critical thinking techniques to consider possible actions and, if desired, write and perform a play based on this scenario. Discuss how this scenario relates to current world politics of overkill, where at least two countries possess a nuclear arsenal great enough to destroy the entire world many times over.

Teacher's Corner

★ Think about this: Each of us is a scientist gathering facts, and an artist dabbling in the creativity of everyday life.

★ Can you think of five ways in which you were called upon to be creative yesterday?

★ Think of three important situations over the course of your life that required a truly creative solution. Choose one to map out using "Response Mapping" and "Critical Thinking Skills" sheets. Notice whether your preferred solution is the same as what you actually did.

★ Take a few minutes to contemplate your own style of facing problems and decisions. Do you stop to think and consider your options? Do you perceive yourself as having choices in your life or feel more at the mercy of circumstances and other people? Do you make your own decisions or rely heavily on others? How does your problem-solving style reflect itself in the classroom?

★ Are there any changes you would like to make in your way of handling problems or decisions?

★ Choose a current problem or decision you face and use "Response Mapping" and "Critical Thinking Skills" sheets to assist you in planning a course of action.

★ Seek creative ways of integrating response mapping, critical thinking, and creative problem solving into your classroom across the curriculum.

Response Mapping

Feelings involve emotions, such as glad, sad, mad, scared, happy, afraid, joyful, jealous, confused, contented, anguished, exuberant, hateful, and peaceful.

Thoughts involve what we think or believe—how we explain or analyze a situation.

Actions involve what we decide to do in response to how we feel and what we think; they are possible solutions to dilemmas or problems.

Fill in the problem situation or dilemma for which a solution is needed. Place four possible feeling responses in the center diamonds. Place eight possible thoughts in the middle-level squares, two for each feeling. Place ten possible courses of action in the outside circles.

Problem Situation: _____

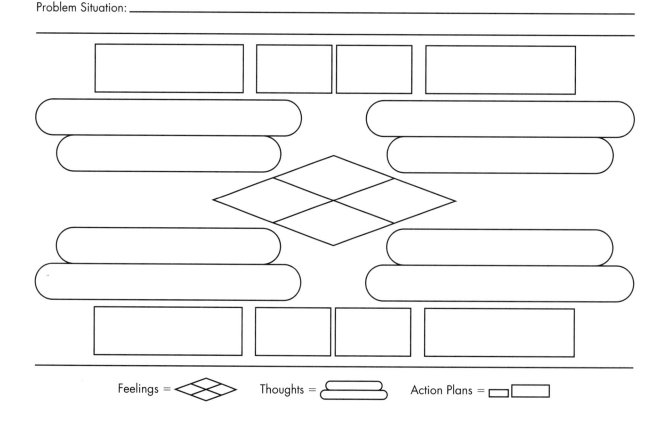

Feelings = ◇◇◇   Thoughts = ⬭⬭   Action Plans = ▭▭

Critical Thinking Skills

Critical thinking involves listing possible action plans, weighing alternatives, and choosing the most desirable solution.

Transfer six action plans from the Response Maps to the numbered boxes on the left. List advantages and disadvantages for each action. Rank actions from most (6) to least (1) desirable (or, rate up to five pluses [+++++] for each set of advantages, and up to five minuses [– – – – –] for each set of disadvantages). Total the score for each action by subtracting minuses from pluses. Circle the top score. In the case of a tie, select one or more favorites.

Action		**±Ratings**
1.	Advantages:	
	Disadvantages:	
		Total:
2.	Advantages:	
	Disadvantages:	
		Total:
3.	Advantages:	
	Disadvantages:	
		Total:
4.	Advantages:	
	Disadvantages:	
		Total:
5.	Advantages:	
	Disadvantages:	
		Total:
6.	Advantages:	
	Disadvantages:	
		Total:

SUM OF THE PARTS
LESSON 27

Creative change often requires group effort, especially at the large-scale level. This is particularly true of modern science, where increasingly sophisticated technology requires the ingenuity and labor of many. Parts and wholes are important to one common definition of creativity: the ability to combine familiar parts into new or different wholes. This lesson explores part and whole relationships and demonstrates the value and necessity of cooperation. In small groups, students face a task involving a number of separate steps. They must assign themselves roles, divide their labor, and organize steps toward a common goal. Students learn that a smoothly operating group can accomplish more than any individual alone. Concepts of *synergy* and *symbiosis* are introduced to explain how the whole is sometimes more than the sum of its parts. You can use "Sum of the Parts" to implement cooperative-learning strategies as well as to explore part and whole relationships across the curriculum.

Preparation

★ Collect a large grab bag of materials (see Materials) for making collages. If desired, enlist students in this process. Before dividing into teams, send everyone on a scavenger hunt at school or home.

Materials

one "Team Roles" sheet (page 171) and one "Team Log" sheet (page 172) per team; large sheets of colored construction paper; scissors; glue; pencils; markers; crayons or paints; an unusual assortment of multimedia materials for collage or mural elements such as tissue paper, material scraps, buttons, illustrated magazines, cardboard, yarn, cotton balls, animal crackers, balloons, pipe cleaners, wire, leaves, dried flowers, pebbles, ice cream sticks, popcorn, toothpicks, and foil

Exercise

1. Divide the class into teams of five or six and introduce "Sum of the Parts" as a cooperative challenge to combine individual efforts toward a team goal: making a multimedia collage or mural.

2. Give each team a "Team Roles" sheet. Review the roles and allow 5 minutes or so for teams to self-assign roles. Emphasize that cooperation, solving, and documenting in the team log the problems that arise are as important as completing the product. Roles may be flexible, with students handling more than one task or switching tasks in midproject. The team engineer must agree to this, while the recorder keeps track of the whole process. Make sure each team has subdivided roles and tasks adequately before beginning collages.

3. Choose a theme for a mural or collage related to the importance of cooperation. Possibilities include Earth Day, ecological concerns, African-American history, and the future of humankind. Choose a simple theme for younger classes, such as an animal collage. Have older students choose their own theme.

In this collage, notice the simplicity and careful placement of objects. These features are often evident in a Japanese cultural aesthetic. Art is a universal language; each of us should take time to understand and appreciate the artistic eye and sensibilities of people from other cultures. This helps us cooperate with others more effectively. As we face the challenges of living in an increasingly interconnected, global community, interpersonal skills of communication, appreciation, and cooperation grow in importance. *Oriental Garden* by Chuck Bowdlear. Photograph courtesy Gary Silk.

4 Allow ample time for preparatory research and completion of collages. For complicated projects, take a second session if necessary. Circulate and remain available to help settle team questions or conflict.

5 Showcase completed student work. Compare and contrast collages in discussion.

Discussion

◆ Did different teams use materials differently?

◆ What were some highlights from team log reports?

◆ What were the cooperative challenges faced by each team?

◆ Did it take much time and energy to handle issues of cooperation?

◆ Where did problems arise?

◆ Were there conflicts about leadership, role or task assignments, or other differences in opinion?

◆ What helped promote creative and productive interchange among team members?

◆ What strategies and creative solutions did you develop?

◆ Did working in a team make the task easier or harder to accomplish?

◆ What is synergy? How does this concept relate to this lesson?

◆ Can you name instances, other than teamwork and cooperation, where the whole is greater than the sum of its parts?

◆ Can you name examples where the whole exactly equals, or is less than, the sum of its parts?

Extensions

27a. Groupthink Divide the class into groups of four to six students. Provide string or yarn and scissors for each "Groupthinker" to cut off 2- to 3-foot sections of yarn. Have one person, the designated Brain, hold one end of all strings. Have each Groupthinker hold one of the other ends. Have Brains begin the groupthink process with an initial sentence or two; for example, "The sun sank over the mountain, as a shadowy figure worked its way toward the big city." After beginning the story, have the leader gently tug the string of one Groupthinker, who then adds the next line or two to the story. Have the Brain keep changing Groupthinkers, creating a group story. If possible, tape record or assign a student to transcribe results. For interesting comparisons, start different groups with the same line.

27b. Animal Goulash Have each student make an animal figure out of clay. Divide the class into groups of four or five students whose animals look very different. Have groups combine parts from each animal to create one or more new animals. Have them make up names for the hybrid animals and a set of facts about their natural habitats. They should describe where each lives, what it eats, what its predators are, what it preys upon, and its habits. Encourage groups to stay consistent with body features. For example, a squirrel-like creature would not prey upon giraffes. Students could make dioramas to display animals in their "natural" environments. If desired, link this Extension with studies of Greek mythology. Students could research hybrid creatures such as Chimera, Gorgon, Centaur, Harpies, Hydra, Minotaur, Scylla, Pegasus, Erinyes, and Sphinx. Or link this Extension with science studies of ecology or hybrid plant and animal species. Study genetic engineering. Let the class debate the pros, cons, and ethics of using genetic engineering to create new life forms.

Synergy is the idea that the whole can be greater than the sum of its parts. Certain tasks, such as cleaning up sick rivers and bad air and feeding the hungry, are so large they can only be tackled through collective, synergistic effort. Yet it does not necessarily take large-group cooperation to achieve synergy. Living organisms are synergistic, requiring cooperation between many cells, nerves, and organs, to create a living whole. This cartoon reminds us that the value in life comes from its wholeness, not its parts. The cost of life in terms of its chemicals alone—water, carbon, nitrogen, and so on—is only a few dollars. The worth of a single human being exceeds any dollar value.

27c. Multicultural Mix-and-Match Books Divide the class into groups of three for creating Mix-and-Match Books. Give each group a flipbook or spiral notepad of five to ten blank pages, with bindings along the side of the pad. Have students divide and cut all pages horizontally into three equal sections, corresponding to head, torso, and leg sections of the body. Have one student in each group draw heads, another torsos, and the third legs, being careful that sections always line up with one another. Have each group choose five to ten different cultures to portray and conduct library research to accurately depict hats, features, and fashion. Have groups mix up the order of cultures represented in each section, letting others guess the culture of origin and which heads, torsos, and legs belong together. Bring multicultural Mix-and-Match Books into younger classrooms and have your students teach a lesson in fashion and custom around the world.

27d. Make Up a Game Have students, in small cooperative groups, use the "Team Roles" and "Team Logs" sheets to organize themselves and design a game related to a language arts, science, multicultural, social studies, or other unit under study. One easy way is to use a board game with a maze to wind through. A toss of the dice determines the number of steps to take. Commands on the squares tell the player when to pick a card. Cards contain questions that players must answer correctly to receive bonuses, with penalties for incorrect answers. Have students participate cooperatively by making up equations, questions, and riddles for the

deck of cards. Challenge groups to create a game where winning depends on a cooperative strategy. Two general resource books on cooperative strategies in the classroom are *Tools for the Cooperative Classroom,* by Susan Marcus and Penny McDonald, and *Student Team Learning: A Practical Guide to Cooperative Learning,* by Robert Slavin.

27e. Words Within Words Prepare a list of words that are frequently part of other words, compound words, or common expressions. Have students select a word from your list and write it in the center of a blank page. Ask them to brainstorm larger "wholes" to which this word could belong and place these around the edges. For example, *foot* is part of football, clubfoot, foothill, off on the wrong foot, and put one's foot in one's mouth. Other good starter words include *leg, fool, butter, table, fly, dog,* and *fruit.* Students could use a circular cluster format (see page 91), and could draw compound words instead of writing them. Or you could diagram the Extension in the format of a star, wheel, or flower, with the starter word in the center. Use this Extension to launch the creation of one or more class books entitled *Does a Loon Fly in a Balloon?* with pages such as, "Should a tailor have a tail?" and "Is a window made of wind?" Have each studensupply one illustrated page.

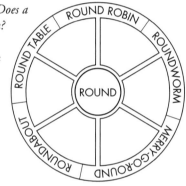

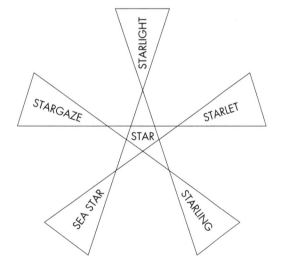

27f. Symbiosis Anyone? Study the concept of *symbiosis* in biology. Have groups research various instances of symbiosis and report to the class. Contrast symbiosis with parasitism. Read *Childhood's End* by Arthur C. Clarke, a story of symbiosis set in the future. Have students write their own science fiction tales centered around science themes of symbiotic or parasitic relationships.

Symbiotic vs. Parasitic

In biology, *symbiosis* is the mutual cooperation between different species in which each promotes the growth of the other. The relationship between a human and dog is symbiotic: dogs are taken care of; humans receive love and affection. Bacteria that inhabit the stomach of a cow are nourished while symbiotically helping the cow digest its food. Another kind of symbiosis exists when animals thrive by eating fruit, and fruit trees benefit by having their seeds spread to areas where they can grow. A different kind of relationship exists with parasitic organisms, such as bacteria and tapeworms. Here, one species, the parasite, feeds off its host, which can eventually lead to the host's sickness or death. In what ways do human beings engage in these two categories of relationships?

27g. The Value of Life When it comes to biological systems and living organisms, the whole is always more than the sum of the parts. Assign groups the task of proving the truth of this statement.

27h. Synergy Think Tank Form a class Synergy Think Tank. Pick an important social problem to address, either in school, the community, or the world, such as garbage on the playground, traffic on the streets, and war in South Africa or the Middle East. Choose issues where the solutions require the cooperation of many individuals.

Brainstorm ideas for addressing the problem and methods to implement student ideas. Carry out at least one solution. For example, hold a contest for the most garbage collected, write a letter about traffic to a local newspaper, protest apartheid in South Africa, or petition a senator to use cooperative strategies toward peace and security in the Middle East.

27i. Earth Day Celebration Discuss James Lovelock's Gaia hypothesis. Form a committee to brainstorm and implement cooperative projects for celebrating Earth Day on March 22. Remember, with enough collective energy, you can accomplish just about anything! This was demonstrated by one European grade school that raised enough money to buy a rain forest in Costa Rica and save it from destruction.

Gaia

The Gaia hypothesis was developed by James Lovelock in 1979. The name is based on the ancient Greek mythological goddess, Gaia, who was Mother Earth. Lovelock's hypothesis is that the earth is not simply a collection of inert and lifeless parts, but more closely resembles a living, breathing, organism; a single entity, symbiotically composed of cooperating parts. If this is true, all aspects of the earth are interconnected, existing in a delicate balance with one another, and our environment and resources are extremely fragile and truly in need of our protection.

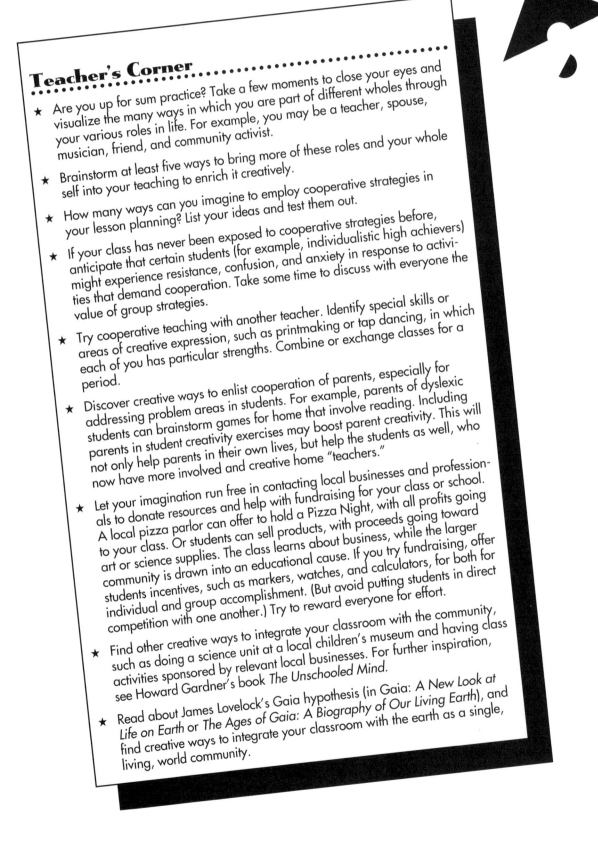

Teacher's Corner

★ Are you up for sum practice? Take a few moments to close your eyes and visualize the many ways in which you are part of different wholes through your various roles in life. For example, you may be a teacher, spouse, musician, friend, and community activist.

★ Brainstorm at least five ways to bring more of these roles and your whole self into your teaching to enrich it creatively.

★ How many ways can you imagine to employ cooperative strategies in your lesson planning? List your ideas and test them out.

★ If your class has never been exposed to cooperative strategies before, anticipate that certain students (for example, individualistic high achievers) might experience resistance, confusion, and anxiety in response to activities that demand cooperation. Take some time to discuss with everyone the value of group strategies.

★ Try cooperative teaching with another teacher. Identify special skills or areas of creative expression, such as printmaking or tap dancing, in which each of you has particular strengths. Combine or exchange classes for a period.

★ Discover creative ways to enlist cooperation of parents, especially for addressing problem areas in students. For example, parents of dyslexic students can brainstorm games for home that involve reading. Including parents in student creativity exercises may boost parent creativity. This will not only help parents in their own lives, but help the students as well, who now have more involved and creative home "teachers."

★ Let your imagination run free in contacting local businesses and professionals to donate resources and help with fundraising for your class or school. A local pizza parlor can offer to hold a Pizza Night, with all profits going to your class. Or students can sell products, with proceeds going toward art or science supplies. The class learns about business, while the larger community is drawn into an educational cause. If you try fundraising, offer students incentives, such as markers, watches, and calculators, for both for individual and group accomplishment. (But avoid putting students in direct competition with one another.) Try to reward everyone for effort.

★ Find other creative ways to integrate your classroom with the community, such as doing a science unit at a local children's museum and having class activities sponsored by relevant local businesses. For further inspiration, see Howard Gardner's book *The Unschooled Mind.*

★ Read about James Lovelock's Gaia hypothesis (in *Gaia: A New Look at Life on Earth* or *The Ages of Gaia: A Biography of Our Living Earth*), and find creative ways to integrate your classroom with the earth as a single, living, world community.

Date _____

Team Roles

To work most efficiently, your team must divide and share tasks among its members. Having defined roles will help team members communicate more effectively and cooperate better. Below are suggested roles for cooperative teams. Use all roles below that suit your project.

Director   Designs overall project and composition; delegates subtasks.

Student(s) designated

_____

Recorder   Keeps a log of team events, recording who did what, which aspects went
smoothly, any conflict encountered and how it was resolved.

Student(s) designated

_____

Troubleshooter   Notices problems in communication or in cooperation strategies.
Finds solutions or seeks help to do so.

Student(s) designated

_____

Artist (or Engineer)   Directs creative ideas and design; dictates materials and methods
needed to carry them out.

Student(s) designated

_____

Resource Expert   Collects materials needed, gets new ideas, circulates among other
teams, and consults with others.

Student(s) designated

_____

Other Roles and Duties

Student(s) designated

_____

Date _____

Team Log

Who did what specific tasks in your team?

How did the team work out?

Did any conflict arise between members? If so, what was it about?

How was the conflict resolved?

Name instances of creativity that occurred in your team, either in the process, discussion, or final product.

What would you do to improve the team's cooperation next time?

SELF IN THE CENTER
LESSON 28

"Self in the Center" touches upon a kind of creativity everyone dabbles in simply by living: the act of self-creation. This is the task of using our talents, shortcomings, and accomplishments to forge the shape our lives. This final lesson circles back to the beginning, to the level of the individual, this time with respect to the big picture. The class creates circles of self-discovery, or personal mandalas, which are used to examine the self and gain perspective on life. The lesson helps students identify values, ambitions, meaning, and direction in life. It promotes cohesion in self-concept, and a sense of validity in one's own vantage point. Use "Self in the Center" to clarify dreams and ambitions, to classify values, to chart a personal future, and to create new directions for the world. The lesson can help strengthen relationships at the end of the year as students learn about, understand, and respect one another at deeper levels.

Preparation

★ Think about your students' understandings of values. Prepare to define and discuss values.

★ Collect a variety of magazines from which students can cut pictures or words.

Materials

white construction paper; pencils; colored markers; glue; variety of illustrated magazines and other collage materials; one "Mandalas Around the World" sheet (page 177) and one "Values Clarification" sheet (page 178) per student; pins or tape for displaying mandalas

Exercise

1 Introduce the class to the concept of a *mandala*. Give students the "Mandalas Around the World" sheet of two examples of mandalas. Describe personal mandalas as circles of self-discovery.

The word *mandala* means "magic circle" in Sanskrit. A mandala is a special circle used to align one's self with the universe. Almost every culture has its own variety of mandala, often connected with philosophical, spiritual, or religious practices. Psychologist Carl Jung proposed that the mandala symbolizes the deepest level of self an individual can have, one that people from all cultures share. Personal mandalas, like the one shown here, help us articulate and communicate our interests, values, ambitions, goals, and plans—in short, what is most important to us. They may reflect recent dreams, current activities, or one's intentions for the future.

2 Hand out "Values Clarification" sheets and give students approximately 10 minutes to complete them. They should use these sheets to identify areas of importance for inclusion in personal mandalas. Note that

The Value of Values

Values help us determine the meaning of right and wrong, good and evil, important and trivial, desirable and harmful, worthwhile and bad. They are the guiding principles in our lives for what we should steer toward and away from. Values arouse strong emotions and are very much tied to culture, with different cultures holding different, sometimes opposing, values. Although we tend to adopt the values of our family, each one of us is ultimately responsible for choosing our own set. It has been suggested that many major problems American society faces today are related to a breakdown in basic values accompanying the fragmentation of the traditional family structure. While the home is the basic place for instilling values, schools and teachers can help strengthen and clarify values as well. This is a controversial issue, and multicultural sensitivity is absolutely critical to addressing it. For a good resource, see William Bennett's *Book of Virtues*.

values clarification is a sensitive topic, especially for students whose families might be lacking basic values. Monitor this activity carefully. If necessary, prepare by teaching students what values are.

(3) Have students choose a symbol or technique to represent each area of importance in their personal mandalas. If desired, use guided imagery to help visualize mandala elements. As students decide what to include, they can look through magazines, collect pictures and words, and create necessary materials. Students may draw, illustrate with photographs, or symbolize by collage the mandala elements. Students may bring materials from home, such as photographs, bits of material, doilies, sawdust, and food wrappers. Preparations could even include discussing the activity and planned elements with parents or other family members.

(4) Have students put together elements to construct personal mandalas. Students should start in the center and work outwards, drawing or attaching the elements. In the center, a self-portrait, photograph, drawing, or object should be placed to symbolize the innermost essence of the student as he or she is or would like to be. Surrounding the center are the most important values, activities, ambitions, political causes, life goals, and so on, layered outwards from greater to lesser significance. Encourage students to represent themselves in as positive light as possible; this is especially important for students with low self-esteem.

(5) With the student's consent, hang personal mandalas side by side, letting the class observe and comment with sensitivity upon images and symbols that appear in each others' productions.

Discussion

◆ What values are reflected in personal mandalas?

◆ What *are* values?

◆ What values are most important to you?

◆ What is the difference between self-centeredness and putting the self in the center of personal mandalas?

◆ Where do our values come from?

◆ How do your values compare with those of your family?

◆ Is it okay for someone else to dictate our values to us? Explain.

◆ What happens when children have values very different from those of their parents, teachers, clergy, or friends?

◆ In the end, why must each of us clarify our own values?

◆ How are values reflected in our everyday decisions?

◆ What are the consequences of not living according to our values?

◆ Can social problems such as crime, violence, drug abuse, and school dropout rates result from the absence of clear values in the home and the self? Why or why not?

◆ How do values relate to self-esteem?

◆ How do values relate to the creation of ourselves?

Extensions

28a. Value Strings Use the following to help younger students articulate their values. Have each student think of a shape to symbolize all important activities and values, such as a football for sports and a heart for health. Have them make two mirror-image shapes for each value. Glue the mirror images together, with a string or cord passing through them. (Or, for simplicity's sake, punch a hole through a single image through which to string the cord.) Have students order the symbols in a meaningful fashion, such as from the most to least important. Display Value Strings on a bulletin board, strung across the classroom, or tied into necklaces. Older students can use more sophisticated techniques, such as paper engineering and jewelry making, to symbolize their values.

28b. Value-Able Sharing Use mandalas to deepen students' understanding of one another. In Magic Circle format (see page 90), have students share, one by one, their value systems, current activities, future aspirations, and goals in life, while the other students draw a mandala reflecting their understanding of the value system of that individual. Afterward, have each student gather the sheets, add his or her own, and bind them into a book of personal mandalas. This Extension can boost student esteem, help bring out the best in students, and teach students how to clarify and communicate their viewpoints. Be careful—this Extension can be emotionally loaded. Feelings of shame and deficiency arise just as easily as pride and accomplishment, especially when students are sharing personal information. If you choose to do this activity, continue the value sharing until every student has had a chance.

28c. Fictional Mandalas Have students make personal mandalas to flesh out and analyze the value systems, goals, and ambitions of characters in a book.

28d. Family Crests Family crests are similar to personal mandalas, with the unique history, values, teachings, and accomplishments of the family symbolically displayed on a shield or coat of arms. Have students design a crest shape and divide it into sections that reflect some aspect of their family's collective history, values, activities, or goals. In preparation, students should interview their parents and other family members. They may discover that a family crest already exists. If not, they should create their own. Create a Family Crest bulletin board, which is a good way to explore multicultural differences and similarities among students and their families. Be sensitive to students who come from adopted, divorced, disrupted, foster, or broken homes, or to students who may be embarrassed or ashamed about revealing their situations. One way to handle this is to give the whole class the choice of making crests about their real families or crests that reflect their ideal family or families they intend to establish for themselves in the future.

28e. Get a Life! As a creative writing task, assign students the role of acting as their own future biographer. Have students write a biography of themselves from the perspective of someone reviewing their lives either in old age or in the future; for example, fifty years after they have died. Students should feel free to write about themselves either as they intend to lead their lives, or as they could lead their lives only in their wildest dreams. You might want to make two separate assignments: have students create one realistic version and one fantastic version. Students should include the values, accomplishments, and major life events—positive and negative—they expect to emerge.

28f. Values and Community Leaders Choose a figure from the community respected by you and your students. Invite this person to your classroom to discuss his or her accomplishments, underlying values, and goals for the future. Have students make personal mandalas that reflect their sense of the essence of this person. Invite the person back to see and discuss the mandalas.

28g. Value Plays With your class, take 5 minutes to brainstorm a list of important positive and negative values, such as honesty, truth, beauty, kindness, dishonesty, ugliness, and cruelty. Divide the class into three groups. Have each group choose at least three values to serve as the names for characters in a play they will create. The play should be a dialogue between the different values, each of whom struggles to define itself and find a place among the others. If desired, students could distinguish between the values of self and the values of culture. Groups may make puppets, masks (see page 56), or special costumes and props to perform Value Plays. If desired, study morality plays from the Middle Ages for inspiration. Make sure groups divide into separate roles—scriptwriters, stagehands, costume or puppet makers.

Tape student performances to show to other classes, administrators, or parents.

28h. Historical Mandalas Have students make mandalas for a particular period of history displaying the circle of values that were the foundation of the period. They could create mandalas for pioneer days or for values at the time of the American Revolution and creation of the U.S. Constitution. Have students use a combination of words and symbols to depict events, dates, and values.

28i. World Problem Mandalas Here is a mandala for world society. Have students rank world problems according to their own values and perspective. They should place a symbol for the central problem of the world in the center of the mandala, with less crucial areas of concern toward the rim. Along with each problem listed, students could include symbols for possible solutions. Compare mandalas. Pick a current political or social problem depicted in more than one mandala. Analyze the problem in terms of values and ideas reflected in the mandalas.

28j. Design-a-Cause Hold a class discussion and select a charity or cause your class believes reflects important values. Design a new logo for the organization, create a poster to advertises its cause, and design an advertising campaign for it. Send class ideas to the organization and wait for a response. Find ways of greater involvement with the organization, such as designing and running a campaign to raise money. Open a bank account for the money raised, and donate the money. Use this Extension to promote a sense of responsibility in students and to develop values.

28k. Tomorrowland Have students design futuristic posters to illustrate times and values of the future.

28l. Time Capsules As a class or in groups, create time capsules, which could be buried and unearthed by people of the future. Have students select five items to include that symbolize our times and communicate current values. Items can range from the manufactured and mundane, such as a can opener and a digital watch, to student-fashioned diagrams of corporate structure or the human body. The only restriction: students cannot use words or numbers.

Teacher's Corner

★ To bring mandala-making to your class all year, set aside a portion of your bulletin board for a class mandala. As a class, list values that underlie your work together, such as honesty, cooperation, and creativity. Identify activities, such as sonnet writing and learning about negative numbers, that you have accomplished. Identify goals for the future. Create and place symbols for values and activities toward the center, and for future ambitions and plans toward the periphery. Symbolize important events throughout the year, and shift mandala elements continually. You could even assign or reward students with responsibility for tracking and representing different aspects in your class mandala. Try to add new elements weekly or monthly. You can combine class mandalas with a yearly or monthly calendar.

★ This final Teacher's Corner ends with you. Gather materials needed to create your own personal mandala. Draw or create symbols for important activities, people, values, ambitions, and goals in your life. One possibility is to make separate mandalas for your real and your ideal selves. One mandala would illustrate how you really lead your life, while the other illustrates your highest ideals.

★ How wide is the gap between the two mandalas? Take several minutes to reflect upon differences between them and how you feel about them.

★ Can you name three ways your values reflect themselves in how you teach and organize your classroom?

★ Take a few minutes to identify factors, internal and external, that may have blocked the full expression of your values in the classroom and in your life.

★ List four changes you could make to come closer to your ideal self and bring your life more in line with your values. Try out at least one.

Mandalas Around the World

Mandala means "magic circle" in Sanskrit. A mandala is a circle of meaning, often used to place ourselves in relation to the universe. This is an example of a Tibetan mandala. It pictures the universe as a palace.

This is a Navajo sand-painting mandala, usually created for spiritual purposes.

European religion also has mandala-like patterns in the stained-glass windows of many churches. A mandala-like description of God is a circle in which the center is everywhere and the circumference is nowhere.

Name _____ Date _____

Values Clarification

Use this sheet to help you clarify people, places, things, activities, goals, and values most important to you.

Which people in your life are most important to you?

What places are most meaningful to you?

What things do you do that are most rewarding to you?

What things are most valuable to you?

What values are most important in your life?

What goals do you have for the future?

Toward what community or world problems do you want to contribute solutions?

THE CREATIVITY INDEXES

In all indexes, Exercises are identified by lesson number (in boldface) rather than page number. Extensions are identified by lesson number and Extension letter. Many activities do not fall neatly under a single index heading: some are under more than one heading, while others are not under any. When an activity falls under many categories of an index, only the major categories are listed.

Einstein is famous for not having spoken until he was three years old and not having done well in school (although his poor school performance may be purely myth—the mistake of biographers). Nonetheless, it can be difficult to recognize the most creative individuals, because they express their talents in unusual ways, or because their weakness in one intelligence overshadows brilliance in another. Never dismiss any child's intelligence across the board, and always consider the full profile of intelligences.

Subject Index

If you are teaching a basic curricular subject—for example, the Industrial Revolution—you could expand the lesson creatively by scanning the listings under Sciences, for example, to find an appropriate Exercise (such as Lesson 25 on inventions) and interesting Extensions (such as 9d, in which students enact various machines).

Arts

1b, 1h, 1i, 1j, 2b, 2d, 2f, **3**, 3a, 3b, 3d, 3e, 3i, **4**, 4a, 4b, 4c, 4d, 4f, **5b**, 5c, 5d, 5e, 5f, 5g, **6**, 6a, 6b, 6c, 6h, 7, 7a, 7b, 7c, 7e, 7f, **8a**, 8b, 8c, 8d, 8h, 8i, **9**, 9a, 9b, 9c, 9d, 9f, 9i, **10**, 10a, 10b, 10c, 10d, 10e, 10f, 10h, **11**, 11a, 11b, 11c, 11d, 11e, 11g, 11h, 11l, **12**, 12a, 12b, 12c, 12e, **13**, 13a, 13b, 13c, 13d, 13e, 13f, 13g, 13h, **14**, 14a, 14b, 14c, 14d, 14h, 14j, 14k, **15**, 15a, 15b, 15c, 15d, 15e, 15f, 15g, 15j, **16**, 16a, 16b, 16c, 16g, 16h, **17**, 17a, 17b, 17c, 17d, 17e, 17f, 17g, 17k, **18**, 18a, 18b, 18c, 18g, 18h, **19**, 19a, 19b, 19c, 19d, 19e, 19f, 19j, 19k, **20**, 20a, 20b, 20c, 20d, 20e, 20f, 20g, 20h, 20i, 20j, **21**, 21c, 21d, 21e, **22c**, 22d, 22e, 22g, 22h, **23**, 23b, 23c, 23d, 23f, 23h, 23i, 23k, **24**, 24a, 24b, 24c, 24d, 24f, 24g, 24i, 24j, **25**, 25b, 25c, 25f, 25g, 25h, 25i, 25j, 25k, **26a**, 26c, **27**, 27b, 27c, 27e, **28**, 28a, 28b, 28c, 28d, 28f, 28g, 28h, 28i, 28j, 28k

Creative Writing

1b, 1h, **2e**, 3b, 3f, 3g, 3i, **4**, 4c, 4f, 4g, **5b**, 5d, 5f, **6a**, 6d, 6e, 6g, 6h, 6i, 6j, 7g, 7j, **8**, 8b, 8d, **9g**, 9h, 9i, **10e**, 10f, 10g, 10h, 10i, **11**, 11c, 11d, 11g, 11i, 11j, 11k, **12e**, 12g, **13d**, 13e, **14a**, 14c, 14d, 14i, 14j, **15i**, 15j, 17f, 17h, 17i, **18**, 18a, 18e, 18f, **19e**, 19f, 19j, **20**, 20a, 20e, 20j, **21c**, 21e, 21g, **22h**, **23**, 23a, 23b, 23e, 23h, 23i, 23j, **24d**, 24f, **25k**, **26a**, 26b, 26c, 26h, 26i, **27a**, 27e, 27f, 27h, **28e**, 28g

Language Arts

1, 1e, 1f, 1j, **2e**, **3a**, 3g, 3i, 4a, 4c, **5a**, 5d, **6a**, 6d, 7g, 7j, **9**, 9e, **10**, 10c, 10d, 10e, 10f, 10g, 10h, 10i, **11**, 11c, 11d, 11f, 11h, 11i, **12**, 12d, 12e, 12f, 12g, **13b**, 13e, **14c**, 14f, 14g, 14j, **15i**, 15j, **16d**, 16g, 16j, **17h**, 17i, **18**, 18a, 18f, **19f**, 19l, **20**, 20a, 20e, **21**, 21a, 21b, 21c, 21d, 21f, 21g, 21h, 21i, **22**, 22a, 22d, 22e, 22i, 22l, **23**, 23c, 23e, 23f, 23g, 23h, 23i, 23j, **24e**, 24f, **25**, 25a, 25b, 25c, 25d, 25e, 25g, 25h, **26**, 26a, 26c, 26d, 26g, 26h, 26i, **27d**, 27e, 27f, **28b**, 28c, 28g

Multicultural

1, 1a, 1b, 1f, 1h, 1i, **2d**, 2i, **3d**, 3i, 4f, 4g, **5f**, **6f**, 6g, 6j, 7c, 7h, **8**, 8a, 8c, 8d, 8g, **9b**, **10h**, **11d**, 11e, 11i, 11l, **12c**, 12f, 12h, **13c**, 13h, **14a**, 14k, **15b**, 15c, 15e, **16b**, 16c, 16d, 17b, 17f, 17k, **18h**, **19a**, 19b, 19d, 19e, 19l, **20b**, 20d, 20g, **21b**, 21i, **22c**, 22f, 22g, 22l, **24e**, 24j, **26a**, 26c, **27**, 27b, 27c, 27d, 27h, **28**, 28b, 28d, 28f

Other Social Sciences

1d, 1f, 1g, **2f**, **3a**, 3d, 3e, 3h, 3i, 4f, 4g, **5e**, 5f, **6i**, 6j, 7c, 7e, 7h, 7i, 7j, **8**, 8b, 8c, 8d, 8g, **9b**, 9i, **10a**, 10c, **11g**, 11l, **12g**, 12h, **13d**, 13h, **14**, 14a, 14c, 14e, 14f, 14g, 14j, 14k, **16b**, 16e, 16f, 16i, **17j**, **18g**, 18h, 18i, **19a**, 19b, 19e, 19j, **20b**, 20d, 20f, **21b**, 21c, 21f, 21g, 21h, 21i, **22e**, 22f, 22g, 22h, 22i, 22l, **23a**, 23c, 23k, **24b**, 24d, 24e, 24f, **25g**, 25h, **26**, 26c, 26d, 26e, 26g, 26h, 26i, **27**, 27b, 27d, 27h, 27i, **28**, 28a, 28b, 28f, 28g, 28h, 28i, 28j, 28k, 28l

Mathematics

5e, 8g, 8i, 9f, **13e**, 13f, **14a**, 14b, 14g, 14k, **15d**, 15f, 15g, **16e**, 16h, 16i, **17c**, 17d, 17g, **18b**, 18c, 18d, 18e, 18h, **19**, 19b, 19g, 19h, 19i, 19j, 19k, **20**, 20h, 20j, **21b**, 21d, **22b**, 22c, **23f**, **24**, 24i, 24j, **25i**, **26**, **27d**

Sciences

1c, **2g**, 2h, 2i, 4b, 4d, 4e, 5e, 5g, 5h, **6h**, 6i, 7d, 7g, **8e**, 8f, 8g, 8h, 8i, **9d**, **10b**, **12b**, 12d, 12h, 12i, 12j, 12k, **13e**, 13f, 13g, **14a**, 14c, 14g, 14k, **15a**, 15e, 15h, 15j, **16f**, 16h, 16i, **17c**, 17d, 17e, 17g, **18e**, 18h, **19a**, 19b, 19e, 19k, **20d**, 20e, 20g, 20h, 20i, **21b**, 21d, **22i**, 22j, 22k, **23a**, 23c, 23k, **24**, 24a, 24c, 24f, 24g, 24h, 24j, **25**, 25a, 25b, 25c, 25d, 25e, 25f, 25g, 25h, 25i, 25j, 25k, **26f**, 26h, **27b**, 27d, 27f, 27g, 27i, **28f**, 28k, 28l

Multiple Intelligences Index

A primary purpose of *Creativity Inside Out* is to enlarge the learning potential of students by engaging multiple intelligences. This index will help you access Exercises and Extensions relevant for each intelligence. Use it to familiarize yourself with concepts and to round out classroom activities. Try to use all the intelligences throughout the year. Each offers not only a new domain for knowledge, expertise, and self-expression, but a different approach toward learning in any domain. You can also use this index to individualize lessons according to learning style based on multiple intelligences (see page 36) and to work with specific learning deficiencies.

Linguistic

1, 1b, 1e, 1h, 1j, **2**e, **3**a, 3e, 3f, 3g, 3i, **4**, 4a, 4c, 4g, **5**a, 5b, 5d, 5e, 5f, **6**a, 6d, 6e, 6g, 6h, 6i, 6j, 7g, 7j, **8**, 8b, 8d, **9**, 9e, 9g, 9h, 9i, **10**, 10c, 10d, 10e, 10f, 10g, 10h, 10i, **11**, 11c, 11d, 11f, 11h, 11i, 11j, 11k, **12**, 12d, 12e, 12f, 12g, 12h, **13**b, 13e, **14**a, 14b, 14c, 14d, 14f, 14g, 14i, 14j, 14k, **15**i, 15j, **16**d, 16g, 16j, **17**f, 17h, 17i, **18**, 18a, 18e, 18f, **19**e, 19f, 19j, 19l, **20**, 20a, 21c, 20d, 20e, **21**, 21a, 21b, 21c, 21f, 21g, 21h, 21i, **22**, 22a, 22d, 22e, 22h, 22i, 22l, **23**, 23b, 23c, 23e, 23f, 23g,

23h, 23i, 23j, 23k, **24**d, 24e, 24f, **25**a, 25b, 25c, 25d, 25e, 25g, 25h, 25k, **26**, 26a, 26b, 26c, 26d, 26g, 26h, 26i, **27**a, 27d, 27e, 27f, **28**b, 28c, 28e, 28g

Spatial

1b, 1i, 1j, **2**b, 2f, 2h, **3**, 3a, 3b, 3d, 3e, 3h, **4**, 4a, 4b, 4c, 4d, 4f, **5**, 5a, 5b, 5c, 5e, 5f, 5g, **6**, 6a, 6b, 6c, 6h, 7, 7a, 7b, 7c, 7e, 7f, **8**b, 8c, 8e, 8f, 8g, 8h, 8i, **9**, 9a, 9b, 9c, 9d, **10**d, 10e, 10h, **11**a, 11b, 11h, **12**j, 12k, **13**c, 13d, **14**, 14a, 14b, 14c, 14d, 14j, 14k, **15**, 15a, 15b, 15c, 15d, 15e, 15f, 15g, 15h, **16**, 16a, 16b, 16c, 16d, 16e, 16g, 16h, 16i, **17**, 17a, 17b, 17c, 17d, 17e, 17f, 17g, 17k, **18**, 18a, 18b, 18c, 18d, 18e, 18g, 18h, **19**, 19a, 19b, 19c, 19d, 19e, 19f, 19g, 19h, 19i, 19k, 19l, **20**, 20a, 20b, 20c, 20d, 20e, 20f, 20g, 20h, 20i, 20j, **21**, 21c, 21d, 21f, **22**, 22c, 22d, 22e, 22f, 22g, 22h, 22j, 22k, **23**, 23b, 23c, 23d, 23h, 23k, **24**, 24a, 24b, 24c, 24d, 24e, 24f, 24g, 24h, 24i, 24j, **25**, 25a, 25b, 25c, 25f, 25g, 25h, 25i, 25j, 25k, **26**c, **27**, 27b, 27c, 27e, **28**, 28a, 28b, 28c, 28d, 28f, 28h, 28i, 28j, 28k, 28l

Kinesthetic

1b, **2**, 2a, 2c, 2f, 2h, **3**, 3a, 3c, 3d, 3h, **5**c, **6**b, 6f, 7, 7a, 7b, 7d, **8**, 8a, 8b, 8e, 8f, 8h, **9**, 9a, 9b, 9c, 9d, 9e, 9f, 9i, **10**, 10a, 10b, 10c, 10e, 10f, **11**, 11d, 11f, 11l, **12**, 12a, 12b, 12d, 12h, 12i, 12j, **13**, 13a, 13b, 13d, 13g, 13h, **14**, 14a, 14b, 14c, 14d, 14h, 14k, **15**b, 15c, 15d, 15h, **16**, 16b, 16c, 16f, 16g, **17**, 17b, 17c, 17d, 17e, 17h,

17k, **18**, 18g, **19**a, 19b, 19d, 19e, 19g, 19l, **20**, 20a, 20c, 20d, 20f, 20g, 20h, 20i, **21**, 21a, 21b, 21c, 21e, 21f, 21h, **22**, 22j, **23**, 23d, 23h, 23i, 23k, **24**, 24a, 24b, 24c, 24f, 24g, 24i, 24j, **25**, 25f, 25g, 25h, 25i, 25j, **26**h, 26i, **27**, 27a, 27b, 27c, 27d, **28**a, 28g, 28l

Knowledge of Self

1, 1a, 1b, 1h, 1i, **2**, 2a, 2b, 2f, **3**, 3b, 3d, 3h, **4**, 4c, **5**, **6**e, 6f, 6g, 7, 7b, 7c, 7e, 7h, 7j, **8**, 8a, **9**, 9h, 9i, **10**, 10i, **11**, 11b, 11c, 11d, 11e, 11g, 11h, 11i, 11j, 11k, 11l, **14**, 14d, 14e, 14f, 14g, 14h, 14k, **17**f, 17j, **18**, **19**h, **20**, 20a, 21, 21c, **21**f, 21g, 21h, 21i, **22**e, **23**a, 23e, **24**d, 24f, **25**, 25d, 25e, 25i, **26**, 26a, 26b, 26c, 26d, 26e, 26f, 26g, 26h, 26i, **27**, 27h, **28**, 28a, 28b, 28d, 28e, 28g, 28i, 28j, 28k, 28l

Knowledge of Others

1, 1a, 1b, 1d, 1f, 1g, 1h, 1i, 2d, 2f, 2i, **3**d, 3h, 3i, 4f, 4g, **5**c, 5f, **6**, 6d, 6e, 6f, 6g, 6i, 6j, 7, 7c, 7e, 7h, 7j, **8**, 8b, 8c, 8d, 8g, **9**g, 9h, 9i, **10**, 10a, 10b, 10d, 10e, 10f, 10h, **11**, 11a, 11b, 11d, 11e, 11f, 11g, 11h, 11i, 11j, 11l, **12**g, 12h, **14**, 14a, 14b, 14c, 14d, 14e, 14f, 14g, 14i, 14j, 14k, **17**f, 17j, **18**i, **19**e, **20**, **21**, 21c, 21f, 21g, 21h, 21i, **22**d, 22e, 22h, 22l, **23**a, 23e, **24**b, 24d, 24e, 24f, **25**, 25d, 25e, 25g, 25h, **26**, 26a, 26b, 26c, 26d, 26e, 26f, 26g, 26h, 26i, **27**, 27h, **28**, 28b, 28c, 28d, 28f, 28g, 28h, 28i, 28j, 28k, 28l

Logical-Mathematical

1c, **2**g, 2h, 2i, **4**b, 4d, 4e, 5e, 5g, 5h, **6**, 6a, 6b, 6c, 6h, 6i, 7d, **8**e, 8f, 8g, 8h, 8i, **9**d, 9f, **10**b, **12**d, 12h, 12i, 12j, 12k, **13**f, 13g, **14**a, 14b, 14g, 14k, **15**a, 15d, 15e, 15f, 15g, 15h, **16**e, 16f, 16h, 16i, 16j, **17**c, 17d, 17e, 17g, 17i, **18**b, 18c, 18d, 18e, 18h, **19**, 19a, 19b, 19e, 19g, 19h, 19i, 19j, 19k, **20**d, 20e, 20g, 20h, 20i, 20j, **21**b, 21d, **22**b, 22c, 22i, 22j, 22k, **23**a, 23c, 23f, 23g, 23k, **24**, 24a, 24c, 24e, 24g, 24h, 24j, **25**, 25a, 25b, 25c, 25d, 25e, 25f, 25g, 25h, 25i, 25j, 25k, **26**f, 26h, 26i, **27**b, 27d, 27f, 27g, 27i, **28**i, 28k, 28l

Musical

2c, 2d, **3**, **11**e, **12**, 12a, 12b, 12c, 12d, 12e, 12f, 12g, 12i, 12j, **13**, 13a, 13b, 13c, 13d, 13e, 13f, 13g, 13h, **14**, 14a, 14b, 14c, 14d, 14k, 22h, **23**f

For One, For All Index

This index allows you to select Exercises and Extensions based on different student configurations. Some activities are designed primarily for the individual student; for example, creating a shape poem and keeping a feelings journal. You will find these activities listed under the Individual Student category even if their introduction and follow-up discussion involve the entire class. Some activities have students do independent research by going to the library or interviewing others. You have the option of doing the research yourself if that is more convenient. Another set of activities focuses on student pairs; for example, peer tutoring and mirroring a partner's movements. There is a category for small cooperative groups; activities include invention teams and human machines. Many activities involve the entire class; for example, full-body orchestras and synchronized movement in patterned formation. Independent Research includes any activity that requires extra research by the students, independent of the teacher.

Individual Students

1a, 1e, 1h, 2e, 3b, 3e, 3f, 4b, 4c, 5c, 6a, 6b, 6c, 6d, 6e, 6h, 6i, 6j, 7, 7a, 7b, 7c, 7d, 7e, 7g, 7j, 8e, 8i, 9h, 10d, 10e, 10f, 10h, 10i, 11a, 11b, 11c, 11i, 11j, 11k, 12d, 12f, 13c, 13e, 13f, 14b, 14c, 14d, 14f, 14h, 14i, 14k, 15, 15a, 15b, 15c, 15d, 15e, 15f, 15j, 16a, 16b, 16c, 16h, 16j, 17, 17a, 17b, 17c, 17d, 17f, 17g, 17h, 17i, 17k, 18a, 18b, 18d, 18e, 18f, 18g, 19a, 19c, 19e, 19f, 19h, 19i, 19j, 20, 20a, 20b, 20c, 20d, 20e, 20g, 20h, 20i, 21d, 21e, 21g, 22, 22a, 22b, 22c, 22d, 22e, 22g, 22h, 22k, 23, 23a, 23b, 23c, 23d, 23e, 23f, 23g, 23h, 23i, 23j, 23k, 24, 24a, 24b, 24c, 24d, 24e, 24f, 24g, 24h, 24i, 24j, 25a, 25c, 25d, 25f, 25g, 25i, 25j, 25k, 26a, 26b, 26c, 26d, 26e, 26f, 26g, 26i, 27e, 27f, 28, 28a, 28c, 28d, 28e, 28f, 28h, 28i, 28k, 28l

Independent Research

1c, 1d, 1g, 1i, 2g, 2h, 2i, 3d, 3e, 3i, 4e, 5h, 6h, 6j, 7c, 7e, 7g, 7i, 7j, 8a, 8c, 8d, 8f, 8g, 8h, 8i, 9b, 9d, 9g, 9i, 10b, 10c, 11b, 11c, 11d, 11j, 12g, 12i, 12j, 12k, 13g, 13h, 14f, 14j, 15b, 15c, 15d, 15e, 15f, 15h, 16b, 16c, 16d, 16e, 16f, 16h, 16i, 17, 17b, 17e, 17g, 18a, 18e, 18g, 18h, 18i, 19c, 19d, 19e, 19k, 20a, 20b, 20d, 20f, 20g, 20h, 20i, 21d, 21h, 22c, 22d, 22e, 22f, 22g, 22i, 22j, 22k, 22l, 23f, 23i, 23j, 23k, 24a, 24d, 24e, 24h, 24j, 25d, 25g, 25h, 25j, 25k, 26d, 26f, 27, 27b, 27c, 27d, 27f, 27g, 27h, 28d, 28h

Student Pairs

1, 1b, 3a, 3g, 6f, 6g, 7g, 8b, 9a, 10d, 10g, 11, 11l, 12b, 14b, 14d, 14g, 15g, 17d, 17e, 17i, 18c, 19, 19e, 20c, 21, 21c, 21f, 21i, 22h, 23i, 24f, 24h, 25, 25d, 25f

Cooperative Groups

1c, 2f, 3i, 4e, 5e, 5f, 5g, 5h, 7c, 7g, 7h, 8a, 8c, 8d, 9, 9b, 9d, 9e, 10, 10a, 10b, 10c, 10e, 10f, 11, 11d, 11l, 12, 12b, 12f, 12g, 12j, 13d, 14, 14a, 14b, 14c, 14d, 14j, 17d, 17e, 17k, 18, 18d, 18h, 19b, 19j, 19k, 20b, 20f, 20j, 21a, 21b, 22g, 21h, 22h, 22i, 22l, 23b, 23i, 24, 25b, 25d, 25e, 25h, 26h, 27, 27a, 27b, 27c, 27d, 27f, 27g, 27h, 27i, 28g, 28l

Whole Class

1e, 1f, 1g, 1h, 1j, 2, 2a, 2c, 2d, 2e, 2f, 3, 3a, 3c, 3d, 3e, 3g, 3h, 3i, 4, 4a, 4b, 4d, 4f, 4g, 5, 5a, 5b, 5d, 5e, 5f, 5g, 6, 6f, 6i, 7a, 7e, 7f, 7h, 7i, 8, 8b, 8d, 8e, 8f, 8g, 8h, 9b, 9c, 9f, 9i, 10a, 10b, 10c, 10e, 11a, 11e, 11f, 11g, 11h, 11i, 11l, 12, 12a, 12c, 12d, 12e, 12g, 12h, 12i, 12j, 12k, 13, 13a, 13b, 13c, 13d, 13e, 13f, 13g, 13h, 14b, 14c, 14e, 14f, 14k, 15, 15d, 15e, 15f, 15g, 15h, 15i, 15j, 16, 16a, 16b, 16c, 16d, 16e, 16f, 16g, 16h, 16i, 16j, 17, 17a, 17d, 17e, 17g, 17h, 17j, 17k, 18, 18a, 18e, 18h, 18i, 19, 19a, 19b, 19c, 19d, 19f, 19g, 19h, 19i, 19j, 19l, 20, 20a, 20e, 20g, 20h, 20i, 21a, 21b, 21d, 21g, 21h, 22, 22a, 22b, 22c, 22d, 22e, 22f, 22i, 22j, 22k, 22l, 23, 23a, 23c, 23e, 23i, 23j, 23k, 24, 24c, 24d, 24e, 24f, 24g, 24h, 24i, 24j, 25, 25a, 25b, 25g, 26, 26c, 26d, 26e, 26g, 26i, 27, 27e, 27f, 27h, 27i, 28, 28b, 28f, 28i, 28l

Time and Activity Planner

Do you ever find yourself with 10 minutes to spare during the school day and wish you could use it wisely? Try the Quickies section of this index to fill, not kill, extra time. Some of the listings refer to an entire Exercise or Extension, while others refer to one aspect of a multiple-part activity. The Ongoing or Reusable Activities listing refers to projects that extend over time and to teaching tools you can use occasionally, over and over. About an Hour refers to activities that last anywhere from a half hour to a couple of hours, depending on whether you stretch or contract them. Asterisks indicate multiple-part activities that can be spread easily over two or more sessions by subdividing component steps or working in shorter time blocks. Entire Units refers to broader activities than those under About an Hour, though not necessarily as broad as units are traditionally defined. This index also identifies activities that work well at the beginning or end of the school year.

Special Populations Index

With this index you can access activities for a broad range of student subpopulations. There is a category for challenging students who can handle divergent thinking or higher-order cognition. Another category addresses students with Attention Deficit Disorder. These activities draw largely upon multimodal techniques and body intelligence for learning. The list for teachers of English as a Second Language includes activities that help build vocabulary or contain nonverbal elements from which to anchor verbal cues. There is no category for students with learning disabilities, as these students are such a diverse group. Look at these students in terms of the Multiple Intelligences Profile (see page 73) to discover their specific disability, learning style, and areas of strength. Then use the Multiple Intelligences index to individualize assignments.

Gifted

1c, 1g, 1j, 2h, 2i, **3e**, 3g, 3i, 4b, 4c, 4e, **5d**, 5h, **6**, 6a, 6c, 6e, 6g, 6h, 6j, 7c, 7e, 7g, 7j, **8c**, 8d, 8f, 8g, 8i, **9d**, 9g, **10b**, 10e, 10i, **11b**, 11d, 11g, 11i, **12c**, 12d, 12g, 12i, 12k, **13d**, 13e, 13g, **14**, 14a, 14b, 14c, 14d, 14f, 14g, 14h, 14k, **15e**, 15f, 15g, 15j, **16d**, 16f, 16h, 16i, 16j, **17a**, 17d, 17f, 17g, 17i, **18**, 18a, 18d, 18e, 18h, 18i, **19h**, 19k, **20**, 20c, 20e, 20g, 20h, 20j, **21b**, 21c, 21d, **22c**, 22d, 22e, 22g, 22h, 22i, **23**, 23a, 23c, 23f, 23j, **24b**, 24e, 24h, 24j, **25**, 25a, 25d, 25c, 25f, 25h, 25i, 25j, 25k, **26d**, 26f, 26h, **27d**, 27h, **28**, 28g, 28i, 28k

Attention Deficit Disorder

1b, **2a**, 2b, 2c, 2d, 2f, **3**, 3a, 3b, 3c, 3h, 4c, **5c**, 5e, 5f, 5g, 7, 7a, 7b, 7c, 7d, 7j, **8**, 8a, 8e, 8f, 8h, **9**, 9a, 9b, 9c, 9d, 9e, 9f, 9i, **10**, 10a, 10c, 10g, **11**, 11d, 11e, 11f, 11l, **12**, 12a, 12b, 12c, 12d, 12f, 12i, **13**, 13a, 13b, 13c, 13d, 13g, **14**, 14a, 14b, 14c, 14d, 14e, 14g, 14h, 14k, **15a**, 15d, 15g, **16**, 16f, **17**, 17a, 17b, 17d, 17k, **18**, 18c, **19a**, 19e, 19g, 19l, **20**, 20c, 20d, 20g, **21**, 21b, 21d, 21f, 21h, 21i, **22e**, 22j, **23d**, **24**, 24a, 24b, 24f, **25h**, 25j, 25k, **26i**, 27b, 27d, **28a**, 28g, 28l

English as a Second Language

1a, 1b, 1h, 1i, 2b, 2d, 2h, **3**, 3a, 3b, 3d, 3f, 3g, 3h, 4a, 4c, **5**, 5a, 5b, 5c, 5e, 5f, 5g, 6a, 6b, 6c, 6f, 7, 7a, 7b, 7c, 7d, 7e, **8a**, 8b, 8e, 8h, **9**, 9a, 9b, 9c, 9d, 9e, 9f, **10**, 10a, 10b, 10c, 10d, 10e, 10g, **11**, 11a, 11b, 11d, 11e, 11f, 11g, 11l, **12**, 12a, 12b, 12c, 12d, 12e, 12f, 12i, 12j, **13**, 13a, 13b, 13c, 13g, 13h, **14**, 14a, 14b, 14c, 14d, 14e, 14g, 14h, 14k, **15**, 15a, 15b, 15c, 15d, 15f, 15g, **16**, 16a, 16b, 16c, 16e, 16h, 16i, **17**, 17a, 17b, 17c, 17d, 17i, 17k, **18**, 18a, 18b, 18g, **19**, 19a, 19b, 19c, 19d, 19e, 19g, 19k, 19l, **20**, 20b, 20c, 20d, 20f, 20g, 20h, 20i, **21**, 21a, 21b, 21c, 21d, 21e, **22**, 22c, 22g, **23c**, 23d, 23h, 23k, **24**, 24a, 24c, 24d, 24f, 24g, 25f, **25i**, 25j, 25k, **26c**, 27b, 27c, **28a**, 28, 28c, 28d, 28i, 28l

Level Grader Index

If a school district implements *Creativity Inside Out,* it will want to partition the lessons and activities according to developmental levels. This way, students have continuity from year to year without repeating creativity studies. This index presents three grade-related levels. Level I corresponds loosely to grades 4 and 5, Level II to grades 6 and 7, and Level III to grades 8 and 9. However, don't assume activities listed under Level I are too easy for grade 8 or those under Level III are too advanced for grade 4. While certain activities are naturally more basic or advanced than others, you can adapt most of them for any level.

Level I

1, 1a, 1b, 1e, 1h, 1i, **2a**, 2b, 2c, 2g, **3**, 3a, 3c, 3h, **4a**, 4g, 5a, 5e, 5g, **6d**, 6f, 6h, 7, 7a, 7b , 7d, 7f, 7h, **8**, 8e, **9a**, 9d, 9e, 9h, 9i, **10d**, 10g, **11a**, 11c, 11f, 11h, 11j, 11l, **12**, 12a, 12b, 12e, 12h, **13**, 13a, 13b, **14b**, 14i, 14k, **15**, 15a, 15d, 15i, **16b**, 16c, 16e, 16, 17a, 17b, 17h, 17j, 17k, **18b**, 18c, 18f, 18g, **19a**, 19d, 19e, 19f, 19i, 19l, **20**, 20g, 20i, **21a**, 21e, 21f, 21h, **22**, 22a, 22f, 22j, **23**, 23b, 23d, 23f, 23g, 23h, 23k, **24**, 24c, 24g, 24i, **25a**, 25c, 25j, 25k, **26**, 26b, 26c, 26g, 27a, 27b, 27d, 27e, **28a**, 28d, 28i

Level II

1d, 1f, **2**, 2e, 2i, 3b, 3f, **4**, 4b, 4d, 4f, **5b**, 5f, **6**, 6b, 6e, 6i, 7c, 7g, 7i, 7j, **8a**, 8b, 8f, 8h, 8i, **9**, 9b, 9c, 9f, 9g, **10**, 10b, 10e, 10h, **11**, 11d, 11e, 11k, **12c**, 12f, 12i, 12j, **13d**, 13f, 13h, **14**, 14c, 14d, 14e, 14g, 14j, **15b**, 15c, 15g, 15j, **16a**, 16f, 16g, **17**, 17c, 17d, 17e, **18**, 18e, **19b**, 19g, 19h, 19k, **20a**, 20d, 20e, **21b**, 21d, 22b, **22d**, 22g, 22k, **23c**, 23e, 23i, **24a**, 24f, 24h, **25**, 25b, 25f, 25g, 25h, 25i, **26d**, 26e, 26i, **27c**, 27i, **28**, 28b, 28g, 28h, 28j, 28k, 28l

Level III

1c, 1g, 1j, **2d**, 2f, 2h, **3d**, 3e, 3g, 3i, **4c**, 4e, **5**, 5c, 5d, 5h, **6a**, 6c, 6f, 6g, 6j, 7e, 7g, **8c**, 8d, 8g, **10a**, 10c, 10f, 10i, **11b**, 11g, 11i, **12d**, 12g, 12k, **13c**, 13e, 13g, **14a**, 14f, 14h, **15e**, 15f, 15h, **16d**, 16h, 16i, 16j, **17f**, 17g, 17i, **18a**, 18d, 18h, 18i, **19**, 19c, 19j, **20b**, 20c, 20f, 20h, 20j, 21, 21c, **21g**, 21i, **22c**, 22e, 22h, 22i, 22l, **23a**, 23j, **24b**, 24d, 24e, 24j, **25d**, 25e, **26a**, 26f, 26h, **27**, 27f, 27g, 27h, **28c**, 28e, 28f

REFERENCES AND RESOURCES

Abbott, E. Flatland: *A Romance of Many Dimensions.* New York: Barnes and Noble Books, 1884, 1983.

Adams, D. *Hitchhiker's Guide to the Galaxy.* New York: Harmony Books, 1980.

Adams, James. *Conceptual Blockbusting: A Guide to Better Ideas,* 3d ed. Menlo Park, Calif.: Addison-Wesley Publishing Company, 1986.

Alexander, K. *Learning to Look and Create: The Spectra Program,* Grade 4. Palo Alto, Calif.: Dale Seymour Publications, 1990.

Alexander, K. *Learning to Look and Create: The Spectra Program,* Grade 5. Palo Alto, Calif.: Dale Seymour Publications, 1990.

Alexander, K., and M. Day *Learning to Look and Create: The Spectra Program,* Grade 7. Palo Alto, Calif.: Dale Seymour Publications, 1994.

Alkema, C. *Alkema's Complete Guide to Creative Art for Young People.* New York: Sterling Publishing Company, 1971.

Amabile, T. *The Social Psychology of Creativity.* New York: Springer-Verlag, 1983.

America and the Future of Man: Courses by Newspaper. University of California, San Diego: CRM Books, 1973.

Armstrong, T. *Multiple Intelligences in the Classroom.* Los Angeles: Jeremy P. Tarcher, 1987.

Arnheim, R. *Visual Thinking.* Berkeley: University of California Press, 1966.

Athey, M., and G. Hotchkiss. *A Galaxy of Games for the Music Class.* New York: Parker Publishing Company, 1975.

Baum, F. *The Wizard of Oz.* New York: Holt, Rhinehart and Winston, 1982.

Bennett, William J. *The Book of Virues.* New York: Simon and Schuster, 1993.

Bruner, J. *The Process of Education.* Cambridge, Mass.: Harvard University Press, 1961.

Bruner, J., et al. *Play: Its Role in Development and Evolution.* New York: Penguin Books, 1976.

Burt, M. *Black Inventors of America.* Portland, Oreg.: National Book Company, 1969.

Carr, R. *See and Be.* Englewood Cliffs, N.J.: Prentice Hall, 1980.

Carroll, L. *Alice in Wonderland.* New York: Grosset and Dunlap, 1946.

Carroll, L. *Through the Looking Glass.* New York: Grosset and Dunlap, 1946.

Clarke, A. C. *Childhood's End.* New York: Ballantine Books, 1987.

Cole, J. *The Magic Schoolbus: Inside the Human Body.* New York: Scholastic, 1988.

Davis, G. *Imagination Express: Saturday Subway Ride.* Buffalo, N.Y.: D.O.K. Publishers, 1970.

De Bono, E. *CoRT Thinking Series.* New York: Pergamon Press, 1976.

De Bono, E. *Masterthinkers II: Six Thinking Hats.* Mamaroneck, N.Y.: International Center for Creative Thinking, 1988.

De Mille, R. *Put Your Mother on the Ceiling.* New York: Walker and Company, 1967.

Dougherty and Evans. *Grokking into the Future.* Parkersburg, W.Va.: Synergetics, 1981.

Eberle, R. Scamper: *Games for Imagination Development.* Buffalo, N.Y.: D.O.K. Publishers, 1971.

Eberle, R., and B. Stanish. *CPS (Creative Problem Solving) for Kids.* Buffalo, N.Y.: D.O.K. Publishers, 1980.

Elder, P., and M. A. Carr. Worldways: *Bringing the World into the Classroom.* Menlo Park, Calif.: Addison-Wesley Publishing Company, 1987.

Felton, B. One of a Kind: *A Compendium of Unique People, Places, and Things.* New York: William Morrow and Company, 1992.

Foster, K. *A Guide for Teaching Creative Thinking Skills and Creative Problem Solving in the Gifted Classroom.* San Diego, Calif.: San Diego City Schools, 1979.

Gardner, H. *Frames of Mind.* New York: Basic Books, 1982.

Ghiselin, B. *The Creative Process.* New York: Mentor, 1952.

Gilbert, A. *Teaching the Three R's Through Movement Experience.* Broken Arrow, Okla.: Burgess Publishing, 1977.

Grimm, G. *It's Me/You'll See.* Buffalo, N.Y.: D.O.K. Publishers, 1973.

Guinness Book of Records. New York: Facts on File, 1994.

Haggerty, B. A. *Nuturing Intelligences: A Guide to Multiple Intelligences Theory and Teaching.* Menlo Park, Calif.: Addison-Wesley Publishing Company, 1995.

Hall, E. *Beyond Culture.* Garden City, N.Y.: Anchor Press, 1976.

Hanks, K., and J. Parry. *Wake Up Your Creative Genius.* Los Altos, Calif.: William Kaufmann, 1983.

Hansen, B. *A Curriculum Model for Theatre in Aesthetic Education.* Somerville, N.J.: Aesthetic Education Program, 1972.

Hendricks, G., and J. Fadiman. *Transpersonal Education: A Curriculum for Feeling and Being.* Englewood Cliffs, N.J.: Prentice Hall, 1976.

Hennessey, B., and T. Amabile. *Creativity and Learning.* Washington, D.C.: National Education Association, 1987.

Herr, S. *Perceptual Communication Skills.* Buena Park, Calif.: Teacher Supplies, 1969.

Hilton, P., and J. Pedersen. *Build Your Own Polyhedra.* Menlo Park, Calif.: Addison-Wesley Publishing Company, 1994.

Hoffman, J. *Backyard Scientist Series*. Irvine, Calif.: Backyard Scientist, 1987.

John-Steiner, V. *Notebooks of the Mind*. Albuquerque, N.M.: University of New Mexico Press, 1985.

Jones, R. *Fantasy and Feeling in Education*. New York: Harper and Row, 1978.

Kandinsky, V. *Point and Line to Plane*. New York: Dover Publications, 1979.

Kauffman, D. *Futurism and Future Studies*. Washington, D.C.: National Educational Association, 1976.

Keller, H. *The Story of My Life*. New York: Doubleday, 1954.

Koestler, A. *The Act of Creation*. New York: Dell Publishing, 1964.

Kuhn, T. *The Structure of Scientific Revolutions*, 2d ed. Chicago: University of Chicago Press, 1970.

Laycock, M. *Bucky for Beginners: Synergetic Geometry*. Hayward, Calif.: Activity Resources Company, 1984.

Lieberman, J. *Playfulness: Its Relationship to Imagination and Creativity*. New York: Academic Press, 1977.

Lomask, M. *Great Lives, Invention and Technology*. New York: Macmillan Children's Book Group, 1991.

Lovelock, J. *Gaia: A New Look at Life on Earth*. New York: Oxford University Press, 1979.

Lovelock, J. *The Ages of Gaia: A Biography of Our Living Earth*. New York: W.W. Norton and Company, 1988.

Marcus, S., and P. McDonald. *Tools for the Cooperative Classroom*. Palatine, Ill.: Skylight Publishing, 1990.

Marks, T. "Creativity Inside Out: From Theory to Practice." Creativity Research Journal, Vol. 2 (1989), pp. 204–220.

McKisson, M. *Chrysalis: Nurturing Creative and Independent Thought in Children*. Tucson: Zephyr Press, 1983.

McMahan, R. *Guide to Classroom Photography*. Lake Hughes, Calif.: The Olive Press, 1985.

Morrison, P., and P. Morrison. *Powers of Ten*. New York: Scientific American Library, 1982.

Nachmanovitch, Stephen. *Free Play: The Role of Improvisation in Life and Art*. Los Angeles: Jeremy P. Tarcher, 1990.

National Foundation for the Improvement of Education. *Cameras in the Curriculum*, Vol. 2. Washington, D.C.: National Education Association, 1985.

Osborn, A. *Applied Imagination: Principles and Procedures of Creative Problem Solving*. Charles Scribner's Sons, 1963.

Pedersen, J., and K. Pedersen. *Geometric Playthings*. Palo Alto, Calif.: Dale Seymour Publications, 1973.

Perkins, D. *The Mind's Best Work*. Cambridge, Mass.: Harvard University Press, 1981.

Renzulli, J. *New Directions in Creativity*. Storrs, Conn.: Creative Learning Press, 1986.

Rucker, R. *The Fourth Dimension: Toward a Geometry of Higher Reality*. Boston: Houghton Mifflin Company, 1984.

Schulz, C. M. *Happiness Is a Warm Puppy*. New York: Ballantine Books, 1987.

Schuman, J. *Art from Many Hands: Multicultural Art.* Englewood Cliffs, N.J.: Prentice Hall, 1981.

Schwartz, L. *Creative Capers: Activities to Stimulate Fluency, Flexibility, Originality and Elaboration,* Grades 3–6. Santa Barbara, Calif.: The Learning Works, 1984.

Sendak, M. *In the Night Kitchen.* New York: Harper and Row, 1970.

Seuss, Dr. *The Sneetches and Other Stories.* New York: Random House, 1961.

Seymour, D. *Visual Patterns in Pascal's Triangle.* Palo Alto, Calif.: Dale Seymour Publications, 1986.

Shaefer, C. *Developing Creativity in Children.* Buffalo, N.Y.: D.O.K. Publishers, 1973.

Simonton, D. *Genius, Creativity, and Leadership.* Cambridge, Mass.: Harvard University Press, 1984.

Sivin, C. *Maskmaking.* Worcester, Mass.: Davis Publications, 1986.

Slavin, R. E. *Student Team Learning: A Practical Guide to Cooperative Learning.* Washington, D.C.: National Education Association, 1991.

Smith, A. G. *Cut and Assemble 3-D Geometrical Shapes.* New York: Dover Publications, 1986.

Stanish, B. *I Believe in Unicorns.* Carthage, Ill.: Good Apple, 1979.

Stanish, B. *Sunflowering: Thinking, Feeling, Doing Activities for Creative Expression.* Carthage, Ill.: Good Apple, 1977.

Stanish, B., and C. Singletary. *Inventioneering.* Carthage, Ill.: Good Apple, 1987.

Stephens, P. S. *Patterns in Nature.* Boston: Little Brown and Company, 1974.

Sullivan, J. *Learning and Creativity with Special Emphasis on Science.* Arlington, Va.: National Science Teachers Association, 1967.

Toneyama, K. *The Popular Arts of Mexico.* New York: Weatherhill, 1974.

Twain, M. *The Prince and the Pauper.* Cutchogue, N.Y.: Buccaneer Books, 1985.

Unseld, T. *Portfolios: African-American Artists.* Palo Alto, Calif.: Dale Seymour Publications, 1994.

Vezza, T., and M. Bagley. *The Investigation of Real Problems: A Teacher's Handbook for Developing Higher Level Thinking Skills in Gifted and Talented Children.* Woodcliff Lake, N.J.: Educational Institutes and Consulting Association, 1979.

Villalpando, E., and K. Kolbe. *Independent Projects.* Phoenix, Ariz.: Think Ink Publications, 1979.

Von Oech, R. *Creative Whack Pack.* Stamford, Conn.: U.S. Games Systems, 1990.

Williams, L. *Teaching for the Two-Sided Mind: A Guide to Right Brain/Left Brain Education.* New York: Simon and Schuster, 1983.

Winner, E. *Invented Worlds: The Psychology of the Arts.* Cambridge, Mass.: Harvard University Press, 1982.

IMPORTANT ADDRESSES

ACTIVITY RESOURCES COMPANY

P.O. Box 4875, Hayward, CA 94540

AMERICAN RADIO RELAY LEAGUE (203) 666-1541

225 Main Street, Newington, CT 06111

FOUNDATION FOR A CREATIVE AMERICA

1755 Jefferson Davis Highway, Suite 400, Arlington, VA 22202 (703) 521-0455

FUTURE MAKERS INVENTOR/MENTOR PROGRAM, SATURDAY ACADEMY (503) 690-1190

Oregon Graduate Institute, 19600 NW Von Neumann Drive
Beaverton, OR 97006

KIDSART

P.O. Box 274, Mt. Shasta, CA 96067

(916) 926-5076

Published quarterly, each unit is filled with information, reproducible worksheets, and hands-on activities on a specific art topic. Available by subscription or by individual copy.

NATIONAL INVENTIVE THINKING ASSOCIATION

c/o The National Invention Center, Inc., 80 West Bowery, Suite 201, Akron, OH 44308

ODYSSEY OF THE MIND
P.O. Box 27, Glassboro, NJ 08028

(609) 881-1603
Fax (609) 881-3596

JON PEARSON
P.O. Box 253367, Los Angeles, CA 90025

PRESIDENT'S COUNCIL ON PHYSICAL FITNESS AND SPORTS
701 Pennsylvania Ave. NW, Washington, DC 20004

(202) 272-3421

PROJECT XL, U.S. PATENT AND TRADEMARK OFFICE
Washington, DC 20231

(703) 557-1610

PUBLIC SERVICE CENTER, U.S. PATENT AND TRADEMARK OFFICE
Washington, DC 20231

(703) 557-HELP

PUBLICATIONS SERVICE, NATIONAL GALLERY OF ART
Washington, DC 20565

U.S. COPYRIGHT OFFICE
Library of Congress, Washington, DC 20559

(202) 707-9100

A CALL FOR FEEDBACK

Now that you've reached the end of *Creativity Inside Out*, I'd like to remind you how important your feedback and reactions to this curriculum are to me. Please let me know which lessons worked best for you, creative ideas you have for other lessons, other extensions, and future revisions or editions. Please write to me at the following address:

TERRY MARKS-TARLOW, PH. D.
1460 Seventh Street, Suite 304, Santa Monica, CA 90401